REPRESENTATIONS OF RAPE AND CONSENT IN MEDIEVAL ENGLISH LAWS AND LITERATURE

GENDER AND POWER IN THE PREMODERN WORLD

Further Information and Publications

www.arc-humanities.org/series/book-series/

REPRESENTATIONS OF RAPE AND CONSENT IN MEDIEVAL ENGLISH LAWS AND LITERATURE

by

MARIAH L. COOPER

ARC HUMANITIES PRESS

British Library Cataloguing in Publication Data
A catalogue record for this book is available from the British Library.

ISBN (Hardback): 9781802700534
ISBN (Paperback): 9781802702743
e-ISBN (PDF): 9781802702170

www.arc-humanities.org
Printed and bound in the UK (by CPI Group [UK] Ltd), USA (by Bookmasters), and elsewhere using print-on-demand technology.

CONTENTS

LIST OF ILLUSTRATIONS

ABBREVIATIONS

AALT	Anglo-American Legal Tradition. University of Huston Law Center. Last Modified August 2015. http://aalt.law.uh.edu/.
Amis and Amiloun	"Amis and Amiloun." In *Amis and Amiloun, Robert of Cisyle, and Sir Amadace*. Edited by Edward Foster. Kalamazoo: Medieval Institute, 2007. https://d.lib.rochester.edu/teams/text/foster-amis-and-amiloun.
Bracton	*Bracton Online*. Harvard Law School Library. Edited by Charles A. Donahue, Thomas R. Bruce, and Terry Martin. Last Modified April 2003. https://amesfoundation.law.harvard.edu/Bracton/.
Britton	*Britton: The French Text Carefully Revised, with an English Translation, Introduction and Notes*. Edited and translated by Francis Morgan Nichols, 2 vols. Oxford: Clarendon, 1865. Reprint Holmes Beach: Graunt, 1983.
Decretum	*Decretum Magistri Gratiani*. Edited by Emil Friedberg. In Corpus Iuris Canonici 1. Leipzig: Tauchnitz, 1879. Reprint Graz: Akademische Druck- u. Verlagsanstalt, 1959.
DMLBS	*Dictionary of Medieval Latin from British Sources*. Edited by Ronald Edward Latham, David R. Howlett, and Richard Ashdowne. Turnhout: Brepols, 2015.
EC	Eyre Courts
Fleta	*Fleta*. Edited and translated by John Selden. 2nd ed. London, 1685.

Glanvill	Glanvill, Ranulf de. *Tractatus de legibus et consuetudinibus regni Anglie qui Glanvilla vocatur* [Treatise on the Laws and Customs of the Realm of England Commonly Called Glanvill]. Edited and translated by G. D. G. Hall. Oxford: Oxford University Press, 1993. Reprint 2002.
Le Bone Florence	*Le Bone Florence of Rome*. Edited by Carol Falvo Heffernan. Manchester: Manchester University Press, 1976.
MED	*Middle English Dictionary*. Edited by Frances McSparran et al. Ann Arbor: University of Michigan Library, 2000–2018. https://quod.lib.umich.edu/m/middle-english-dictionary/dictionary.
MER	Middle English Romance
Sir Degare	"Sir Degare." In *The Middle English Breton Lays*. Edited by Anne Laskaya and Eve Salisbury. Kalamazoo: Medieval Institute, 1995. https://d.lib.rochester.edu/teams/text/laskaya-and-salisbury-middle-english-breton-lays-sir-degare.
Sir Gowther	"Sir Gowther." In *The Middle English Breton Lays*. Edited by Anne Laskaya and Eve Salisbury. Kalamazoo: Medieval Institute, 1995. https://d.lib.rochester.edu/teams/text/laskaya-and-salisbury-middle-english-breton-lays-sir-gowther.
Sir Orfeo	"Sir Orfeo." In *The Middle English Breton Lays*. Edited by Anne Laskaya and Eve Salisbury. Kalamazoo: Medieval Institute, 1995. https://d.lib.rochester.edu/teams/text/laskaya-and-salisbury-middle-english-breton-lays-sir-orfeo.
TNA	Kew, The National Archives

ACKNOWLEDGEMENTS

I AM INDEBTED to the support of many people over many years. I began thinking about this project as an undergraduate student at Trent University and submitted my first paper on this topic to Fiona Harris-Stoertz in 2014. Thanks to her encouragement, I pursued this project at the graduate level. I must thank my doctoral supervisory committee, Marica Cassis, John Geck, Sébastien Rossignol, and Katherine Weikert. Their suggestions and guidance were instrumental to my development as a scholar and the fruition of this research project. The feedback I received from members of my doctoral examination committee, Edwin Bezzina, Sonja Boon, and Kathleen Cawsey, helped me refine my arguments. Sonja's insightful observations provided the foundation for this book. Sara Butler helped answer my questions and generously reviewed an early version of this project. Hannah Wood, my friend and conference buddy, has kept me laughing throughout this process, even when it was difficult. This book would not exist without Katherine Weikert's incredible support and mentorship. I cannot accurately express my appreciation for Kate's kindness and reassurance over the years.

Research funding that I received through the Social Sciences and Humanities Research Council, Memorial University of Newfoundland's Scholarship in the Arts, Memorial's Funding for Doctoral Studies, Memorial's President's Doctoral Student Invest Fund, and Acadia University's Research Fund all made this project possible.

I am indebted to my family who have continually cheered me on throughout my academic career. None of this would have been possible without the support from my Grandpa Orval Cooper and Aunt Brenda. To my parents, Steve and Brenda, and my husband, Ian, thank you all for listening to me as I talked about the ideas in this book for the past decade. Ian, thank you for your patience as I spent many nights tucked away in the office writing. My most profound thank you goes to my mom, Brenda: my personal editor, conference buddy, and research trip assistant. Her unwavering support has been invaluable.

Lastly, I want to acknowledge the women and girls whose stories I have attempted to tell. This book stands as a testament to their strength and perseverance in going to court and having their truth written down and preserved for future generations.

Introduction

RAPE AND CONSENT IN MEDIEVAL ENGLAND

A YOUNG, POOR girl named Juliana le Hare was raped by a man named Richard.[1] Despite being poor, unmarried, and still living in her father's modest home, young Juliana demanded to have her day in court. She told the authorities that Richard violently, with force, raped her of her virginity. But Richard did not act alone. Juliana explained to the court that another man, Stephen, helped Richard. Juliana said that it was Stephen, not Richard, who forcibly grabbed her against her will, pulled her into a dark cellar, and closed the door on her. There was no way out of the cellar. Juliana was stuck. She was alone, and there was nothing she could do when Richard came in and raped her. Speculatively, Richard heard rumours that Juliana launched a formal appeal of rape against him, and instead of pleading his innocence, Richard fled from the authorities. Perhaps this was a victory for Juliana; she may have known that the chances of securing a full felony conviction were minimal, so Richard fleeing into outlawry may have given her some satisfaction. Or perhaps Juliana was angry and upset that Richard fled; maybe Richard's evading of criminal prosecution made Juliana determined to still bring a case forward against Stephen. Despite following the expected legal processes, such as notifying the authorities in due time and appearing in court when scheduled, the jurors did not believe young Juliana. The jurors, who were all local men from Juliana's community, said that Stephen was not guilty, and that Richard didn't even rape Juliana of her virginity. Perhaps the jurors debated whether Juliana was a virgin at the time or if she *actually* consented to the alleged rape. Perhaps they discussed her past sexual history, and maybe they judged her poor socio-economic status as grounds for someone who might lie about these sorts of things.[2] Either way, Juliana was probably devastated by the court's decision, but it got worse. She was deemed to have essentially wasted the court's time and, in the end, it was only Juliana who was to be imprisoned for false appeal.

---

1 TNA, JUST1/62 m5d.

2 Carissa Harris explains how in Chaucer's texts "poor women, because of their material disadvantage, bear the brunt of societal judgement against women who are 'dishonest' 'of hir bod[ies].'" See *Obscene Pedagogies*, 34.

The case of Juliana—which comes to us from the 1232 Buckinghamshire eyre—is not remarkable or unique. Rather, its unexceptional status is indicative of the larger trend that this book examines, which is mainly how people in medieval England viewed rape and consent. In this book I consider what cultural ideologies of medieval England promoted a "rape culture"; that is, what societal beliefs contributed to victim-blaming stereotypes and common rape myths, such as the application of pressure to change a "no" into a "yes"? I know that using the term "rape culture" immediately makes some readers skeptical, but its historicity is important to acknowledge.[3] To help answer this question, this book looks at a wide range of source material including laws, legal and medical treatises, trial records, hagiography, conduct literature, and popular Middle English Romance (MER). This book focuses on the representations of rape and (non-)consent in England from the twelfth to the fourteenth century through a social historical analysis of legal and literary sources. Unlike previous research, this book does not seek to examine the legal history of rape, nor is it a book on the literary studies of rape narratives. Rather, this book looks at the social, legal, and literary representations of rape and (non-)consent. I aim to show how these different sources have commonalities and how, by viewing them together, we can observe the reoccurring themes of the physicality of (non-)consent, the duality of mental and physical (non-)consent, and the expectations of resistance. Here, the research reveals new aspects of medieval English rape culture. Together, I argue that the cumulative impact of these various sources is that medieval English culture was characterized by a common belief that the minds and bodies of both rape victims and, similarly, rapists could operate independently of one another, which ensured the legal and social requirement of resistance to prove non-consent. This duality of mental and physical (non-) consent perpetuated a hesitancy to believe women's accusations of rape.

Scholars have explored medieval histories of rape and sexual assault for decades and, more recently, scholarship has addressed the limitations of binary distinctions between rape and consensual sex.[4] This book builds on the foundational work of previous legal scholars—particularly Kim Phillips's emphasis on the medieval English interpretation of rape as "the assaulted body" and Patricia Orr's study of wounding and rape in the legal treatises

3 Harris, *Obscene Pedagogies*, 1–25, 114.

4 For an overview of the historiography, see Piercy, *Resistance to Love*, 4–32. See also Gavey, *Just Sex?*, 1–14. For consent studies in medieval scholarship, see Harris and Somerset, eds., "Colloquium: Historicizing Consent," 268–367. See also Lett, "Women Victims of Sexual Assault and Rape," 45–70.

of *Glanvill* and *Bracton*.[5] This book considers how non-legal sources complicate or reinforce Phillips's and Orr's findings. While Phillips argues that "consent is of only peripheral interest"[6] to the legal treatise known as *Bracton*, I offer alternative sources and interpretations to suggest that (non-) consent was actually central to the common and legal understandings of rape and sexual violence, including within *Bracton*. As Orr notes, the crime of rape was a crime of violence, but what does this violence represent?[7] As discussed throughout this book, the inclusion of physical force and blood was more than legal or hagiographic rhetoric; it was indicative of that what had occurred was, indeed, a crime against the woman's will, as she tried to physically resist the rape and can "prove" it by her bodily injury. However, the belief that the body could act against the will of the mind significantly complicated this requirement of physical "proof" of non-consent.

There is no single definition of the Latin legal term *raptus*. It does not perfectly map onto our modern understandings of the crime of rape, and its exact meaning has been debated by scholars for decades.[8] *Raptus* is

---

5 Orr, "Men's Theory and Women's Reality," 121–62; Phillips, "Written on the Body," 125–44.

6 Phillips, "Written on the Body," 129.

7 Orr, "Men's Theory and Women's Reality," 131, 140.

8 For example: Brown, "*Inaudito exemplo*," 21–34; Cannon, "*Raptus* in the Chaumpaigne Release and a Newly Discovered Document Concerning the Life of Geoffrey Chaucer," 74–94; Dunn, *Stolen Women in Medieval England*, 10–14; Dunn, "The Language of Ravishment in Medieval England," 79–116; Edwards, "Beyond *Raptus*," 1–8; Gravdal, *Ravishing Maidens*, 4–9; Gravdal, "Camouflaging Rape," 361–73; Hanawalt, "Whose Story Was This?," 126; Harvey, *The Fires of Lust*, 187–201; Hawkes, "Female Consent in Rape and Ravishment in Later Medieval England," 47–53; Histed, "Medieval Rape," 743–69; Kelly, "Meanings and Uses of *Raptus* in Chaucer's Time," 101–65; Kelly, "Statute of Rapes and Alleged Ravishers of Wives," 361–419; Musson, "Crossing Boundaries," 84–101; Orr, "Men's Theory and Women's Reality," 121–62; Plucknett, *Legislation of Edward I*, 114–16; Pollock and Maitland, *The History of the English Law before the Time of Edward I*, vol. 2, pp. 490–92; Post, "Ravishment of Women and the Statutes of Westminster," 150–64; Post, "Sir Thomas West and the Statute of Rapes, 1382," 24–30; Robertson and Rose, "Introduction," in *Representing Rape in Medieval and Early Modern Literature*, 1–20; Seabourne, "Rape and Law in Medieval Western Europe," 342–57; Seabourne, *Imprisoning Medieval Women*, 91–96; Walker, "Common Law Juries and Feudal Marriage Customs in Medieval England," 705–18. For a close linguistic interpretation of *raptus*, or *rapuit et abduxit*, see Dunn, "The Language of Ravishment," 87–89; Dunn, *Stolen Women*, 17–19, 24. Dunn provides an example from the gaol delivery rolls (1375–1376) where *raptus* was used in a case of theft (TNA, JUST3/165A m6d). For an overview of sexual laws in Europe more generally, see Brundage, *Law, Sex and Christian Society*. The legal

defined as the "(act of) snatching away" or "taking away (property)," and subsequently came to be understood as "abduction (of a woman, us[ually] accompanied by sexual assault or coercion), rape."[9] Originating from Roman law, *raptus* (which Brundage defines as "carrying off by force") was primarily "the abduction of a woman against the will of the person under whose authority she lived," and it did not necessarily indicate coitus.[10] As the Middle Ages progressed, *raptus* became synonymous with abduction and/or sexual violence, which has led Caroline Dunn to claim that that *raptus* is "one of the most ambiguous legal terms in medieval England."[11] However, the legal sources are explicit in that rape is a crime that can only be committed by a man onto a woman. In medieval England, it was legally impossible for a man to be the victim of rape.[12]

In trial records and court proceedings of rape cases, there are complex layers of power relations: victim and perpetrator; woman and man; complainant and defendant; complainant and judge; the individual and the court system. Gender is intrinsically a part of these power relations, and consent is inherently about power.[13] Women were excluded from medieval English

---

understanding of *raptus* was recently broadened to include employee procurement. This was brought to light by Euan Roger and Sebastian Sobecki's archival discovery on the Geoffrey Chaucer and Cecily Chaumpaigne case. See Roger and Sobecki, "Geoffrey Chaucer, Cecily Chaumpaigne, and the Statute of Laborers," 407–37. For a discussion on the use of "legal fiction" in elopement cases disguised as ravishment cases, see Musson, "Crossing Boundaries," 92–93; Pope and McSheffrey, "Ravishment, Legal Narratives, and Chivalric Culture in Fifteenth-Century England," 818–36.

9 DMLBS, "raptus," articles 1–3.

10 Brundage, "Rape and Seduction in the Medieval Canon Law," 141.

11 For an overview of this change in meaning, see Brundage, *Law, Sex and Christian Society*. For medieval England specifically see Dunn, "The Language of Ravishment," 80; Pollock and Maitland, *The History of the English Law*, vol. 2, p. 490.

12 For a discussion on male-victim rape cases made through sodomy charges, see Harvey, *The Fires of Lust*, 197–200. In theory, married women could only make two felony appeals, that of rape and the murder of their husbands, but women made up about one-third of all appeals in thirteenth-century England appealing crimes such as homicide, theft, and assault. See Klerman, "Women Prosecutors in Thirteenth-Century England," 287–88.

13 While "woman" is used as the default to describe medieval victims of rape in this book, because medieval sources require a female victim and male perpetrator, this research is grounded in gender theory's rejection of biological essentialism and instead places masculinities and femininities as part of a social construct that can be occupied by any sexed bodies. The complexities of gender identity as being performed, often unconsciously, is assumed throughout this research. Judith Butler's explanation that gender only gains social meaning when understood within the

juries and, consequently, there is a fundamental gendered component of male judgement and gaze in the medieval English criminal courts.[14] Upon hearing an accusation of rape, the presenting jurors had to decide whether to bring the private appeal to the officials. One can speculate that once an accusation of felony was made, "the rumors and suspicions that circulated" in the community "became the governing perceptions of the truth of the matter," leading to a "complex process of community judgement" before any case was brought to the courts.[15] The exclusive selection of local men to serve as jurors—who in turn enforced a standard of community policing in the form of jury presentments and verdicts—forced women attempting to appeal rape to face not only legal and medical impediments but also implicit social judgements. It is important to recognize the immense number of social hurdles that women like young Juliana le Hare overcame to even get to trial.

James Brundage suggests that theologians defined rape based on four conditions: violence, abduction, sexual intercourse, and non-consent of one individual. But what did the condition of non-consent entail?[16] While Brundage notes that violence could range from wounding and physical assault to "moderate force" used to intimidate someone into acquiescing, this leads one to question how theologians perceived the legitimacy of such coercive consent. Unlike the secular criminal courts, "strenuous resistance" was not necessary to prove non-consent in the eyes of theologians/canonists, as "active combat by the victim was not something that they expected" but rather, according to Brundage, raising the hue and cry were acceptable grounds to prove non-consent.[17] Building on this analysis of the centrality of

---

cultural context of a given society grounds the following research by exploring how medieval English culture perceived normative masculinity and femininity. See Butler, *Gender Trouble*, 180; Butler, *Undoing Gender*, 20. For a discussion on contextualizing consent based on power dynamics, see Akard and Raw, "Global Response," 363.

14 For an overview on jury selection see Bellamy, *Crime and Public Order*, 121–22; Butler, *The Language of Abuse*, 6, 96, 105; Butler, *Forensic Medicine*; Green, *Verdict According to Conscience*, 11, 15; Musson, *Medieval Law in Context*, 91, 110–17. See also *Glanvill*, book 13, chaps. 3–7.

15 Green, *Verdict According to Conscience*, 16–17.

16 Brundage, "Rape and Seduction in the Medieval Canon Law," 143. For analyses on the overrepresentation of clergymen as defendants in *raptus* cases see Dunn, *Stolen Women*, 181–83; Gravdal, *Ravishing Maidens*, 212–13; Musson, *Medieval Law in Context*, 100. Contrary, Robin Storey suggests that clergymen were maliciously accused of rape to ensure they maintained their vow of celibacy in "Malicious Indictments of Clergy in the Fifteenth Century," 221–40.

17 Brundage, "Rape and Seduction in the Medieval Canon Law," 144.

verbal non-consent (as indicative of mental non-consent) through the hue and cry, this book examines the role of mental non-consent, the so-called steadfast will, and its alleged internal fight with the consent of the flesh of the violated woman.

The notion of moral elevation through surviving rape is contrary to hagiography where female saints are willing to sacrifice their life to escape rape.[18] Since the virgin martyrs are obviously virgins when they are martyred, rape is always threatened in hagiography and never completed, or, as Howard Bloch, bluntly states, "the only real virgin—that is, the only true virgin—is a dead virgin."[19] This Christ-like bodily sacrifice was, as Suzanne Edwards argues, all dependent on preserving the chastity of the mind, which required constant mental non-consent during the rape. Stretching Edwards' analysis further, I consider how the weakness of the flesh believed to be biologically inherent in female anatomy seemingly overpowers the mental non-consent. In turn, I interrogate what power this conceptualization held outside theological debates.

To develop this analysis, I turn to literary sources and their representations of rape and consent. Scholars have established the common trope of rape in romance, and the legal realities of trial by oath and trial by ordeal in romance have already been recognized.[20] However, what has yet to be fully discussed is the correlation between real legal expectations of rape survivors and the physical proof of non-consent in romance as being consistent with the legal doctrine. This research is indebted to the work of literary scholars who have emphasized the limitations of legal sources and, as Samantha Katz Seal argues, made clear the need to consider "legacies of misogyny and sexual violence" in medieval literature.[21] Carissa Harris's foundational research on the use of obscenity in premodern English and Scottish literature to teach

18 Edwards, *The Afterlives of Rape*, 2, 45.

19 Bloch, *Medieval Misogyny and the Invention of Western Romantic Love*, 108.

20 For example: Baechle, Harris, and Strakhov, "Reassessing the Pastourelle"; Butler, *Language of Abuse*; Cooper, *The English Romance in Time*; Dinshaw, *Chaucer's Sexual Poetics*; Duby, *The Knight, the Lady and the Priest*; Edwards, *The Afterlives of Rape*; Gravdal, *Ravishing Maidens*; Higgins and Silver, eds., *Rape and Representation*; Hopkins, Rouse, and Rushton, eds., *Sexual Culture in the Literature of Medieval Britain*; Kaeuper, *Chivalry and Violence;* Menuge, ed., *Medieval Women and the Law*; Putter and Gilbert, eds., *The Spirit of Medieval English Popular Romance*; Robertson and Rose, eds., *Representing Rape in Medieval and Early Modern Literature*; Saunders, *Rape and Ravishment*; Wolfthal, *Images of Rape*.

21 Seal, "Whose Chaucer?," 487. See also Piercy, *Resistance to Love*, 6–7. For a discussion on "the limitations of legal frameworks," see Franklin et al., eds., *Consent*.

"felawe masculinity"—and, particularly, to recognize survival speech in pastourelles—informs the present research, especially as we are still living with many of these seemingly *medieval* ideologies when it comes to rape and consent.[22] Building on this research, I examine a wide range of source material which I argue contribute to sustaining conflicting ideologies around mental and physical (non-)consent.

By combining the analysis of romance narratives with legal histories, this research allows for a flourishing opportunity to study societal anxieties "largely invisible from more conventional historical records."[23] In this way, these sources become mirrors—however distorted they may be—reflecting a relatable experience to the audiences.[24] As scholars have noted, medieval literature was a platform for discussion and debate about the realities of rape.[25] Rape, as an event which occurs in the select romances, is not necessarily the focus of the following analysis. Rather, it is the social attitudes, legal influences, and realities intruding into the fictional which are of primary concern here. In alignment with the legal texts, this book will further argue that romances were beyond fanciful entertainment or hagiographic rhetoric, but rather they had the capacity to be legally instructive. As will become evident in the following chapters, romance is reflecting a reality but does not necessarily intend to be realistic.

There are, of course, limitations to a heterosexual lens of study, as medieval sexual practices were not exclusively heterosexual, and such generalizations run the risk of obscuring the diversity of same-sex sexual practices of the period. I am cognizant of the fact that the source material—which defines rape as a crime committed by a man onto a woman—carries with it an assumption of heteronormativity, and this does not reflect the realities of sexuality and sexual violence of the medieval past. In an attempt to combat this, I follow queer theorists' critiques of heteronormativity. Here, rape is not viewed as the product of "toxic masculinity" but as a product of hegemonic masculinity and femininity—an act which is not outside the cultural bounds of acceptability but firmly entrenched within them.[26] This critique of

22 Harris, *Obscene Pedagogies*, 10.

23 Goldberg, "Introduction," in *Medieval Women and the Law*, x.

24 For a discussion on the relationship between romance and reality, see Galloway, *Medieval Literature and Culture*, 82; Harris, "Pastourelle Fictionalities," 239–42; Piercy, *Resistance to Love*, 14–30.

25 Harris, "Pastourelle Fictionalities"; Kaeuper, *Chivalry and Violence*, 35; Raw, "Readers Then and Now," 313.

26 Connell, *Masculinities*, 77. For more on queer theory, see Gavey, *Just Sex?*, 1–14.

normative cultural practices enables us to consider medieval England's cultural toleration of sexual violence.[27] Tracey Nicholls defines "rape culture" as a culture "that normalizes and excuses rape, a social context in which the desires of privileged aggressors are prioritized over the comfort, safety, and dignity of marginalized populations that are seen as targets, prey."[28] These cultural ideologies make rape appear tolerable, perhaps even inevitable, and they are largely unquestioned cultural markers that are upheld by larger cultural structures, such as laws and gender norms. Through my analysis of this medieval evidence, I acknowledge what we now define as traits of a rape culture in the modern era are also evident in the Middle Ages.[29]

As Harris states, "neither rape nor consensual sex follows a single paradigm."[30] As such, the sources are at times contradictory, which is often unsettling for historians. I am okay with the conflict; I am at ease with this ambiguity because I believe that the ambiguity of sexual (non-)consent is emblematic of larger contemporaneous cultural beliefs about women's sexuality. I want to explore these contradictions; I want to pause in the uncertainty and consider how medieval thinkers—theologians, writers, and readers—sought to harmonize conflicting ideologies around mental and physical (non-)consent and, in turn, consider how these conflicts enabled victim-blaming ideologies. Sadly, this is not a new topic. The longevity of victim-blaming can be traced back to the high and late Middle Ages.[31] Medi-

27 See Akard, "Unequal Power and Sexual Consent," 288; Harris, "On Servant Women, Rape Culture, and Endurance," 475–83; Harris, *Obscene Pedagogies*; Seal, "Whose Chaucer?," 487; Piercy, *Resistance to Love*, 15; Schwebel, "Chaucer and the Fantasy of Retroactive Consent," 338; Torres and McNamara, "Female Consent and Affective Resistance in Romance," 44.

28 Nicholls, *Dismantling Rape Culture*, 9–10, 26. See also Brownmiller, *Against our Will*, 391. For an overview of rape myths, see Payne et al., "Rape Myth Acceptance," 27–68.

29 For a discussion on "the toxicity of normative masculinity" see Mardorossian, *Framing the Rape Victim*, 10–28. For an analysis of the current "cultural coupling" of sex and violence, see Fraser and Seymour, *Understanding Violence and Abuse*, 19–23, 74, 87.

30 Harris, *Obscene Pedagogies*, 105, 123.

31 I am not saying that victim-blaming began in the Middle Ages. See Brundage, *Law, Sex and Christian Society*, 55–174. For a discussion on victim-blaming as a part of "invulnerability theory" see Canadian Resource Center for Victims of Crime, *Victim Blaming*, 3. For an analysis of victim-blaming ideologies, see Grubb and Turner, "Attribution of Blame in Rape Cases," 443–52. For a discussion on the positive correlation between physical injury and victim-blaming, see Andrews et al., "Gender, Social Support, and PTSD in Victims of Violent Crime," 422.

eval English jurors, defendants, and authors belittled accusations made by rape survivors with questions which are all too familiar to us today: What was she doing there alone? Was she drinking? Was she asking for it? Did she enjoy the assault? The common tropes include fears of false rape accusations, the binary construction of the "true rape victim" and the blame-worthy woman, and the perceived defence that the survivor's body can enjoy the sexual assault. While this research is firmly focused on the medieval past, comparisons to modern culture are inescapable (dare I say necessary) and will be discussed in the final chapter.

Modern understandings that consensual sex does not necessarily mean ethical, mutually agreed upon sexual contact enables scholars to explore the multivalent understandings of rape and (non-)consent in the medieval past.[32] Heeding Sarah Baechle's advice, this book takes a structural approach to the source material in order to gain a deeper understanding of the "cultural scripts that foster violation," that enable victim-blaming mentalities, and that support the assumed verisimilitude of rape mythologies to better understand medieval English cultural beliefs around notions of rape and consent.[33] Louise Sylvester's work on feminine passivity requiring the performance of reluctance—the so-called "token no"—allows for the understanding that certain cultural markers around expected gendered behaviour may have not only contributed to a hesitancy to believe rape survivors but also perhaps contributed to the frequency at which seduction could apparently lead to rape.[34] This eroticization of the reluctant lady, which works to enhance the male desire to turn rejection into submission, has been noted by various scholars. Simultaneously, scholars have challenged the "token no" to develop a perspective on such vocal non-consent as more than performative reluctance.[35] Instead of viewing a woman's change of a "no" to a "yes" as flippant or formulaic, Alice Raw reminds us that "coerced consent" can be an act

---

32 Recent scholarship in the field of historical consent has emphasized the inadequacies of a "consent only" framework that ignores the limitations of freely given consent. However, as Harris, Piercy, and others have noted, consent is discussed in the source material and thus we ought to consider its "linguistic 'historicity.'" See Piercy, *Resistance to Love*, 4–8; Harris, *Obscene Pedagogies*, 34; Harris and Somerset, eds., "Colloquium: Historicizing Consent," 268–367.

33 Baechle, "Speaking Survival," 468.

34 Sylvester, *Medieval Romance and the Construction of Heterosexuality*, 2, 30–39, 41.

35 Harris, "Pastourelle Fictionalities," 240; Moss, "#NotAllMen," 295; Piercy, *Resistance to Love*, 31; Seal, "Chasing the Consent of Alice Chaucer," 277; Torres and McNamara, "Female Consent and Affective Resistance in Romance," 34–49.

of survival.[36] As Suzanne Edwards states, "consent is thus the switch-point between misogyny's carrot and stick" in that if the woman gives her consent, she will escape violence, and if she withholds her consent, she will "suffer harm."[37] Contextualizing consent within the power dynamics and cultural norms of medieval England is thus paramount to reading past the "token no" and viewing reluctance and acquiescence as a form of endurance.[38] I agree with the scholarly critiques of Sylvester's "token no" in that saying "no" is not just a performance of reluctance or a performance of ideal femininity. This book is grounded in the understanding that "no" is verbal non-consent, and sometimes saying nothing at all is indicative of mental non-consent. I understand the consequences of saying "no" and how quickly a "seduction" can turn physically violent.

Throughout this book I use the term "identity," and it is important to remember that women "were active in negotiating and creating their own identities alongside commonly recognized stereotypes and norms of gender expectations."[39] I consider how both real and fictional women were assumed to be innocent, guilty, or a reluctance accomplice in their own rapes, and how these *legal identities* were constructed, upheld, and usurped. I use the term "identity" to consider the legal caricatures placed on women while acknowledging that they were not necessarily performing these "identities." This is largely due to the nature of the archives as produced by and for the king's court. I can only view the courts' rendition of events and how the judges or jurors viewed these individuals as guilty or victimized. I consider how ideal masculinity and femininity influenced the legal rhetoric of rape cases and potentially disadvantaged women appealing rape.[40] The symbolic representations of "woman" in rape narratives as either Mary or Eve, pure or corrupted, innocent or guilty are binaries consistent in the laws themselves, the

---

36 Raw, "Readers Then and Now," 307–14. See also Akard and Raw, "Global Response," 363–67.

37 Edwards, "Consent and Misogyny," 335.

38 For a discussion on the contextualization of consent see Akard and Raw, "Global Response," 363–67. For an examination of (non-)consent in Chaucer, see Baechle, "Speaking Survival," 463–74. For an analysis of "endurance," particularly around the role of servant women, see Harris, "On Servant Women, Rape Culture, and Endurance," 475–83.

39 Kane and Williamson, "Introduction," 16.

40 My methodology is similar to Amanda McVittty's in her analysis of treason and masculinity, in that gendered identities in felony trials were connected to broader cultural understandings of "manhood" and "womanhood." See McVitty, *Treason and Masculinity in Medieval England*, 5.

trial records, medical texts, conduct literature, hagiography, and the literary sources of popular MER. These symbolic representations are both explicitly mentioned and implicitly hinted at in the primary sources' discussions of rape victims. Here, I argue that the duality of mental and physical (non-) consent was sustained by the cultural symbols employed in rape narratives wherein a woman as either Mary or Eve, pure or polluted, virgin or temptress, innocent or guilty. Importantly, power allows space for resistance, and, indeed, there are resistance narratives in the primary sources discussed.

Sources and Structure

This book is divided into two primary fields of study: medieval English laws and popular MER. First discussed in turn, these will be brought together at the end of this book for a discussion which will ultimately show that the polarity of mental and physical (non-)consent enabled the cultural space for belittling a woman's accusations of rape and thus ensured the necessity of physical resistance to prove her non-consent. In this analysis, I am building on the extensive EC archival research completed by Harold Schneebeck and Barbara Hanawalt while including new cases, new translations, and shifting my lens of focus away from statistical analysis and instead looking at the use of language—blood, injury, virginity, pollution, corruption—to describe the alleged victims and perpetrators.[41] I recognize that applying statistical findings of medieval court records is a speculative endeavour; not all crimes make it to authorities, not all authorities follow up on criminal accusations, and records get lost or purposefully destroyed. Studying legal records can frustrate historians, as verdicts are frequently left unmentioned or concord was made out of court, and thus there are inevitable gaps in the records themselves.[42] Just like today, many instances of rape in the Middle Ages were never reported to authorities. We cannot know whether women chose not to appeal because of the financial penalty they would endure if their appeal failed, the potential for a damaged reputation or blame being placed on them, or the fact that convictions were rare, and the prosecution process seemed pointless.[43]

41 Hanawalt, "The Female Felon in Fourteenth-Century England," 253–68; Hanawalt, *Crime and Conflict*; Hanawalt, "Women Before the Law," 165–96; Schneebeck, "The Law of Felony in Medieval England," vol. 2.

42 For a discussion on the issues of using medieval trial records for statistical data see Butler, "Getting Medieval on Steven Pinker," 29–40.

43 For a statistical analysis of conviction rates see Bellamy, *Crime and Public Order*, 158; Carter, *Rape in Medieval England*, 108; Groot, "The Crime of Rape," 329;

I draw on 179 *raptus* cases, which includes sixty-one rape cases in the court of the general eyre, from 1201 to 1330, as well as records from the King's Bench, coroners' rolls, goal delivery rolls, calendar of close and patent rolls. Furthermore, I explore the meaning of *raptus* in the legal treatises *Glanvill*, *Bracton*, *Britton*, *Mirror of Justices*, *Placita Corone*, and *Fleta*, as well as in the legal statutes of Westminster I, II, and the Statute of Rapes. Together, with these legal sources, I explore representations of rape and (non-)consent in medical and ecclesiastical treatises, such as those by William of Conches, Augustine, and Gratian alongside hagiography, conduct literature, and MER to weave together a social historical prospective of rape and (non-)consent in medieval England. By looking at a wide range of sources and how they interpreted rape, consent, and the "causes" of rape, we can see connections, reoccurring themes, and "textual hauntings."[44] I do not offer a singular, definitive, definition of medieval English interpretations of consent, as it was indeed a "flexible concept." [45] However, it is clear that consent, assent, and will mattered to legal, ecclesiastical, medical, and literary authors in the medieval period. When we consider the propinquity between these varying sources, we can gain a comprehensive—albeit often contradictory—appreciation for the reoccurring theme of the duality of mental and physical (non-)consent.

Looking at legal and literary sources together, seeing how they reinforce certain tropes, and recognizing how they conflict with one another offers scholars the vantage point by which to see "how medieval ideas about consent were far more complex, dynamic, and nuanced than we typically acknowledge."[46] Medievalist have long debated the meaning of "consent," and Gwen Seabourne cautions against historical speculation, as the legal terms used for consent "are nowhere defined."[47] While recognizing the "slip-

---

Hanawalt, *Crime and Conflict*, 59; Hanawalt, "Women Before the Law," 186; Kittel, "Rape in Thirteenth-Century England," 106–10; Schneebeck, "The Law of Felony in Medieval England," 219n120. For discussions on the limitations of legal records see Davis, *Fiction in the Archives*.

44 Following Piercy, I am not suggesting that these are "direct lines of influence" but rather they offer "implications for understanding contemporaneous views." Piercy, *Resistance to Love*, 7–8. Like Harris's use of "linkages," I am not arguing causality between source material, but rather the "notion of 'partial connection'" between the sources. Harris, *Obscene Pedagogies*, 9.

45 Piercy, *Resistance to Love*, 12–13.

46 Harris and Somerset, "Introduction," 270–71.

47 Seabourne, *Imprisoning Medieval Women*, 153. See also Youngs, "Reading Ravishment," 56.

periness" of defining consent in medieval England, the various sources show a persistent attempt to classify (non-)consent and to harmonize conflicting notions of mental and physical consent. In short, "medieval people were curious about consent."[48] This research contributes to the ongoing discussion concerning the way that (non-)consent was viewed through physical injury, not separate from it, which led to a legal and social expectation of resistance to rape. However, I contend that the "legible flesh"[49] was seemingly insufficient, as medical, ecclesiastical, and literary texts argue for a more nuanced interpretation of mental and physical (non-)consent. The two conflicting consent models enabled the theoretical space for a cultural hesitancy to believe women's accusations of rape, as the body and mind could seemingly operate independently of one another. The blurriness between physical and mental (non-)consent appears throughout the source material covered in the remaining chapters, and this blurriness allowed for the weaponization of (non-)consent against victim-survivors.[50]

I follow the structure presented in Sara Ahmed's *Willful Subjects*, offering "threads of arguments that are woven together and tied up somewhat loosely" and considering how "echoes and repetitions" of mental and physical (non-)consent reappear in the primary sources.[51] As will be discussed at length in the next chapter, medieval English laws generally defined rape as when a man overpowers a woman with force, leading to her "corruption." In this overview of England's *raptus* laws from *Glanvill* to the Statute of Rapes, I provide close readings of the legal texts to offer new interpretations about the physicality of non-consent in the criminal courts. The next chapter moves from the secular to the sacred and explores ecclesiastical perspectives. Rape was technically the only sexual crime not to be tried in church courts. However, canon texts offer nuanced perspectives of mental non-consent to rape versus the physicality of non-consent which were paramount in the secular criminal courts. This analysis will demonstrate that men of law (secular and ecclesiastic) were highly interested in debating the possibility of mental and physical (non-)consent of rape victims. With the background of legal understandings (both secular and ecclesiastical) around rape and consent,

---

48 Akard and Raw, "Global Response," 363, 365.

49 Phillips, "The Breasts of Virgins," 1.

50 For more on male-authored texts and their use of "weaponized consent" see Akard and Raw, "Global Response," 363–67. Despite modern usage of "survivors" of sexual assault, I use the term "victim" throughout the remainder of the book as it more accurately reflects medieval mentalities towards rape.

51 Ahmed, *Willful Subjects*, 19.

Chapter Three examines new translations of rape cases from the EC. These trial records allow for exploration of the criminal courts' interpretations of relevant laws and demonstrate the existence of a schism between the laws in theory—that is how they were written—and the laws in practice—that is how they were applied in presented cases. Here I offer new, literal translations of the primary sources which may at times appear jarring and unsettling to modern readers, but I aim to reproduce as accurately as possible the meaning of the sources. Such "realistic" interpretation of *raptus* laws, as Gwen Seabourne states,[52] allows scholars to consider the broad applications of the laws and how they reinforce certain tropes not explicitly stated within the prevailing legal doctrine. Even though at times the application of the laws appears to be incongruent with the laws themselves, they were not necessarily seen as incompatible with the legal statutes. The third chapter will demonstrate that the courts continually exploited the lack of physical injury and virginity to question the (non-)consent of the woman and downgrade the offence. This analysis will focus on the language around blood, force, corruption, and virginity within the court records which legitimized the duality of physical and mental (non-)consent within the EC.

Chapter Four provides the crucial analysis of the physicality of (non-) consent as operating independently and, at times, in contradiction of mental non-consent. Here, medical assumptions about conception and the consequences of pregnancy occurring from rape are discussed as providing the scientific framework supporting the legal system. This chapter explores the bodily victimization of both rapists and rape victims, and I consider the relationship between rape, irrationality, and monstrosity. I offer three legal identities that women could have when appealing rape: either the innocent victim (based on physical injuries as proof of non-consent), the reluctant but willing accomplice (mental non-consent but physical consent proven by pregnancy from rape), or the culpable woman (no physical injuries to prove that a crime occurred).

The following two chapters combine MER with the previous analyses of legal and ecclesiastic texts. By looking at how narratives of rape and sexual violence are represented in select romances, these chapters present inferences about medieval English popular opinions and cultural norms surrounding sexual violence. This is a difficult task, in that the "relation of fiction and reality in Middle English romance is notoriously difficult to assess ... romance

52 Seabourne, *Women in the Medieval Common Law*, 6–7.

straddles the actual and the fantastical."[53] However, this task is crucial as romance demonstrates the legal ambiguities of mental and physical (non-) consent and thus offers a platform to consider the larger cultural ideologies of rape and consent. Chapters Five and Six provide close readings and new interpretations of scenes of sexual violence in *Sir Orfeo*, *Amis and Amiloun*, *Sir Degare*, *Sir Gowther*, and *Le Bone Florence of Rome*. These texts were selected for their broad representations of sexual violence, (non-)consent, and rape which enable us to examine how the threat of rape, and the rapeable body,[54] were integral to cultural interpretations of licit or illicit sex. These chapters will demonstrate how popular romances have striking consistencies in their representations of the legal responsibilities of women to resist their own rape, and when they are not able to, the apparatus of legal identities is employed, by way of conception and marriage, to "erase" the rapes.

The final chapter draws these threads of diverse sets of evidence together, to emphasize how medieval English legal, literary, medical, and ecclesiastical sources viewed consent and non-consent to rape based on the belief that the mind and body of both rape victims and rapists could function in contradiction to one another. This ensured a legal and social expectation of resistance to prove non-consent. This chapter also more specifically examines the cultural expectations of masculinity and femininity which allowed for the persistent threat of rape, as discussed above. Finally, this chapter considers the long-lasting impacts of these medieval conceptualizations.

Overall, this research provides new insights into medieval cultural understandings of sexual consent and the duality of mental and physical (non-)consent. This research deconstructs the legal identities of women in the medieval English criminal courts, which continue to be upheld in modern Western courts. By weaving these threads of diverse sources together, I contribute to the conversation about medieval England's rape culture and the cultural ideologies around consent of the flesh which allowed for, or even encouraged, sexual violence against women.

---

53 Saunders, "A Matter of Consent," 105.

54 I use the term "rapeable" based on the framework provided by Andreasen, "'Rapeable' and 'Unrapeable' Women," 102–13.

Chapter I

THE PHYSICALITY OF (NON-)CONSENT

SECULAR *RAPTUS* LAWS

ROSE HERVY WAS a young unmarried woman still living with her father, John, when a local man in the village, Adam de Bassingborn, raped her.[1] Young Rose did not want to notify the authorities; perhaps she was scared or felt guilty for somehow causing her own rape. Either way, Rose didn't want to go to court. Nonetheless, the authorities ordered the indictment of Adam for raping Rose. But Adam was nowhere to be found. So, the judge asked the jurors something along the lines of: "do you think that Rose was a virgin when Adam raped her?" The local men of the community who made up the jury probably heard rumours and scuttlebutt that Rose and Adam were flirtatious with one another. Perhaps the jurors even saw Rose speaking to Adam in the past and thought it looked a little *too* friendly. The jurors told the judge that, with certainty, Rose was not a virgin at the time of the rape, and she even had consensual sex with Adam in the past. The jurors went further, claiming something in the manner of: "Rose and Adam were frequently having sex, everyone knows this." Speculatively, jury deliberations went something like "well, if Rose wasn't a virgin at the time, and if she agreed to have sex with Adam in the past, then this isn't *really* a crime even if she was raped this time around." All charges were dropped.

Rose's case (1285) demonstrates the multiple concerns that the EC took into consideration when distinguishing sex from rape, including past relationships, past consensual sex, and virginal status. The criminal courts cared about consent to coitus, but, as in the cae of Rose, past consensual relationships were used as a legally legitimate excuse to drop an indictment of rape against the accused, like Adam. I use this case to begin this chapter on medieval England's secular *raptus* laws, as it is indicative of the multivalent interpretations of licit and illicit coitus. This chapter covers the "golden age of English common law" and the five ages of medieval England's *raptus* laws beginning with two legal treatises, *Glanvill* and *Bracton*, which are followed by three statutes, Westminster I and II and the Statute of Rapes.[2]

---

1 TNA, JUST1/242 m93d.

2 For more on the periodization see Bellamy, *Crime and Public Order*, 1–2; Dunn, *Stolen Women in Medieval England*, 18–51; Kelly, "Statute of Rapes and Alleged

The primary aim of this chapter is to not only provide the legal understanding necessary for interpretation of romances and cases, but, more importantly to emphasize the legal inferences of mental and physical (non-)consent.

Glanvill

The legal treatise known as *Glanvill* was composed around 1187–1189.[3] According to this text, the two felony appeals that a married woman could make herself were rape (book 14, chap. 6) and the death of her husband (book 14, chap. 3), because both were assumed to cause injury to her body. Concerning the latter appeal, *Glanvill* states *quia una caro sunt vir et uxor* (because husband and wife are one flesh). This is interpreted both as her own flesh and, through the matrimonial rights of a husband and wife, the flesh of her husband. This *una caro*, or "one flesh," of husband and wife both enables women to appeal the murder of their husbands while also prohibiting women from appealing rape by their husbands, as a single flesh cannot rape itself. The emphasis that *Glanvill* places on the flesh of the woman becomes especially problematic for the appeal of the crime of rape. *Glanvill* states:

> In the crime of rape [*Raptus crimen*] a woman charges a man with violating her by force [*viro vi oppressam*] in the peace of the lord king. A woman who suffers [*patitur*] in this way must go, soon after the [crime][4] [*maleficium*] is done, to the nearest vill and there show to trustworthy men [*probis hominibus*] the injury [*iniuriam*] done to her, and any effusion of the blood [*sanguinem si quis fuerit effusus*] there may be and any tearing of her clothes [*vestium scissiones*]. She should then do the same to the reeve of the hundred. Afterwards she should proclaim it publicly in the next county court; and when she has made her complaint, the form of proceeding to judgement shall be stated as above. In such a case a woman is allowed to make an accusation just as in every case of injury done to her body [*iniuria corpori suo illata*]. It should be known that in such a case it is for the accused to choose whether he will submit to the burden of the ordeal, or will rely on disproving the accusation of the woman.

Ravishers of Wives," 361–419; Musson, *Medieval Law in Context*; Post "Ravishment of Women and the Statutes of Westminster," 150–64.

3 I have personally consulted London, British Library (hereafter BL), MS Additional 24066 (ca. 1200) and London, Lincoln's Inn Library (hereafter LI), MS Misc. 3 (ca. 1200–1225) and compared them to Hall's edited and translated text which is derived from these manuscripts. I also viewed London, BL, MS Harley 1119.

4 DMLBS, "maleficium," article 1a.

> Moreover, it should be known that if anyone is convicted in this kind of plea the judgement against him shall be the same as in the crimes discussed earlier. Nor can the wrongdoer escape this by expressing his willingness, after judgement, to marry the [corrupted woman] [*corruptam illam*]. For if he could it would frequently happen as a result of a single defilement [*pollutionis*] that men of servile status [*seruilis conditionis homines*] disgraced [forever] [*perpetuo fedare*[5]] women of good birth, or that men of good birth were disgraced by women of low estate, and thus the fair repute of their families would be [shamefully][6] blackened [*indecenter denigrari*]. But before judgement is given the woman and the accused can be reconciled to each other by marriage, if they have licence from the king or his justices and the [agreement] [*assensu*] of their families.[7]

The initial definition of the crime is when a "woman charges a man with violating her by force," and so there are explicitly gendered roles of the female victim and the male rapist. The use of *raptus* in *Glanvill* seems to only imply forcible coitus and not abduction, as the *maleficium*—the sexual crime—leads to *corruptam*—the damaged sexual purity of the woman. The importance of physical domination of the woman's body, the *viro vi oppressam* (by physical force), is critical to the definition and proof of the crime. Unlike modern interpretations of rape which include the mental non-consent of the victim, *Glanvill* shows that the twelfth-century definition was based on the physical domination of the woman's body as proof of her non-consent. There is the assumption that if the man violates the woman by force, then she will inevitably have physical scars, bruises, bleeding, or torn clothes. Physical force leading to physical bodily injury of the woman is the critical proof which *Glanvill* states the woman needs to show trusted men. As Kim Phillips argues, *Glanvill* is primarily concerned with the injured female body.[8]

The legal requirement of the woman to immediately display her bloody and bruised body to "trustworthy men" ensures that for her to be believed, she must have physical bodily proof of the rape. Despite Barbara Hanawalt's claim that the *effusio* ("effusion of blood") was referring to "the breaking of the hymen,"[9] it is a common phrase used throughout Europe's medieval criminal courts, and, consequently, it must be cautiously regarded as a legal topos, meaning that it did not necessarily relate to virginal blood associated

---

5 DMLBS, "fedare (v. foedare)."

6 DMLBS, "indecenter," article 3b.

7 *Glanvill*, book 14, chap. 6. Translations adapted from Hall.

8 Phillips, "Written on the Body," 140.

9 Hanawalt, "Whose Story Was This?," 126.

with the hymen. While blood was associated with loss of virginity in the Middle Ages, virginity was not solely viewed by an intact hymen.[10] *Glanvill* uses *f[o]edare* to describe the perpetual "disgrace" that men of servile status inflict upon elite women. However, *foedare* is more accurately translated as to "pollute," "corrupt, make impure," or "disfigure, mar the appearance of," and, subsequently, as to "dishonour, [or] shame."[11] Here, rape is considered a crime of sexual pollution, physical injury, and shame. Under *Glanvill*, if a woman acquiesces to the rape in fear of her life and she does not physically try to fight off her attacker, then she has no physical bodily proof of injury done to her. As a result, *Glanvill* leads one to suspect that she could be considered a culpable woman, for she did not physically resist her own rape. The "true victim" of rape, according to this analysis of *Glanvill*, has bruising, bleeding, and torn clothes. Here we see the formation of dualistic legal identities which the laws created for women in rape cases; there is this binary construction of the truly innocent victim (with physical bodily injury) and the blame-worthy, culpable woman (with no physical injury to show as proof of resistance).

Once the woman has shown the *probis hominibus* (good men) her bodily injuries, she then must do it again at the court of the hundred. If she misremembers, the appeal fails (as with all felony appeals, not just rape), and the woman could be accused of false appeal and thus be imprisoned or fined. The retelling of the rape to the hundred must be identical, *idem faciat*, word for word, to the statement given to the trustworthy men, such as the local sheriff or coroner, immediately after the assault. If the retelling at the hundred is identical to the initial appeal, then the woman has the duty to make her accusation public at the next court hearing. This was a huge risk for a woman. In a period when a woman's sexual purity was critical to her marriage prospects, proclaiming sexual defilement publicly in the courts could ruin her marriage potential and the probable income that her marriage would generate for her family. The importance of sexual reputation was brought up specifically in *Glanvill* with regards to the option of concord through marriage. This marriage clause demonstrates that a woman could procure a marriage even though her sexual reputation may have been damaged by the rape. *Glanvill* states that the marriage clause could not be claimed "after judgment." This was a safeguard, according to *Glanvill*, against low-status

---

10 Kelly, *Performing Virginity*, 28–38. For a discussion on the shape and firmness of breasts to determine sexual experience see Phillips, "The Breasts of Virgins," 1–19.

11 DMLBS, "foedare," article 1a, 1b, 2a, 4a.

women accusing high-born men of rape strictly for the purposes of trapping the accused into marriage. *Glanvill* was careful to protect the reputations of noblemen and noblewomen in stating that only "before judgement" could this marriage clause be claimed. Implicitly, but not so subtly, *Glanvill* warns the reader that frequently (*frequenter*) low-status women (*mulieres ignobiles*) would maliciously claim rape by elite men (*generosos homines*) in the hopes of securing a favourable marriage, and low-status men (*seruilis conditionis homines*) would rape high-status women (*generosissimas mulieres*) to trap them into marriage. When rape claims were made between people of vastly different socio-economic classes, *Glanvill* warns that one should be cautious of false and malicious claims for marriage purposes. The inequity of status between defendant and complainant could, according to *Glanvill*, not only ruin the reputation of the individuals involved but also that of their families and kinship group, as through the rape trial "the fair repute of their families would be shamefully blackened." Rape allegations held widespread, communal implications.

The marriage clause, with the consent of the king and the families, could theoretically erase the rape. By reason of *uno caro*—when the husband and wife become one flesh through matrimony—the acceptance of marriage between the female complainant and male defendant turned the crime of rape into a consensual sexual encounter. If the marriage clause was not claimed, then the accused could undergo either a trial by ordeal (which was becoming increasingly less popular throughout the high Middle Ages) or opt for a trial jury. The lack of archival records on jurors' deliberations leaves much speculation as to how jurors reached a verdict. Potentially, disproving the "accusations of the woman" relied on the reputations (sexual, social, economic, and moral among other factors) of both the complainant and the defendant. Speculatively, community policing in terms of the individual's reputation and the assumed believability of the woman was a large factor contributing to the jury's verdict.

The appeal process was to be initiated by the woman herself, not her male kin, for she was the victim of the crime because *alia iniuria corpori suo illata solet audiri*—the "injury [is] done to her body." Rape was considered a physical crime only with no consideration of the mental trauma to the victim.[12] *Glanvill* emphasizes the corporality of the crime by using the word *cor-*

12 Of interest, felony proceedings did consider "intentionality" of the alleged offender, considering their "state of mind" both during and after the crime. See Kamali, *Felony and the Guilty Mind in Medieval England.*

rupta, defined as "the spoiled parts (of the body)" which are "injured."[13] The damaged body belongs to the woman, as *Glanvill* writes *corruptam illam* in the feminine accusative singular. Additional definitions of *corrupta* include the "mutilated" or "marred" body, which underlines the physicality of the *viro vi oppressam*. Alternatively, *corrupta* can be defined as "immoral," which demonstrates the complexity of *raptus* as both a sexual sin and a secular felony. In this reading, the immorality is not the actions of the man, but rather the woman is immoral due to her sexual defilement. We see the binary legal identities of the innocent victim and the culpable woman beginning to form. These legal identities are not necessarily the lived experiences of the female victims. The criminal courts told the women (through verdicts) which "identity" they ought to be: a victim of a crime or guilty of a crime. Such identities are entirely dependent on the physical injuries of the woman, which are visible proof of her non-consent. *Glanvill* implicitly suggests that the truly innocent victim did not consent to the rape, as was evident by the injuries done to her body. On the contrary, *Glanvill* indicates that the blame-worthy woman was scheming and possessed no physical injury to prove her malicious accusations. According to *Glanvill*, it was feared that false accusations of rape were made to trap good honest men into marriage. The lineage of attitudes and assumptions towards rape victims continued from *Glanvill* to *Bracton* and evolved into constructed binary identities of the "true victim" and the "lying woman." This was dependent on the physical proof of (non-) consent.

Bracton[14]

The legal treatise known as *Bracton*, composed within the first half of the thirteenth century, shifts focus to the rape of virgins.[15] This is explicit in the opening discussion of the appeal of rape, as *Bracton* begins with *appellum de raptus virginum*, or "appeal of the rape of virgins." The treatise states the definition of the crime in very similar terms as *Glanvill*: "the rape of virgins [*raptus virginum*] is a certain crime accused by a woman to some man, by whom she says that she has been violently overwhelmed [*violenter oppres-*

13 Lewis and Short, *A Latin Dictionary*, "cor-rumpo."

14 I have personally consulted London, LI, MS Hale 135 and compared it to Harvard Law School's transcription and translation on *Bracton Online*.

15 For contextual information see McSweeney, *Priests of the Law*, 1–3.

sam] against the peace of the lord king."[16] Once again the crime is defined using force, or *violenter*, against the woman, as it was in *Glanvill*. *Opprimere* can be broadly defined as to "overpower," "oppress," or "molest," but when coupled with *virginum* and *violenter*, *oppressam* is more accurately read as "rape."[17] But unlike *Glanvill*, where *raptus* implied forced coitus with any woman, here *raptus* means exclusively the violent rape of virgins.

Next, *Bracton* describes the rational for the punishment of the man who is convicted of raping a virgin: "the loss of members, that there be member for member, for when a virgin is [corrupted] [*corrumpitur*] she loses her member and therefore let her [seducer][18] [*corruptor*] be punished in the parts in which he offended."[19] *Corrumpere* means "to corrupt (morally or doctrinally)," or "to violate" or "harm."[20] However, the contemporaneous late thirteenth-century philosophical text, *De secretis mulierum*, "Secrets of Women," describes "corruption" as either the "emission of the [female] seed," or "a wound in the skin of virginity," suggesting that "corruption" is the loss of virginity, not moral corruption or harm.[21] It is important to note that *Bracton* states the *oppressam* of the virgin leads to her corruption. This perceived corruption could be her loss of virginity and thus deteriorated marriage market value, her *fama*, or her injured body, but either way it is the woman who is "damaged."

Next, *Bracton* suggests the assumed causes of rape by its choice of punishment: "let him thus lose his eyes which gave him sight of the maiden's beauty for which he coveted her. And let him lose as well [his] testicles which excited his hot lust."[22] In taking away the rapist's vision, *Bracton* connects the woman's beauty with the cause of her own rape. The sight of a beautiful young virgin could cause men to become rapists. This is suggestive of the belief that rape is done spontaneously out of passion and lust, and it is not a crime of predetermined violence and domination.[23] As Samantha Katz

---

16 *Bracton*, vol. 2, p. 414, ll. 27–29.

17 DMLBS, "opprimere," articles 4a, 6a, 7a.

18 DMLBS, "corruptor," article 1c.

19 Translation adapted from *Bracton*, vol. 2, p. 414, ll. 29–31.

20 DMLBS, "corrumpere," articles 1a, 2a, 3a.

21 Lemay, *Women's Secrets*, 67.

22 *Bracton*, vol. 2, p. 414–15, ll. 31–34, l. 1: "Oculos igitur amittat propter aspectum decoris quo virginem concupivit. Amittat etiam testiculos qui calorem stupri induxerunt."

23 Harris's analysis of the thoughtful decision-making process to rape within

Seal notes, there is a "simulacrum of consent," in that the woman's beauty instigates the man's seduction and that this all-consuming "male desire, once kindled by female beauty ... cannot be contained."[24] According to *Bracton*, the man's "passion of rape,"[25] or "hot lust" (*calorem stupri*), originates in the male testicles, and consequently, every man was susceptible to this all-consuming desire. This meant that "good" men were assumed to have been able to control this impulsive urge for coitus at the sight of a beautiful woman, as it was weaker, less worthy men who were not able to control their impulses and who would succumb to these urges. From the medieval perspective, this illustrates a distinct socio-economic class division in perceptions about "which type of men" rape. It also demonstrates the belief that a potential rapist's body initiates the desire to rape which could lead to an internal struggle between the mind and body. Depending on the strength of mind to overcome the body's "hot lust," as suggested by *Bracton*, a man will or will not rape.

The punitive loss of testicles and vision was a unique punishment imposed on the rapists of the most vulnerable women, according to *Bracton*, while the forcible rape of all other women received a different punishment. *Bracton* states that all women, even concubines and sex workers, are worthy of legal recourse, but there is most definitely a hierarchy of victimhood:[26]

> Punishment of this kind does not follow in the case of every woman, though she is oppressed by force [*vi opprimatur*], but some other severe punishment does follow, according as she is married or a widow living a respectable life, a nun or a matron, a recognized concubine or a prostitute plying

---

Chaucer's *Reeve's Tale* provides us with another medieval perspective as to why men rape. Yet, even within this text Harris notes that John upholds "the myth that men are incapable of preventing themselves from raping when they are tempted by women's intoxication, revealing clothing, or irresistible beauty," thus reaffirming *Bracton*'s reasoning as to why men rape. The conflicting ideologies, that is *Bracton*'s assumed loss of control and Chaucer's detailed passages of "thought and deliberation," further emphasize the complex (and conflicting) medieval English understandings and ideas about rape victims, rapists, and (non-)consent. See Harris, *Obscene Pedagogies*, 49–50, 54, 59.

24 Seal, "Chasing the Consent of Alice Chaucer," 278.

25 DMLBS, "calor," article 1c; "stuprum," article 1a.

26 In general, common law grouped women together based on several factors beyond martial status, so although it is not surprising to see this type of categorization, it is still worthy of consideration since virginal rape appears to hold a unique place in appeal prosecutions (discussed in Chapter 3). See Seabourne, *Women in the Medieval Common Law*, 12–13.

> her trade without discrimination of person, all of whom the king must protect for the preservation of his peace, though a like punishment will not be imposed for each.[27]

The forcible nature of the crime is restated, and if force was applied in the rape and the victim's socio-economic status and *fama* considered, then an appropriate punishment would be applied. The worthiest victim was the raped virgin, followed by nuns and widows (who must be living a respectable, chaste life), married women (who were sexually honest to their husbands), loyal concubines (who slept with only one man), and, lastly, the necessary sex workers. Although *Bracton* states that some other punishment is prescribed to men convicted of raping these holy or non-virginal women, the treatise does not indulge with any further information as to what the punishment is. Even though *Bracton* allowed all women to be victims of rape, there was a clear hierarchy of those who were considered worthy victims. The rationale for the victimhood hierarchy is simple: *virginitas et castitas restitui non possint*, or "virginity and chastity cannot be restored."[28] Virginity was key to the marriage market; there were real economic implications to the rape of virgins. Once gone, virginity could not be restored. The woman was considered forever changed. She was considered corrupted.

In very similar language and procedure to *Glanvill*, *Bracton* explains how the woman could initiate the appeal process and the prescribed proof she must show:

> When thus a virgin has been corrupted [*virgo sic corrupta*] and oppressed [*oppressa*] against the peace of the lord king, she must go at once and while the deed is newly done, with the hue and cry [*clamore et huthesio*], to the neighbouring townships and there show the injury done to her [*iniuriam sibi illatam*] to men of good repute, the blood and her clothing stained with blood [*sanguinem et vestes suas sanguine tinctas*], and her torn garments [*vestium scissiones*]. And in the same way she ought to go to the reeve of the hundred, the king's serjeant, the coroners and the sheriff.[29]

The process requires that the woman has physical proof of non-consent in almost identical terms to *Glanvill*: physical bodily injury, blood, and bruising as well as physical signs of force and struggle, such as torn and stained garments. The immediacy of the hue and cry is a further legal requirement echoing *Glanvill*. The woman must not waste any time in telling good, trust-

27 *Bracton*, vol. 2, p. 415, ll. 1–6.

28 *Bracton*, vol. 2, p. 415, ll. 8–9.

29 *Bracton*, vol. 2, p. 415, ll. 15–20.

worthy men of her rape or else it is suspicious that she waited to make it known.[30] If a woman had little physical proof of non-consent to the crime, the likelihood of her reporting the rape to all the men (the neighbouring men, the reeve of the hundred, the king's serjeant, the coroner, and the local sheriff) is significantly diminished, as her reputation could suffer immensely if her plea should fail in court, not to mention the threat of imprisonment and amercement from a failed appeal.

It was the duty of the local coroner to inspect the woman's body and record her accusation for *si raptus virginum* (where there is rape of virgins). First, the coroner had to determine *factum recens fuerit*—that the rape occurred recently "by certain indications."[31]The *signa praesumptionem inducant*, or the "signs which lead to presumption" of rape, include if the woman diligently raised the hue and cry immediately after the crime, "or her garments are torn, or if not torn, stained with blood."[32] Here we see the either/or construction of mental and physical non-consent. The immediacy of the hue and cry was verification of mental and verbal non-consent, and the torn and stained clothes were evidence of resistance and thus were used as confirmation of physical non-consent. However, there was still the expectation that the true victim of rape would have physical, bodily proof of their victimization, as *Bracton* states that the woman must "show the injury [*iniuriam*] done to her ... the blood and her clothing stained with blood."[33] So, while acknowledging the possibility (and necessity) of mental and physical non-consent, *Bracton* upholds the paramount importance of physical proof of non-consent to initiate the appeal process. *Bracton* continues with the words of the woman's appeal by then offering a new definition of the crime of *raptus*: "The said B. [perpetrator] came with his force [*cum vi sua*] and wickedly [*nequiter*] and against the king's peace laid with her [*concubuit*][34] and took [*abstulit*] from her, her maidenhood (or 'virginity') [*pucelagium suum sive virginitatem*] and kept her with him for so many nights (and let

30 Raising the hue and cry was not unique to rape cases, as it was included in other English felony laws. The "feminization" of the hue and cry has been noted by scholars as becoming an increasingly womanly activity in the fourteenth century. See Bennett, *Women in the Medieval English Countryside*, 26, 41; Sagui, "The Hue and Cry in Medieval English Towns," 186–87.

31 *Bracton*, vol. 2, p. 344–45, ll. 33–34, ll. 1–3.

32 *Bracton*, vol. 2, p. 345, ll. 3–7: "et ruptum vestimentum, et si non ruptum, sanguine tamen intinctum."

33 *Bracton*, vol. 2, p. 415, ll. 17–19.

34 DMLBS, "concumbere," article 1a.

her thus set out all the facts and the truth)."[35] *Bracton* is now explicitly referring to rape and loss of virginity by the inclusion of the words *concubuit, abstulit,* and *virginitatem. Bracton*'s inclusion of the adverb "wickedly" reinforces the assumed intent of the felony, indicating that this was not a crime of accident or "misadventure."[36] However spontaneous it may be—due to the randomness of seeing beautiful virgins which initiates the "hot lust"—the ultimate choice to rape and abduct the woman was wickedly acted upon.

The use of force (*cum vi*) is once again stated, as the proof of violence must be evident to determine that the woman did not consent to the coitus. It is logical to presume that violence is indicative of resistance and that the application of force is used to overpower the victim. This suggests, according to *Bracton*, that the woman resisted the rape, and the physical injury was proof of her non-consent. This is the most direct definition of rape presented in both *Glanvill* and *Bracton*. The notion of theft—the stealing the maiden's virginity by force—was crucial to the crime. However, *Bracton* also claims that she must have also been held prisoner (*detinuit*) for an extended period after the rape, *per tot noctes* (for so many nights). This is a shift from *Glanvill*'s definition of the crime of *raptus*. Not only does *Bracton* separate the rape of women from the violent rape of virgins, but *raptus* also now includes abduction.

Bracton claims that the man could avoid the woman's appeal entirely under certain "exceptions."[37] The most obvious exception to the charges is *quia adhuc virgo est*—the woman is still a virgin. The female body was once again placed at the centre of the crime, as *Bracton* states: "in that case let the truth be proven by an examination of her body, made by four legal women sworn to tell the truth as to whether she is a virgin or corrupted."[38] *Bracton* clearly states that *corrupta* is the opposite of *virgo*— corruption is the opposite of virginity. This is congruent with the definition of corruption in *De secretis mulierum* previously discussed. Here, corruption is apparently visibly evident to these "legal women who make an oath." *Concubuit* leads to the visible *corruptio* of the woman, and if she is visibly corrupted, she is not a virgin.

35 *Bracton*, vol. 2, p. 416, ll. 4–7.

36 Kamali, *Felony and the Guilty Mind in Medieval England*, 50–59.

37 *Bracton*, vol. 2, p. 416, ll. 13–14.

38 *Bracton*, vol. 2, p. 416, ll. 18–20: "et quo casu probetur veritas per aspectum corporis, et per quatuor legales feminas iuratas de dicenda veritate utrum virgo sit vel corrupta."

The inspection of the woman's body was done by other women, and this was a unique legal-medical scenario where men relied on the testimony of law-abiding women in medieval England's criminal courts. It is not surprising that these "legal women" were most often called on to examine the female body for loss of virginity and "the rupture of young children's genitals."[39] But we do not know exactly what these women inspected. They could have, perhaps, looked for ruptured genitals now associated with the breaking of the hymen, but there were numerous methods to determine virginity at this time, including inspecting "the size of the uterus ... whether it seemed open or constricted" as well as urine tests, fumigation tests, position and firmness of breasts, and "behavioural indicators."[40] *De secretis mulierum* states "On the Signs of Corruption of Virginity" that an enlarged vagina or urine tests with "flowers of a lily" demonstrate this corruption, while "shame, modesty, [and] fear" are "Signs of Chastity."[41] Sara Butler correctly warns that despite the popularity of urine tests, we should not assume their use in *Bracton* because the text does not mention it.[42] However, *Bracton* does not tell us anything about the process of inspecting the alleged rape victim. In a different context, on determining the validity of a pregnancy, *Bracton* states that *legales et discretas mulieres*—these "lawful and discreet women"—examine a woman *per ubera et per ventrem*—"by feeling her breasts and abdomen" to determine if she is pregnant.[43] Whatever it was they inspected, the testimony of these "legal women" determined what happened next: "if they say that she is a virgin [*virginem*], the appellee will depart quit of that appeal and the woman be placed in custody [*femina custodiatur*],"[44] meaning that she would be imprisoned for false appeal. Evidently, the testimony of the *legales feminas* chosen to inspect the body of the alleged rape victim was upheld as absolute law. If, however, the women determined that the maiden was corrupted (*corruptam*) then the all-male jury is tasked with determining whether the accused man was responsible for the corruption.[45] The woman's body, as the physical proof of her corruption, relied on the authority of other women, and it is arguable that this was the only time in criminal

---

39 Kümper, "Learned Men and Skilful Matrons," 108.

40 Kelly, *Performing Virginity*, 1–38; Phillips, "The Breasts of Virgins," 1–19.

41 Lemay, *Women's Secrets*, 127–28.

42 Butler, "More than Mothers," 376.

43 *Bracton*, vol. 2, p. 202, ll. 3–6.

44 *Bracton*, vol. 2, p. 416, ll. 20–22.

45 *Bracton*, vol. 2, p. 416, ll. 22–24.

trials that female testimony held such legal implications and authority in the king's court.

Alternative exceptions available to the accused were to claim that he did indeed corrupt her (*corrupit*); that is, he took her virginity, but *de voluntate sua et non contra voluntatem*—he did so "of her own will and not against her will."[46] The question of the woman's will, or *voluntatem*, is thus central to *Bracton*'s definition of whether a crime of rape occurred. *Voluntas* in the ablative form translates to "voluntarily, freely, of one's own (free) will."[47] This appears to offer a glimpse into what we now consider mental or verbal affirmative consent, in that the individual freely and under no coercive pressure agrees to the coitus. However, this is at odds with the expectation that the woman has proof of resistance through physical bodily injury to get this far in the legal process. The inconsistency— that a woman must have physical proof of non-consent (injury) to obtain a trial, but at the trial the man can state that he acted in accordance with the woman's will which (if freely given) should not result in physical injury—is demonstrating two contradictory consent models in *Bracton*. The treatise acknowledges that a woman can have two different types of (non-)consent: mental consent through her *voluntatem* and physical non-consent through her bodily injury. In turn, physical consent was evident through the absence of bodily injury.

If the defendant pleaded that *voluntatem* was given, then *Bracton* concludes that the woman now accuses the man of rape due to "hatred of another woman whom he has as his concubine, or whom he has married, and at the instigation of one of her kinsmen."[48] The male defendant's claim of the woman's consent clearly held a much higher degree of truth than the accusations of non-consent made by the woman herself. The maliciously false appeal of a woman made to disgrace an honest man out of sexual jealousy and at the provocation of her family is explicitly stated. As a legal treatise with wide circulation, this was devastatingly suspicious of women's accusations of rape. This was not just rhetoric, but rather a legal reality which women faced in the courts.[49] Secular lawmakers were fearful of women's fake rape claims, and when coupled with the belief that women could be nat-

---

46 *Bracton*, vol. 2, p. 416, ll. 26–30.

47 DMLBS, "voluntas," article 1d.

48 *Bracton*, vol. 2, p. 416, ll. 30–32.

49 The case of Isabella de Chadeston (1275) is a prime example of an assumed malicious appeal made by a jealous woman. See TNA, C54/93 m17. Translation available in *Calendar of Close Rolls, Edward I, 1272–1279*, 262.

urally vindictive, simply claiming unfounded rape accusations was a viable avenue for the accused to be acquitted.

In group rape cases,[50] the primary perpetrator of virginal rape ought to "lose their member" and "their abettors suffer severe corporal punishment but without loss of life or members."[51] The only way a convicted rapist of a virgin could be excused from this punishment was if the woman wished to marry the man who raped her. *Bracton* is restating the marriage clause in *Glanvill*: "unless, before judgement rendered, the woman thus corrupted [*femina sic corrupta*] claims him for her husband, for this lies wholly in her discretion, not in that of the man."[52] As in *Glanvill*, the woman has the ability to claim her rapist as her husband and thus legally erase the crime of rape, as there was no punishment prescribed once this marriage clause was claimed. This figurative erasure of rape transformed it into premarital consensual coitus by way of the marriage clause.

If the man convicted of rape could, after judgement, choose to marry the woman, *Bracton* echoes *Glanvill* in warning of the evil that would come: "for if this were in the man's will [*voluntate viri*] this wrongful act [*inconveniens*][53] would follow, namely, that a villein or a common person [*ignobilem*] might bring perpetual shame [*perpetuo foedare*][54] upon a noblewoman [*mulierem nobilem*] and good family by a single act of defilement [*pollutionis*] and take her to wife to the disgrace [*opprobrium*] of her family."[55] The *pollutio* is "defilement caused by physical or moral contamination," which suggests that the woman has been physically or morally "contaminated" or polluted through the act of rape.[56] As stated in the analysis of *Glanvill*, *foedare* implies pollution, corruption, and disfigurement.[57] The connotations of impurity through rape are connected with physical bodily disfigurement which underpin the notion of physical proof of resistance and non-consent. The language used to describe a rape victim as corrupted and contaminated is

50 I have written elsewhere on the difference between "group rape" and "gang rape." See Cooper, "'Let's Bring the Boys In'"; Cooper, "Re-Reading Medieval English Cases of *Raptus*."

51 *Bracton*, vol. 2, p. 415, ll. 10–11.

52 *Bracton*, vol. 2, p. 417, ll. 10–12.

53 DMLBS, "inconueniens," article 2b.

54 DMLBS, "foedare," article 4a.

55 Translation adapted from *Bracton*, vol. 2, p. 417, ll. 12–15.

56 DMLBS, "pollutio," article 2a.

57 DMLBS, "foedare," articles 1a, 1b, 2a.

reinforcing the idea that the victim is the one who should feel shame, for she is the one who is now polluted, disgraced, disfigured, and defiled.

The explicit fear of sexual defilement or pollution of noblewomen by unworthy, lower-class men is once again stated in *Bracton*. The marriage of vastly different social classes was not acceptable in thirteenth-century England, and it imputed a bad reputation not only on the woman but on her entire family. This is an important point: the damaged sexual reputation of the maiden—the young and presumably unmarried daughter of the family—could bring much shame to the entire family group. By including the marriage clause at the sole discretion of the woman, *Bracton* protected noblewomen from rape by opportunistic men seeking social mobility. This implicitly suggests that if men were legally able to choose to marry the women they raped, then rape would be a much more common crime. The narrative logic here is founded on the belief that all men are potential rapists due to their innate "hot lust." *Bracton* even switches the role of nobility in the following lines: if *vir raptor sit nobilis*, a nobleman rapes an *ignobilis* (a peasant woman), the law remains the same, as the choice of marriage always belongs to the woman.

If, however, the woman decides to continue with the punitive mutilation, *Bracton* describes the appeal process of those who were accessories to the crime, with the careful distinction that one man can be culpable of the rape of a virgin—that is "*corruptione*"—but "many men can be accused of lying [*de concubitu*] with her after"[58] her virginity has been stolen. *Corruptio* is the opposite of virginity, thus once the corruption occurs, the other men are guilty of *concubitus* (having laid with her) but not the corruption of her virginal status. *Bracton* then outlines *de appellatis de forcia*, or the appeal of those accessories to the crime of rape:

> The said A. [woman] appeals C. [secondary offender] for that on the same day and the same year etc. on which the aforesaid B [primary offender] [etc.] and at the same hour that the said B. took her maidenhood [*abstulit pucelagium*], the said C. was an accessory [*in forcia*], that is, he held her [*tenuit eam*] while the said B. took her maidenhood [*abstulit ei pucelagium*] (or "he lay [*concubuit*] with her after [*cum ea postquam*] etc." or aided [*axulio*] in some other way). And that he did this wickedly [*nequiter*] and in felony [*in felonia*] she offers to prove [*offert probare*] against him as the court may award. The appellee may here be set free by the county [or convicted] though the principal is convicted.[59]

58 *Bracton*, vol. 2, p. 417, ll. 25–26.

59 *Bracton*, vol. 2, p. 417–18, ll. 33–34, ll. 1–5.

Presumably the proof is the same bodily proof of non-consent required to make the original appeal against the primary offender. *Bracton* is not concerned about the exact nature of how these people aided in the rape but states that their involvement in any way enables the woman to appeal them directly. *Bracton* notes that the construction of appeals requires the primary offender to be listed first, followed by the "accessory" to the crime, and, finally, by the "instigator." *Bracton* claims that all these actors have a part to play in the felony:

> Giving assistance and instigating are (so to speak) the accompaniments of the principal deed and are so conjoined and connected with it that they are not separable ... for the wound, the assistance and the instigation form a single deed: there would be no wound had there been no assistance, and neither wound nor assistance without the instigation.[60]

This is not unique to rape, as the appeal of other felonies distinguish primary culprits and accomplices, but what is of note is how historians thus far have overlooked accomplices in rape appeals.[61] The collective nature of the sexual violence (what I call "group rape") is extremely understudied among *raptus* scholars, but *Bracton* makes it clear that even those who are charged as accessories to the crime are still liable for felony rape.[62]

At this point in the treatise there is an *addicio*, as *Bracton* explains the extent of punitive mutilation in "ancient times":

> by the law of the Romans, the Franks and the English, even his horse shall to his ignominy be put to shame upon its scrotum and its tail, which shall be cut off as close as possible to the buttocks. If he has a dog with him, a greyhound or some other, it shall be put to shame in the same way; if a hawk, let it lose its beak, its claws and its tail.[63]

The mutilation of the animals indicates that they were considered accomplices to the crime, which leads to the assumption that the animals were used to aid in "hunting" the woman.[64] *Bracton*'s description of the blatant

---

60 *Bracton*, vol. 2, p. 392, ll. 11–12, 16–21.

61 The "other men" involved in rape appeals are briefly mentioned in Dunn, *Stolen Women*, 62–63 and Gravdal, *Ravishing Maidens*, 125–26. They are not mentioned in Saunders, *Rape and Ravishment*, nor Robertson and Rose, eds., *Representing Rape*. Harris discusses homosociality in literary depictions of rape in *Obscene Pedagogies*, 26–66.

62 Cooper, "Re-Reading Medieval English Cases of *Raptus*."

63 *Bracton*, vol. 2, p. 418, ll. 15–19.

64 Thank you, Sara Butler, for pointing this out to me.

de-masculinization of the rapist and his animals paints a vivid image of the humiliating and public punishment of men convicted of virginal rape. By taking away the man's genitalia, the rapist was unarmed and his masculinity (and that of his animals) was further degraded. The crime of rape was defined by the physical bodily injury of the woman and the punishment was defined in the physical bodily mutilation of the man (and his horse, dog, or hawk). The anonymous legal commentary *Placita Corone*, composed in 1274–1275, states that a woman married to a convicted rapist may "claim her husband's testicles as her own property" and thus save him from genital mutilation, and instead he would only be blinded.[65] While the urge to rape derives in the testicle's "hot lust," the lust originates from the sight of beautiful women. So, while the rapist's eyes and testicles could betray his inner reason, it was believed that simply blinding the rapist while leaving his testicles intact would ensure that he will never rape again while still being able to perform the conjugal debt owed to his wife.

Bracton further complicates the expectation of physical proof of non-consent, as the so-called ancient laws claimed that even if the woman was a *meretrix* (a sex worker), she was still an equal victim, because *nequitiæ eius reclamando consentire noluit*, "by protesting against his wickedness she refused to consent." *Consentire*, or "to consent, agree, [or] comply"[66] is once again central to *Bracton*'s determination of licit or illicit coitus. The woman's non-consent is evident by her *reclamando*—her crying out in protest.[67] The verbal non-consent, which was understood as as indicative of the woman's mental non-consent, was apparently all that was needed to prove the rape of sex-workers in these "ancient times," and yet *Bracton* states earlier that in thirteenth-century England, women must have bleeding, bruising, and torn or stained clothing. While acknowledging the existence of mental (and verbal) non-consent, *Bracton* stresses the importance of physical proof of non-consent and thus undermines the legitimacy of mental non-consent in medieval England's criminal courts.

Overall, the legal age of *Bracton* generally follows *Glanvill*, wherein there is an emphasis on the physical injuries from the rape. The physical harm (*iniuria et violentia*) done to the woman's body (*corporis sui illata*) is not only justification for her right to appeal rape,[68] but it is the necessary

---

65 Kaye, ed., *Placita Corone*, 9.

66 DMLBS, "consentire," article 1a.

67 DMLBS, "reclamare," articles 1a and 2a.

68 *Bracton*, vol. 2, p. 419, l. 26.

proof to show that rape occurred. Despite the acknowledgment of mental non-consent to rape, *Bracton* reiterates the need for proof of resistance, as suggested in *Glanvill*, which ensures that physical non-consent was legally paramount.

The First Statute of Westminster

Enacted in 1275, the Statute of Westminster I was the first royal statute pertaining to rape and/or abduction, and it was one of King Edward I's first legislative acts. *Glanvill* and *Bracton* were not statutes. The treatises were written commentaries on the laws practiced, and, unlike the statutes, they were not officially approved by the king. Most relevant here is chapter thirteen, "Ravishment of Women," in which the statute states: "And The King prohibits that none do ravish [*ravie*], nor take away by force [*ne prenge a force*], any Maiden [*damoysele*] within Age, neither by her own consent [*gré*] nor without; nor any Wife or Maiden of full age, nor any other Woman, against her Will."[69] The use of *damoysele*, or maiden, is likely referring to an unmarried virgin. The use of force is once again stated in the definition of the crime, as in *Glanvill* and *Bracton*. However, unlike *Glanvill* and *Bracton*, where *raptus* was used to mean forced coitus, *raptus* is more ambiguous under Westminster I.

While the definition of *raptus* under Westminster I was (and still is) a debated point among legal scholars, that is not of concern here.[70] In the first clause of chapter thirteen, there is evidence of the constructed legal identity of a culpable woman, as it states that "the woman may be willing to participate."[71] Previous definitions of *raptus* included *contra voluntatem* (against her will), but here the crime might not be entirely against her will. The fact that the crime still occurred even with the woman's mental and verbal consent shows a shift in the legal understanding of the crime, in that her consent was becoming irrelevant to the courts. J. B. Post argues that this first

---

69 Translation from Luders, ed., "Statute of Westminster the First," in *The Statutes of the Realm*, vol. 1, chap. 13, p. 29.

70 See Cannon, "*Raptus* in the Chaumpaigne Release," 80; Carter, *Rape in Medieval England*, 46; Coke, *The Second Part of the Institutes of the Laws of England*, 180; Dunn, *Stolen Women*, 30; Kelly, "Statute of Rapes and Alleged Ravishers of Wives," 365–66, 383, 390; Pollock and Maitland, *The History of English Law*, vol. 2, pp. 490–91; Post, "Ravishment of Women and the Statutes of Westminster," 150–64; Walker, "Wrongdoing and Compensation," 286.

71 Saunders, "A Matter of Consent," 109.

clause effectively makes the consent of minors irrelevant to the fulfilment of the crime, and, as such, he claims that "this may be the first secular prohibition of coition with a minor."[72] The definition of a minor in medieval England was fluid and differed for boys and girls, ranging from young children to the age of about twelve or fourteen, as suggested by ecclesiastical doctrine. Gwen Seabourne discusses the various considerations of minor age in England's common law, and she notes that there was a debate about the "capacity to endure penetration and capacity to conceive." Referencing the treatise *Fleta*, Seabourne indicates that "below 9 ½ was too young for a girl" to perform marital consummation.[73] This first clause, which prohibits sex with minors regardless of their consent, indicates the fallibility of a "consent only" model to determining "what is pleasurable, healthy sex and what constitutes unhealthy, possibly violative sex."[74] This signals that medieval English laws recognized that consent was not the only thing that mattered when determining licit or illicit coitus, as there could be limitations to one's ability and capacity to give affirmative consent.

The French verb *ravir* (to ravish) is derived from the Latin verb *rapere*, meaning primarily "to seize and carry off." Although different from early medieval interpretations of *raptus*, both *ravie* and *raptus* originate from *rapere*, defined as "to seize and carry off; woman carried off for sexual purpose." However, a third meaning of *rapere* is "to bring to ecstasy," which further emphasizes medieval suspicions of the woman's hidden sexual desires within the very word used to define the sexual assault.[75] That is, a woman may have physical enjoyment from the rape despite her mental trauma and non-consent. The statute claims that the crime of being *ravie* is applicable to a maiden (virgin), wife, damsel of full age (that is, available for marriage, likely older than fourteen), or any other woman who is ravished against her will. These first two clauses ensure that a minor cannot give sexual consent, and when a woman of marriageable age does not give consent, it is still a crime. The importance of "will" and age are crucial to the definition of the crime of *ravie* under Westminster I. Here, there is no indication that this

72 Post, "Ravishment of Women and the Statutes of Westminster," 150.

73 Seabourne, *Women in the Medieval Common Law*, 31n100. Cites *Fleta*, bk. 5, chap. 27. Piercy offers an alternative age for consent stating that it was twelve years old for girls and fourteen years old for boys. See Piercy, *Resistance to Love*, 10.

74 Akard, "Unequal Power and Sexual Consent," 291.

75 DMLBS, "rapere" articles 1a, 1b.

is dependent on physical proof of non-consent, but rather the verbal and mental non-consent—the violated will of the victim—is of primary concern.

The statute continues:

> and if any do, at his Suit that will sue within Forty Days, the King shall do common right; and if none commence his Suit within Forty Days, the King shall sue; and such as be found culpable, shall have Two Years Imprisonment, and after shall fine at the King's Pleasure; and if they have not whereof they shall be punished by longer Imprisonment, according as the Trespass requireth.[76]

If the women did not appeal, the king could still indict. Speculatively, this could show compassion and protection for women who were afraid of the repercussions of appealing. The social stigma of openly claiming to be a survivor of rape and the potential loss of assumed value on the marriage market are just a few of the deterrents (not to mention the psychological trauma of being inspected by the coroner and of bringing a rapist to trial). These factors among others, such as lack of physical injury or a missed menstrual cycle that may lead to suspicion of pregnancy from rape, could all worked to deter women from reporting rapes, as is evident in the lack of rape appeals in coroners' rolls during the fourteenth century.[77] It is in this way that Westminster I can be interpreted as protecting those women who did not want to publicly go to trial, as it still brought them some sort of justice through the king's suit.

The time limit of forty days to appeal was considerably shorter than that for other felonies, such as homicide, which allowed an appeal to be made anytime within the year of the crime. Sir Matthew Hale, a chief justice in the court of the King's Bench in the late seventeenth century, commented that the forty-day rule was a result of the suspicion that if the woman delayed in bringing the appeal forward, "it carries a presumption that her suit is but malicious and feigned."[78] The forty-day rule could also be pragmatic, in the sense that the woman must still show trusted men the physical proof of non-consent (i.e., her physical bodily injuries and any torn or blood-stained clothing). If she waited any longer than forty days, proof of the crime could disappear, as the wounds and bruises might be healed. However, if the woman consented to the *ravie* and wished to marry the accused man, this clause in the statute eclipsed her consent, as the man could still be indicted

76 "Statute of Westminster the First," chap. 13, p. 29.

77 Hanawalt, "Women Before the Law," 182.

78 Hale, *The History of the Pleas of the Crown*, vol. 1, p. 632.

and tried at the king's suit. This effectively made the woman's consent irrelevant if the king's suit proceeded.

The allowance of the king's indictment gave the crown unprecedented legal power to interfere in the marriage clause. Since the legal ages of *Glanvill* and *Bracton*, the use of marriage as a theoretical erasure of rape was a legal option available to women. Westminster I took that away through the king's indictment, which speculatively suggests—as supported by Frederick Pollock and Frederic William Maitland—that "an appeal of rape was not unfrequently the prelude to a marriage."[79] Marriage was used as concord between plaintiffs and defendants, and it could be the result of scheming couples or it could be the tragic ending for women who failed to properly appeal and were left with few other options. There were many reasons cases failed, including vagueness of detail, mixed up dates, if the woman did not remember "the door by which her assailant entered, or which member the rape of her virginity had ruptured," or if a woman was "raped on the road between two named vills [she] had the strict words of the statute cited against her, for failing to specify a single vill."[80] Although there is evidence that some couples used the marriage clause to form their own marriages without parental consent, there is equally evidence of the opposite in the plea rolls. A woman could have been left in the extremely difficult position of having her appeal fail, being fined by the courts, and potentially having to endure a diminished reputation while facing the threat of imprisonment of one year for false appeal, and her only option out was to marry the very man that raped her.

Following Westminster I, Edward I published the Office of the Coroner sometime between 1275 and 1276. Here the duties of the coroner in the appeal of rape are outlined:

> Further, if any be appealed of rape [*raptu*], he must be attached, if the appeal be fresh, and if they see apparent sign of truth [*signum veritatis*] by effusion of blood [*ampnum sanguinolentum*], or an open Cry made [*vel hutesium levatum*]; and such shall be attached by four or six pledges, if they can find them. If the appeal were without cry [*sine hutesio*], or without any manifest sign or token [*sine signo manifesto*], two pledges shall be sufficient.[81]

79 Pollock and Maitland, *The History of the English Law*, 491.

80 Post, "Ravishment of Women and the Statutes of Westminster," 155.

81 Transcription and translation from Kelly, "Statute of Rapes and Alleged Ravishers of Wives," 367. See also Luders, ed., "The Office of the Coroner," in *The Statutes of the Realm*, vol. 1, p. 41.

The physical bodily injury of the woman—the effusion of the blood—is here explicitly connected to the truth that the crime occurred and, in turn, proof of non-consent. Yet the "effusion of blood, *or* an open Cry made" clearly indicates that non-consent was either physical (through bodily injury) *or* verbal and thus mental non-consent (through crying out in protest). The expectation of physical proof of non-consent is following *Glanvill* and *Bracton*, and thus during the legal era of Westminster I, the binary concept of the truly innocent victim (with bodily injury) and the culpable blame-worthy woman (without bodily injury) is once again upheld. Notably, only two pledges were needed if the woman did not make her accusation known right away, if she did not properly raise the hue and cry, or if there were minimal "signs" of truth—that is bodily injury.

Overall, the legal age of Westminster I shows a greater concern for mental non-consent than *Glanvill* and *Bracton*, particularly with minors, and yet the Office of the Coroner indicates that physical bodily proof of non-consent was still legally important. The two consent models were put in opposition to one another: the woman can show either effusion of blood *or* cry out in protest. The binary construction of mental and physical (non-)consent—either this or that, but not both—demonstrates that the mind and body of rape victims can apparently be in conflict.

The Second Statute of Westminster

Westminster I was evidently considered insufficient, as it was quickly replaced by the Statute of Westminster II just ten years later in 1285. Chapter thirty-four of Westminster II, "Judgement of Life and Member for Rape," is of concern here.[82] The statute states, in part:

> [A1] It is provided that if a man from henceforth do ravish [*ravist*] a woman – married, maid, or other – where she did not [agree] [*assentue*], neither before [*ne avaunt*] nor after [*ne apres*], he shall have judgement of life and of member. [A2] And likewise where a man ravisheth [*ravist*] a woman – married lady, damosel, or other – with force [*a force*], although she [agree] after [*assente apres*], he shall have such judgement as before is said, if he be attainted at the king's suit, and there the king shall have the suit.[83]

---

82 For the subsequent discussion, I follow the designation of sections of the statute as suggested by Henry Ansgar Kelly, "Statute of Rapes and Alleged Ravishers of Wives," 367.

83 Transcription and translation from Kelly, "Statute of Rapes and Alleged Ravishers

The first clause defines the victim broadly as any woman, virgin, maiden, or wife. However, the statute's inclusion of her non-consent either before or after the time of the crime is a new addition which works to make the temporality of consent legally important. This enabled the woman to change her mind about her consent. For example, if a woman consented to a fictious abduction but under family pressure she was forced to publicly declare non-consent after the attack, then the man was still criminally liable even though he may have acted under the pretenses that she was a willing participant. This effectively erases the woman's consent to marriage, as indicated in clause A2, as the king could still indict the man and if he were found guilty, he could be punished with the loss of life or member. By disregarding the woman's consent, her male kin could indict, and thus they were, according to Post, "allowed to override her own [wishes], despite her nominal status as victim, and the time-honoured concord by marriage was removed."[84] However, contrary to Post's argument, the marriage clause was not entirely obliterated.

The anonymously authored, late-thirteenth-century legal treatise *Britton* is useful to historians in understanding how people at the time interpreted the new statute. *Britton* explains that in the crime of *rape,* the laws were applicable to any woman *quele qe ele soit pucele ou autre* (whether she be a virgin or not) who experienced violence (*de violence*) on her body.[85] *Britton* repeated that the crime was a felony regardless of "the suit of the woman by appeal of felony, or at our suit."[86] Men convicted of rape were, according to *Britton*, prescribed the same punitive measures as men convicted of homicide: the death penalty. The punishment was applied to all men convicted of rape, according to *Britton*, "whether the woman have [agreed] [*assentue*] after commission of the felony or not, as is contained in our Statutes of Westminster [*nos estatutz de Westmoster*]."[87] The apparent cohesion between the first and second statute is highlighted by the use of the plural *estatutz*, and it was justified by the continued irrelevance of the woman's consent. *Britton* claims that regardless of whether the woman agrees to the rape after the crime, it is still an indictable felony.

---

of Wives," 369. Kelly translates *assentue* as "consent." See also Luders, ed., "The Statute of Westminster Sec.," in *The Statutes of the Realm*,vol. 1, chap. 34, p. 87.

84 Post, "Ravishment of Women and the Statutes of Westminster," 158.

85 *Britton*, vol. 1, bk. 1, chap. 15, p. 55.

86 *Britton*, vol. 1, bk. 1, chap. 15, p. 55.

87 *Britton*, vol. 1, bk. 1, chap. 15, p. 55. Nicholas translated *assentue* as "consent."

The other major legal treatise known as *Fleta*—written in Latin by an anonymous author around 1290 and heavily influenced by *Bracton*—also emphasizes physical violence in stating *de raptu et violentia copori suo illata* (about *raptus* and violence done to her body).[88] Although *raptus* is still ambiguous here, the heavy influence of *Bracton* and the reiteration of only two appeals married women can make strongly indicates that *raptus* is referring to forced coitus. This analysis of *Britton* and *Fleta* allows various assumptions to be made about medieval men in the legal profession and their interpretations of rape and non-consent. Medieval lawmakers and legal professionals were considering the temporality of non-consent and the legal implications of verbal non-consent after the fact, and yet the treatises are still reiterating that rape is a crime of violence on the woman's body. Thus, they are upholding the expectation of physical proof of non-consent. Even if physical non-consent was evident immediately after rape, the possibility of changing mental non-consent to consent sometime after the crime was clearly of concern, and the treatises claim that this unsettledness of when and what type of consent occurred was largely irrelevant to the legal prosecution under Westminster II. The statute imposed capital punishment if the man was convicted at the king's suit, regardless of whether the woman consented before, during, or after the alleged crime.

The Statute of Rapes

Westminster II gradually eroded the legal importance of the woman's (non-) consent in favour of her kin's right to appeal. At the same time, the entire process of appeal was generally in decline in English common law, which came to favour indictments. The legal age of Westminster II lasted nearly one hundred years from 1285 until 1382, when it was replaced by the Statute of Rapes. In this new age, the woman's legal right to appeal her own rape was taken away from her. I Instead, this right was given to her male next of kin—primarily her father or husband. This statute protected the patriarchal wealth of the family by eradicating the marriage clause and legally treating "eloping couples as dead, in order to maintain the integrity of family estates."[89] Unsurprisingly, this piece of royal legislation came to fruition from the petitions of one angry father, Sir Thomas West, whose daughter Eleanor forged her own independent marriage using *raptus*. It is because of

88 *Fleta*, trans. Selden, bk. 1, chap. 35.

89 Post, "Ravishment of Women and the Statutes of Westminster," 160.

this father's wrath that the new legal age of *raptus* emerged, and thus it is a reminder of the importance of the social community to the legal infrastructure of medieval England.

The Statute of Rapes was initiated with a petition made in the summer of 1382 by Sir Thomas West to John of Gaunt, a royal magnate. This petition includes the retelling of the abduction of his daughter, Eleanor, by Nicholas Clifton. This is the first of two petitions made by West, and it reads:

> To the most honourable and dread lord the king of Castile and Leon, duke of Lancaster, Thomas West and Alice his wife humbly pray, that whereas Nicholas Clifton was lately with the retinue of the said Thomas on the last voyage to France and Brittany; and then the said Nicholas was familiar with the said Thomas for some time, until the Sunday after the feast of the translation of Saint Thomas [7 July] last past, on which day he came to the said Alice at her manor of Testwood in the county of Southampton, to ride with the said Alice to a certain place; and upon this the aforesaid Alice, with her son Thomas and her daughter Eleanor and others of their meinie, went towards this same place, by abetment and counsel of the said Nicholas, the said Alice having faith in him; and the said Nicholas led the said Alice to a great wood in the New Forest, where the said Nicholas, who was armed, had several other men at arms and archers by his ordinance and arrangement [*makement*] in ambush with the intention of ravishing [*ravyser*] the said Eleanor; and he went and approached the said ambush, taking them with him, and they made assault upon the said Alice and Eleanor and their meinie with drawn swords, bows and arrows drawn back to the ear, and ravished the said Eleanor, with most evil affray to the said Alice and her company, who thought that the great and treacherous insurrection had been renewed; from which affray the said Alice has taken such illness that it is likely to be the cause of her death; for which they pray remedy.[90]

The petition is focused on the harm done to Alice West, the wife of Sir Thomas, more so than the abduction of his daughter Eleanor. Nicholas Clifton was known to the West family, as he was in the retinue of Thomas West. On August 19, 1382, Thomas received a warrant to arrest Nicholas and his eight accomplices, who were all named, and the goods that were seized during Eleanor's "ravishment" were listed as worth £45.[91] The arrest was based explicitly on the robbery of goods taken, described in the gaol

90 Translation from Post, "Sir Thomas West and the Statute of Rapes 1382," 25–26. I have viewed both the French translation TNA, PRO31/7/109, and the original Latin petition at TNA, Special Collections: Ancient Petitions SC8/147, no. 7347. The French *ravyser* [*ravisseur*] is the basis of the translation for Post. The Latin petition uses *r[apu]er[unt]*.

91 *Calendar of Patent Rolls, Richard II*, vol. 2, p. 197, m. 26d.

delivery roll as *cepit et abduxit* (seized and abducted). Eleanor's name is not mentioned, nor is the term *raptus*.[92] These goods are listed in the *Calendar of Patent Rolls*, and the abduction of Eleanor is mentioned only as an *additio*:

> Commission to Thomas West, Ivo Fitz Waryn, John Daunteseye, Thomas Blount the elder, Thomas Blount the younger and John Butusthron to arrest and deliver to the gaol of Winchester Nicholas Clyfton, Philip Oldefrende, Richard Attefelde, servant of Nicholas Pauncefot, John Hobeldod, Roger Bordeaux of London, tailor, John Kelfeld, John Skypton, Goucelyn, servant of Nicholas Clyfton, and William Parkere, who lately rose in insurrection with a great company at Lynhurst, co. Southampton, assaulted Alice the wife of Thomas West, knight, Thomas their son and Eleanor their daughter, and others, at Mallewod in the New Forest, and robbed them of a horse, value 19*l.*, a saddle, value 60*s.*, a silver-gilt girdle, value 60*s.*, pearls and other precious stones, value 13*l.* 6*s.* 8*d.*, and linen and woollen clothes, value 6*l.* 13*s.* 4*d.*, in addition to which Nicholas Clyfton ravished Eleanor.[93]

Fictitious abductions of wealthy women were not uncommon, as wealthy daughters were rarely given their choice in marital partner, and thus the *raptus* marriage clause was an attractive and legally binding alternative.[94] The Statute of Rapes was passed during the next parliament session, in October of 1382, and although it does not specifically name the case of Eleanor West, scholars believe that it undoubtedly was passed because of her elopement and her father's petition. The statute states:

> Against the Offenders and Ravishers [*malefacores & raptores*] of Ladies, and the Daughters of the Noblemen, and other Women, in every Part of the said Realm, in these Days offending more violently [*violencius*], and much more than they were wont; It is ordained and stablished, That wheresoever and whensoever Ladies, Daughters, and other Women aforesaid be ravished [*rapiant*], and after such Rape [*et post hic raptum*] do consent [*consenserint*] to such Ravishers [*Raptorib3*], that as well the Ravishers [*Raptores*], as they that be ravished [*quam rapte*], and every of them, be from thenceforth disabled, and by the same Deed be unable to have or challenge all Inheritance, Dower, or Joint Feoffment after the Death of their Husbands and Ancestors; and that incontinently in this Case the next of the Blood of those Ravishers [*sanguine eodem Rapienciū*], or of them that be ravished, to whom such Inheritance, Dower, or Joint Feoffment ought to revert, remain, or fall after the Death of the Ravisher [*repientis*], or of her that is so ravished [*rapte*],

92 TNA, JUST3/174 m1d.

93 *CPR, Richard II*, vol. 2, p. 197.

94 Bellamy, *Crime and Public Order*, 58; Pope and McSheffrey, "Ravishment, Legal Narratives, and Chivalric Culture in Fifteenth-Century England," 818–36.

> shall have Title immediately, that is to say, after the Rape [*post raptū*], to enter upon the Ravisher, or her that is ravished [*raptam*], and their Assigns, and Land-Tenants in the same Inheritance, Dower, or Join-Feoffment, and the same to hold in State of Inheritance; and that the Husbands of such Women, if they have Husbands, or if they have no Husbands in Life, that then the Fathers or other next of their Blood, have from henceforth the Suit to pursue, and may sue against the same Offenders and Ravishers [*malefactores & raptores*] in this Behalf, and to have them thereof convict of Life, and of Member, although the same Women after such Rape do consent to the said Ravishers [*mulieres post hujusmodi raptum decis raptoribȝ consenserint de vita & membro convincendi*]. And further it is accorded, That the Defendant in this Case shall not be received to wage Battle, but that the Truth of the Matter be thereof tried by Inquisition of the Country. Saving always to our Lord the King, and to other Lords of the said Realm, all their Escheats of the said Ravishers, if peradventure they be thereof convict.[95]

The statute was applicable to all women by its inclusion of damsels, daughters, and wives. The patriarchal control of women was greatly extended in this statute by effectively taking away women's economic independence and thus making the marriage clause ever more difficult. This was the likely intent and focus of Thomas West's first petition, as it was not the unwilling abduction of Eleanor that was of primary concern, but rather the violation of her guardian—her mother—and her master—her father.[96] The legal ability to bring an appeal forward—which in previous legal ages was exclusively the right of the woman—was now entirely the right of the woman's male kin. The parliament roll states the reason for the new statute in the opening clause, where it claims that many ravishers were not facing judicial punishment of life and member because women "after such Rape [*et post hic raptum*] do consent [*consenserint*]." Shannon McSheffrey and Julia Pope argue that the "sequential nature of the consent" is at the heart of this statute, as the previous Westminster II only allowed for an indictment if the woman consented after the crime, but this new statute granted the right to appeal to male kin if the woman consented after.[97] Suzanne Edwards agrees that the statute was concerned that women would consent after the alleged crime

95 Transcription and translation from Luders, ed., "6 Rich. II, Stat. I," in *The Statutes of the Realm*, vol. 2, chap. 6, p. 27. See Post, "Sir Thomas West and the Statute of Rapes 1382," 26–27.

96 For a detailed discussion of this statute and its implications see Kelly, "Statute of Rapes and Alleged Ravishers of Wives," 361–419.

97 Pope and McSheffrey, "Ravishment, Legal Narratives, and Chivalric Culture in Fifteenth-Century England," 821–24.

and "that the *raptus* itself was the sign of her consent," which "affirms the central importance of consent [and] a mutable feminine will."[98] This statute thus seems to be primarily concerned with mental and verbal (non-)consent.

This did not necessarily help Thomas West, and thus, sometime before the next parliament sat in February of 1383, Thomas made his second petition directly to King Richard II, in which he asked that the statute be applied to his daughter. This second petition states:

> To our most gracious and dread lord the king, and to his lords of this present parliament, we your humble lieges Thomas West and Alice his wife pray, that whereas the said Thomas and Alice, at the last parliament held at Westminster the Monday after Michaelmas last past, showed how Nicholas Clifton, with others, lately made horrible assault upon the said Alice, at Malwood in the New Forest, and feloniously ravished and deflowered [*felonousement ravist et defuissolla*] their daughter Eleanor, and because of their suit a statute was made in the said parliament for punishing severely such rapes [*rapeo fortement*] in time to come: may it please your most gracious and dread lordship that, because this statute and the penalty therein comprised were ordained because of the said felonious rape [*felonius rap*] and at the suit of the said Thomas and Alice, that the said Nicholas and Eleanor be especially included in the said statute, to bear the penalty of the aforesaid statute prompted by themselves [*comensant en lour persones*], as the intent of our lords was thus in parliament, and that they be disabled from having any manner of estate in land or rent as regards Nicholas, and Eleanor if she [assent] at any time, and that her father, or any other of her blood, can have suit to attaint him according to the form of the statute, notwithstanding that the said Eleanor be now covet of the said Nicholas.[99]

Unlike his first petition, which focused almost entirely on the harm done to his wife Alice, Thomas's second petition includes the rape and loss of virginity of his daughter Eleanor. Thomas admits that his daughter may be the wife of Nicholas Clifton, which—perhaps unknown to him—was in fact true. The ambiguity about Eleanor's (non-)consent to the marriage and when the defloration occurred—whether it was during the time of the abduction or part of the consummation of the marriage—was likely intentional. Despite the second petition focusing more on the loss of virginity through the rape and abduction of Eleanor, it was the marriage of his daughter, who may have given her consent to Nicholas, that was of primary concern. The inclusion

98 Edwards, "The Rhetoric of Rape," 11.

99 TNA, Ancient Petitions, SC8/146, no. 7252. Translation from Post, "Sir Thomas West and the Statute of Rapes 1382," 27.

of Eleanor's consent, which can be given "at any time" in her life until she is dead, further ensured that, by the law, Thomas was *himself* the victim. Even if Thomas was not the victim during the time that he wrote the second petition, the inclusion of Eleanor's potential consent at any point in her life ensured that anytime in the future, if and when Eleanor consented, Thomas was the victim of the ravishment. The seizure of the father's property during the abduction, as mentioned in the first petition, was seemingly conflated with the father's ownership over his daughter's virginity and marriage contract.

In May 1384, just over a year after the Statute of Rapes was passed, the Commons debated the harsh penalties of the law and asked for it to be replaced by the less severe punishments in Westminster II. This appeal was refused. The 1382 Statute of Rapes remained in place until the Statute of 31 Henry VI in 1453, which gave women the ability to get out of marriages that they were forced into by their ravishers. The Statute of Rapes was clearly concerned about the apparent fickleness of women's mental (non-)consent while also acknowledging that ravishers are "in these Days offending more violently [*violencius*]."

Concluding Thoughts

The transition from *Glanvill* to *Bracton* to Westminster I and II and, finally, to the Statute of Rapes, was accompanied by a slow erasure of the woman's legal right to appeal her own rape. By the final legal age, the right to appeal was given to her male kin—primarily her father or husband. As I have shown throughout this chapter, there was a clear indication that rape was a physical crime, with the expectation of force and injury written into the laws and treatises. Such physical injury strongly implies the legal expectation of the woman to physically resist the rape in order to prove her non-consent. Despite the importance of bodily injury, the treatises and statutes recognize the potential of verbal and mental (non-)consent through crying out in protest, raising the hue and cry, and consenting after the crime occurred. The duality of the two consent models is routinely emphasized throughout the secular laws—the woman can show bodily injury or cry out—while at the same time there is the expectation that the woman shows physical injury to initiate the appeal process. Eventually, throughout the course of the thirteenth and fourteenth centuries, there is an increasing worry about the variability of a woman's mental (non-)consent, which becomes the primary legal concern. However, this debate was not confined to the secular courts, as the conflicting consent models were of outmost concern to theologians who were debating the duality of mental and physical (non-)consent.

Chapter 2

THE DUALITY OF MENTAL AND PHYSICAL (NON-)CONSENT

ECCLESIASTICAL PERSPECTIVES

AN UNMARRIED WOMAN named Margaret de Lawheie, who lived with her father, William, was expected to go to church regularly.[1] Perhaps she did not particularly enjoy going to church, whether it was because the Latin mass made no sense to her and it was boring, or perhaps because the local deacon creeped her out. Maybe she noticed that Arnald, the deacon, kept staring at her while she was in church. Arnald did notice the unmarried Margaret. He lusted over her, he thought about her, and, one day, he kidnapped and raped her. Margaret told the authorities that Arnald abducted her, kept her in his home, and raped her, but the jury did not believe her. They agreed that Arnald did forcibly abduct Margaret, and he did have sex with her, but the jurors claimed that Margaret and Arnald had a past sexual relationship. Maybe the jurors heard a rumour around town that Margert slept with the deacon a couple of years ago. The jurors agreed that Margert previously had a relationship with Arnald and that she now no longer wanted that relationship. So, the jurors claimed, Arnald took it upon himself to kidnap Margaret and have sex with her, but this was no crime. The all-male jury said that Margaret did not consent to sex with Arnald this time, but because she had consented to sleep with him in the past, this was not *really* rape.

The case of Margaret demonstrates the weaponization of past consensual relationships and the abuse of power by a member of the clergy. Shifting focus from the secular to the sacred, this chapter provides a more holistic understanding of the rape culture that existed in medieval England from the perspective of church doctrine. This includes an analysis of the ecclesiastical debates about the sanctity of rape survivors and the questionable legitimacy of suicide as defence against rape. This chapter further demonstrates the nuanced—and at times contradictory—interpretations of the duality of mental and physical (non-)consent within ecclesiastical texts. Despite discussions about mental non-consent in canon texts, there was an inherent paradox in ecclesiastical debates about women's expected resistance and acceptance of suffering.

1 TNA, JUST1/174 m32d.

While secular courts were developing a systematic form of common law, the ecclesiastical courts were undergoing their own revisions of texts to try and make a unified and comprehensive canon law code. It is no coincidence that the foundational canon law treatise Gratian's *Decretum*, written by 1140, occurred around the same time as *Glanvill*. Although the *Decretum* was not officially confirmed by any pope, it was the accepted authoritative text on medieval canon law and was used in universities. The *Decretum* is divided into three sections. The first is *distinctiones*, regarding elections for ecclesiastical office, while the third section is dedicated to the sacraments. Part two, the *causae*, deals with criminal legal matters of both clerics and the laity. Each *causa* is subdivided into various questions which are further divided into various chapters, or answers. The following analysis explores Gratian's interpretations of *raptus* and how the works of Sts. Jerome and Augustine contributed to complex ecclesiastical perspectives on the possibility of consent of the flesh overpowering mental non-consent of rape victims.

Raptus in Canon Law

In *causa* thirty-six of the *Decretum*, Gratian discusses the various scenarios of rape and abduction leading to marriage, and it is here that he includes the use of *raptus* as meaning both forcible coitus and abduction. In the first question, Gratian asks, "Indeed, Isidore [of Seville] says, in book II of his *Etymologies* c. 33: What is *raptus*."[2] The answer is "*Raptus* is actually, having been said, illicit coitus [*illicitus coitus*], which is called after the verb *corrumpere* [to corrupt]; hence, whoever controls [*potitur*] [a woman] by *raptus* delights in illicit sexual intercourse [*stupro fruitur*]."[3] The emphasis on possession, illicit coitus, and corruption is explicit. Gratian's inclusion of *corrumpendo* is strikingly similar to the inclusion of *corrupta* in *Glanvill* and *Bracton*. To Gratian, *raptus* is primarily a sexual crime which pollutes or corrupts the woman's pure body. However, in the next answer to question one, Gratian delivers another definition of *raptus*:

> Therefore, since she was corrupted [*corrupta*] by illicit coitus [*illicito coitu*], and since she was in this way abducted [*abducta*], that is having been led from the home of [her] father, [and] because no action of her marriage had been [settled] before [the abduction and coitus], it cannot be denied that she should be called *rapta*.[4]

---

2 *Decretum*, C. 36, q. 1, cap. 1, p. 1288. All *Decretum* translations are my own.

3 *Decretum*, C. 36, q. 1, cap. 1, p. 1288.

4 *Decretum*, C. 36, q. 1, cap. 2, pp. 1288–89.

The definition is now stricter. Instead of applying to any woman who endures illicit sexual intercourse, answer two of question one clarifies that it is strictly applied to young maidens who are abducted from their father's homes and suffer rape. The condition that the woman must be abducted from her father's home implies that Gratian's use of *raptus* was under the narrow interpretation of an unmarried daughter. The truly innocent victim is a young daughter who is not yet married or in her husband's home and is, therefore, most likely a virgin seized from her father's house.[5] The crime is both against her and, equally, against her father, as the father is the victim of loss of valuable property through the seizure of his daughter's body and the loss of her virginity for the marriage market. Financial compensation for the lost marital value was made as satisfaction—the so-called "price of chastity" (*precium pudicitiae*)—between an accused rapist and the girl's father.[6]

While the use of violence in the definition of *raptus* is not explicit, the consequence of corruption is. *Corrumpere* is defined as primarily "to destroy, ruin, [or] waste," although, it can also mean "injury."[7] With reference to *raptus*, *corrupta* can indicate someone who is "marred, corrupted," or "mutilated,"[8] and *corrupta* as a neuter plural noun refers to the specific "spoiled parts (of the body)."[9] While the inclusion of violence in the canonical definition of *raptus* may initially seem to be a scholarly interpretation, violence is actually part of the definition of *corrupta*.[10] Since the mutilated or spoiled body parts of the woman imply physical injury, it is reasonable to conclude that such mutilated body parts were a consequence of physical violence. Only if all four of these conditions are met (illicit sex, abduction, violence, and no pre-arranged betrothal) would Gratian then view the crime as *raptus*. Contrary to other crimes of sexual violence, Gratian claims that rape is measured by the visible violence used against the female victim or her legal guardian.[11] This legal necessity of violence was not (unlike in the

5 James Brundage notes that this was not unanimously accepted. See Brundage, "Rape and Seduction in the Medieval Canon Law," 143.

6 *Decretum*, C. 36, q. 2, cap. 8, p. 1291.

7 Lewis and Short, *A Latin Dictionary*, "cor-rump (conrump), rui, ruptum," articles 1, 2; DMLBS, "corrupmere," article 1a: "to harm."

8 Lewis and Short, *A Latin Dictionary*, "cor-rump (conrump), rui, ruptum," articles 1a, 1b.

9 Lewis and Short, *A Latin Dictionary*, "cor-rump (conrump), rui, ruptum," article 2b.

10 Gravdal claims that the Decretum includes four elements for raptus, See Gravdal, *Ravishing Maidens*, 8.

11 *Decretum*, C. 36, q. 1, cap. 2–3, p. 1289.

secular courts) restricted to visible signs of violence and resistance on the woman's body. It also applied to her kin and any violence her family may have endured. This reiterates the familial impact of rape as stated in the secular laws, in that it is not only a violation of the woman's rights, but it is equally a violation of her family—primarily her father's—rights.

If a felon claimed to be a member of the church, then he fell under the "benefit of the clergy," and his case would be heard in the ecclesiastical courts. Gratian states, "if indeed, they are clerics, let them fall from [their] very own positions [in the church]."[12] This clause enables any man accused of *raptus* who is of clerical status exemption from a secular criminal trial. This was a favourable option for the accused, as the punishment for felons in the ecclesiastical courts was relatively soft compared to that of the secular courts. A loss of rank in the church, possible excommunication, penance, and amercement were the primary punitive measures which must have seemed favourable compared to possible (although highly unlikely) mutilation and death under the king's law. If, according to Gratian, he was *vero laici* (in truth a layman), the punishment was excommunication.[13] The church acted as a sanctuary for criminals (not just rapists) who sought to avoid secular criminal trials: "but if he sought refuge in a church with the *rapta* [woman], by the privilege of the church he is deserving of impunity from death."[14] The rapist and/or abductor "had to stay in the church continuously [for] forty days and forty nights," and "villagers guarded the church" to ensure that he did not attempt to flee.[15] Only after the completion of the forty days and nights was the man able to leave without injury, at which point he was forced to leave England. If he did not promptly abjure, he could receive capital punishment.

In canon law, a lack of marital consummation could be grounds for an annulment, and, consequently, marital sex was an important element to a legal marriage. This consummation requirement theoretically enabled the validity of the *raptus* marriage clause, as consummation of the union was already established through the woman's appeal of rape, and the only other ingredient needed for a valid marriage was the freely given consent of the two individuals. This consent would (in theory) overcome the invalidity of marriage made by force in canon law. In 1200, Pope Innocent III explicitly allowed marriage by abduction or after rape if both parties gave voluntary

12 *Decretum*, C. 36, q. 2, cap. 4, p. 1290.

13 *Decretum*, C. 36, q. 2, cap. 4, p. 1290.

14 *Decretum*, C. 36, q. 1, cap. 2, p. 1289.

15 Hanawalt, *Crime and Conflict*, 37.

consent to the marriage, but the woman's consent to marry her rapist could not be obtained by coercion or force. Alternatively, rape could be used to coerce a reluctant bride into matrimony by leveraging her decreased marriage market value. So, despite theologians' insistence on freely given consent to matrimony, rape could be weaponized to obtain coercive consent. Either way, rape was a viable means to secure a valid marriage in canon law. There was, however, a distinction between future and present consent. The intention to marry was simply a betrothal and was easily broken. Alternatively, present consent—said in the present tense (*I thee wed*)—constituted a legally binding marriage, as ordained in the ca.1160 decretals of Pope Alexander III. If a case includes future consent and then coitus resulting in the loss of virginity, the church courts deemed that the marriage was legally valid, and the future consent was transformed into present consent with carnal knowledge. Thus, if a woman agrees to marry a man in the future, and he then rapes her virginity, it is not legally defined as rape in church courts despite the brutality of the crime.

Ecclesiastical consent theory to marriage, in which only the freely given consent of the bride and bridegroom was necessary, conflicted with the necessity of non-consent in appealing rape. Here the issue of temporality is evident. According to Gratian, *raptus* requires non-consent at the time of the crime, but marriage requires consent at the time of the marital vow. Consequently, secular lawmakers were forced to accept scheming women who could claim a fictitious rape and/or abduction (apparently not consenting) and then, as allowed by the law, consent to marry the man after the "crime" was committed. The ecclesiastical demand to a valid marriage—one in which both the bride and bridegroom give free consent and consummate the union—made the fictitious claim of rape and/or abduction a viable avenue to marriage in both the ecclesiastical and the secular courts. Canon law suggests that however troubling the marriage clause in *raptus* may be in the secular world, there was no legal objection to it in the ecclesiastical realm.

In *causa* thirty-six, Gratian introduces the hypothetical scenario of a man who seduces a virginal maiden with gifts, lures her "without her father knowing" into his house where they have intercourse, and subsequently "in public calls [her] wife."[16] Gratian asks in question one whether or not this is still considered *raptus* and, in question two, if the man is able to marry the girl if her father gives his consent? To question one, Gratian states *sit raptus*

16 *Decretum*, C. 36, p. 1288.

(it is *raptus*) because *raptus quoque est illicitus coitus* (for *raptus* is illicit coitus).[17] However, Gratian clarifies the various forms of illicit coitus:

> Therefore, since she was corrupted by illicit coitus [*illicito coitu sit corrupta*], and since she was in this way abducted [*abducta*], that is having been led from the home of [her] father, [and] because no action of her marriage had been [settled] before [the abduction and coitus], it cannot be denied that she should be called *rapta.* But not all [acts of] illicit coitus, nor of every illicit deflowering, is called *raptus. Fornicatio* [fornication] is one thing, *stuprum* another, *adulterium* [adultery] another, *incestus* [incest] another, [and] *raptus* another. §1. *Fornicatio*, seems to be any kind of illicit coitus, that is without [one's] legitimate wife, however it is especially understood [as illicit coitus] of widows, or prostitutes, or concubines. §2. *Stuprum*, however, is especially the illicit deflowering of a virgin [*virginum illicta defloratio*] when it appears both the maiden is corrupted with both of their consent [*utriusque voluntate virgo corrumpitur*] [and there is] no proceeding conjugal agreement, [her] father immediately after learning [about this] is not returning this wrongdoing to his heart... §5. *Raptus* is committed, when a girl is violently [*violenter*] led [*ducitur*] from the house of her father, so that she is corrupted and had [as his] wife [*ut corrupta in uxorem habeatur*], it will be undisputed that if the violence [*vis*] is brought to the girl only, or to the parents only, or to both; this is punished by death. But, if he sought refuge in a church with the woman [*rapta*], by the privilege of the church he is deserving immunity from death.[18]

Here we see the distinction between rape with the use of force and rape through seduction—with gifts and promises—as two distinct sexual acts. *Stuprum* is illicit sex with a virgin, but this is not considered rape because the man and woman agree to the sex. However, it is still viewed as "illicit" because the woman's father did not agree and there was no prearranged marriage betrothal. In this definition of *raptus*, rape must be violent. This echoes the expectation of physical resistance to the rape, in that violence is used to restrain the victim because the victim will apparently not acquiesce. This in turn leads to bodily proof of non-consent. However, Gratian claims that the force used does not necessarily have to be against the woman herself, but it could be against her family and would still be considered *raptus.* This ensures that the woman and her family are both victims. To answer question two, if this is a lawful marriage, Gratian says it is not, for Gratian requires consent to be given before coitus. But in *causa* thirty-six question two, Gratian allows marriage between victim and rapist to occur only if the

17 *Decretum*, C. 36, q. 1 cap. 1, p. 1288.

18 *Decretum*, C. 36, q. 1 cap. 2, pp. 1288–89.

woman consents, her family consents, and the rapist repents to the church and does penance.[19]

Gratian's *Decretum* was the primary source for canon law curriculum in European universities until around 1230, when it was supplemented with the decretals of Pope Gregory IX known collectively as the *Liber extra*.[20] The *Decretals*, or papal letters, quickly became the main source of curriculum once they were published. In the influential *Liber extra*, Gregory IX explicitly made the marriage clause in *raptus* cases legally binding:

> Even though it is said to be a question of rape [*raptus*] when nothing is done about nuptials beforehand, a man should not be called a rapist [*raptor*] who had the woman's assent [*mulieris assensum*] and who betrothed or married her before he knew her sexually [*quam cognoverit*], even though the parents might object and claim that he raped [*rapuisse*] her.[21]

Gregory IX's statement agrees with Gratian's, who stated previously that it cannot be called *raptus* if there was a prearranged betrothal. However, the *Liber extra* makes it much clearer that parental consent is irrelevant to the validity of a marriage. This marriage clause of the ecclesiastical courts—and the church's insistence on present consent as the prelude to a valid marriage—made the secular legal identity of the scheming woman all the more real. The fear of the conniving woman—one who arranges her own marriage through the appeal of *raptus* and is supported by the church's consent theory to marriage—was increasingly problematic to secular lawmakers and male kin throughout the twelfth and thirteenth centuries, as is evident by the continued statutory restrictions. Although the ecclesiastical courts held jurisdiction over the legality of a valid marriage—and the secular courts could not take that away—they could and did contravene it by taking away the woman's inheritance through the Statute of Rapes. Thus, by the late fourteenth century, a woman could obtain her own valid marriage through *raptus*, but the secular courts allowed her male kin to ensure that she was disinherited to protect the patrimony.

Gratian's definition of rape ensures that it excludes the ability to have marital rape, since the conjugal debt requires sexual consent. The marital debt was mentioned by St. Paul in I Corinthians 7:3–4, which states that upon marriage both a husband and wife share a "marital duty" to consent to intercourse. As stated in Genesis 2:24 (and reiterated in legal

---

19 *Decretum*, C. 36, q. 2, cap. 7, p. 1291.

20 Brundage, "The Teaching and Study of Canon Law in the Law Schools," 110–11.

21 Translated by Kelly, "Statute of Rapes and Alleged Ravishers of Wives," 407.

treatises already discussed), upon marital vows and consummation, a man and woman are *duo in carne una* (two in one flesh). Bluntly, in secular and ecclesiastical courts, marital rape was a non-existent crime, as a single flesh could not rape itself. Furthermore, with the conjugal debt owed mutually by both spouses, there should be no refusal of intercourse between a husband and wife. Marriage had an immensely powerful transformative role in medieval English understandings of rape and consensual sex. The marriage clause within *raptus* laws was upheld in ecclesiastical texts as legally binding, transforming rape into consensual sex, and once enacted, rape between husband and wife could legally never occur. Despite Gratian's expectation of physical violence to define *raptus*, the woman's mental consent to choose to marry her rapist led to the legal erasure of the violent crime.

Consent of the Flesh-Mind Debate

The duality of mental and physical (non-)consent was heavily debated in ecclesiastical texts and undoubtedly would have been known by criminal court justices. The idea that the body of a rape victim could operate independently of the mind troubled the secular courts, but canon texts had little issue with the two theories of consent. Indeed, stories of virgin martyrs suggested a separation between the body and mind of the potential rape survivor, and these narratives were extremely powerful didactic tools. Part of the ecclesiastical campaign of controlling sexuality was indoctrination through saints' lives. As a popular literary genre, saints' lives (hagiography) were instrumental in idealizing certain attributes, behaviours, and gender roles which the listening and reading audiences were expected to learn from and imitate in the real world. Hagiography was a powerful tool to normalize virginal purity and venerate women and men who exercised extreme control over their bodies. When written or translated into the vernacular, hagiography had a unique synergistic relationship with social practices, being influenced by the social world and heavily influencing the construction of ideal masculinity and femininity. Female saints were frequently threatened with rape and sexual violence, and these narratives describe the physical sexual violence in more graphic detail than we find in secular romance or legal trial documents. According to ecclesiastical doctrine and traditional church rhetoric, the female body was the locus of sexual temptation. As all women were deemed the descendants of Eve, the female body needed to be controlled, and the church played a vital role in this social, community-based policing of female sexuality.

The medieval religious experience was heavily influenced by age and gender. The female life cycle shaped the expected behaviour of women, as maidens, wives, and mothers were given different role models to praise. The Virgin Mary—as the holy mother—and St. Margaret—as the patron saint of childbirth—primarily targeted women who entered marriage. Young maidens not yet married were targeted with the hagiographic tales of virgin martyrs, such as Sts. Lucy, Cecilia, and Katherine. Hagiography was extremely popular in the high Middle Ages, influencing not only the spiritual realm but also legal texts, as St. Lucy is referenced in Gratian's *Decretum* and thus directly guiding ecclesiastic legal thought. Archbishop of Genoa, Jacobus de Voragine, composed his *Golden Legend* around the 1260s and there are nearly a thousand extant copies "of the Latin text alone," and "another five hundred or so" manuscripts in vernacular translations all over Europe.[22] The popularity of saints' lives in England is evident by the fact that over two-hundred years after Jacobus's text was written, it was printed in English by William Caxton in 1483. The longevity of popularity of Jacobus's *Golden Legend* in England provides historians with the opportunity to explore the polarity of mental and physical non-consent of virgin martyrs. Jacobus tended to elaborate on the gruesome details of torture and titillation from his earlier source material, suggesting a fascination with the horrors of martyrdom to contemporaneous audiences.

Jacobus uses the same language to describe St. Lucy as the secular legal texts describe rape—that is she "possessed the beauty of virginity without trace of corruption."[23] Once again, virginity is in opposition to corruption. Lucy dedicated herself to God, and, according to Jacobus, her betrothed was furious about her rejection and declared to the consul Paschasius that she was a Christian. Under interrogation, Lucy refused to submit to idol worship, and Paschasius claimed that she "talk[s] like a whore." According to the *Legend*, Lucy refuted this insult by claiming that she "never have had anything to do with any seducers of the body or of the mind." According to Jacobus, speaking as Lucy, the seduction of the mind is any temptation away from the Christian God, whereas the seduction of the body "are those who would have us put the pleasure of the flesh ahead of eternal joys."[24] The language here is verbatim to medical texts, such as by William of Conches,[25] in

22 Duffy, "Introduction," xii.

23 *The Golden Legend*, 27.

24 *The Golden Legend*, 27–28.

25 Discussed at length in Chapter 4.

which the pleasure of the flesh leads to corruption. Paschasius proposes to take Lucy to a brothel, so that her "body will be defiled and [she] will lose the Holy Spirit." In Jacobus's *Golden Legend*, Lucy defiantly replies:

> The body is not defiled ... unless the mind consents. If you have me ravished against my will, my chastity will be doubled and the crown will be mine. You will never be able to force my will. As for my body, here it is, ready for every torture. What are you waiting for?[26]

Lucy explicitly states that her body cannot be truly corrupted or defiled so long as she maintains mental non-consent to the attack. Her mental non-consent throughout any rape ensures her chastity of the mind and soul. Paschasius then "invite[s] a crowd to take their pleasure" with Lucy, thus inviting a group rape "until she is dead." However, when a group of men try to carry Lucy off, she could not be moved due to Holy intervention. After urinating on Lucy and pouring boiling oil over her, she eventually has her throat slit.[27]

This hagiographic narrative invites several nuanced considerations about rape and consent that are seemingly absent from secular sources. This rendition of Lucy's life clearly states that "the body is not defiled" so long as there is mental non-consent. The bodily "corruption" is thus not applicable to the mentally steadfast maiden, despite any rape that may occur. The judicial application of group rape as an acceptable punishment for a defiant Christian who upset a betrothed suitor is striking. Lucy's bodily autonomy leads not only to her death but to her authorized group rape. Of course, the group rape never happens, as Lucy dies a virgin martyr, but we should read past the rhetoric and read the violence back into the text. In this re-reading, the judicial application of group rape as a punitive measure is like war tactics as expressed by Augustine of Hippo (discussed below), in that the victors of war may justly be entitled to rape the women of the newly conquered lands.

This analysis of Jacobus's *Legend* of Saint Lucy may seem purely theoretical, but even Gratian references the virgin martyr in his *Decretum*. In *causa* thirty-two, question five, on loss of innocence, he states:

> That purity [*pudicitia*] is not able to be taken by violence [*violenter*] is proven by many authorities. For it is a virtue of the soul [*virtus animi*], which cannot suffer violence [*violentiam non sentit*]. For force [*vis*] can be inflicted upon the body [*corpori*] but cannot be inflicted upon the soul [*non*

26 *The Golden Legend*, 28.

27 *The Golden Legend*, 29.

animo]. Therefore, even if the body is corrupted by violence [*corpus violenter corrumpatur*], if chastity of the mind [*pudicitia mentis*] is kept intact then one's chastity is doubled [*castitas duplicatur*]. Thus St. Lucy is reported to have said to Paschasius, "if you cause me to be violated [*violari*] against my will [*invitam*], my chastity [*castitas*] will be doubled, and you will bring me closer to salvation [the crown of a martyr]. For God judges my thoughts and intentions [*sensibus et voluntatibus*]."

Hence, Ambrose writes in book 5 *On Virgins*:

C. 1. Virginity of the soul [*virginitas mentis*] is better than virginity of the flesh [*quam carnis*].

It is more tolerable to have a virgin mind [*mentem virginem*] than a virgin flesh [*quam carnem*]. Both mental and physical virginity are good, if possible; if it is not possible, if we cannot be chaste [*casti*] unto man, let us at least be chaste unto God. §1. A virgin [*virgo*] can be prostituted [*prostitui*], but she cannot be an adulteress [*adulterari*]. Wherever there is a virgin of God, there is a temple of God. Indeed, brothels [*lupanaria*] do not bring chastity into disrepute, but chastity in a place removes all disgrace [*infamiam*].

C. 2. Flesh [*caro*] cannot be corrupted [*non corrumpitur*] by a mind [*mente*] that is not corrupted [*incorrupta*]. The same authority [Ambrose, speaking about] fallen virgins:

In reality, the flesh [*caro*] cannot be corrupted [*corrumpi*] unless the mind [*mens*] is corrupted [*corrupta*] first.

C. 3. A stranger's lust [*aliena libido*] pollutes [*polluit*] no one. Augustine, in City of God [book 1, chapter 18]:

Is she afraid that foreign lust [*aliena libido*] can pollute [*polluat*] someone? Lust will not pollute [*non polluet*], if it is another's lust, if however it pollutes, it is not another's [*non aliena*] lust. But because purity [*pudicitia*] is a virtue of the soul [*virtus animi*], and it has that power as a companion, by which it might choose to tolerate a given evil rather than to consent [*consentire*] to evil, moreover because no one who is noble in spirit and chaste has it in their power what may become of their flesh [*carne*], but only that she might assent with her mind [*annuat mente*] or refuse [*vel rennuat*]: I ask you, who in their right mind would think that they would be losing their purity [*pudicitiam*], if a desire [*libido*] that is not their own [*non sua*] is being exercised [*exerceatur*] and fulfilled with their restrained [*apprehensa*] or overwhelmed flesh [*oppressa carne*]?

C. 4. The same authority [Augustine, speaking on:]

When an intention of the soul endures, by which the body [*corpus*] has also merited sanctification, the violence [*violentia*] of another's lust [*libidinis alienae*] does not take away the sanctity of the body itself [*ipsi corpori*], which the steadfastness [*perseverantia*] of one's self-restraint [*continentia*]

> preserves. Can it truly be the case, if a given woman whose mind has been corrupted [*mente corrupta*] and who has violated the vow that she gave to God, is going to her seducer [deceptorem] to be violated [*vicianda*], that we still call her holy with respect to her body [*corpore*] as she is going, when that sanctity of her soul, by which her body is sanctified, has been lost and destroyed? Let us dispense with this error and instead keep in mind that the sanctity of the body is lost even though the body itself remains untouched [*intacto*]. The same authority: §1. They will hold Lucretia, a noble and old Roman matron, up with great praises of purity. When in his lust, the violent son of the king Tarquinius had conquered her body, she exposed the crime of that most wicked young man to her husband Collatinus, and to her uncle Brutus, two most brave and illustrious men, and she bound them [by oath] to avenge her. Afterwards, disgusted [*aegra*] by the foul thing [*foedi*] that was done to her and not able to bear it [*inpatiens*], she killed herself. What are we saying? Is she an adulteress, or should she be declared chaste? This is not a hard question. A certain man speaking well and truthfully therefore said: "it is a marvel; there were two, and only one committed adultery." Well said and most truly. For seeing in the mixing [*conmixtione*] of those two bodies, the most polluted desire [*inquinatissimam cupiditatem*] of the one and the chastest will [*castissimam voluntatem*] of the other, and understanding that it was not a matter of two bodies being joined, but two minds disagreeing [*animorum diversitate*]: "There were two," he said, "and only one committed adultery."
>
> **C. 14**. Those who have been oppressed [*opprimuntur*] should not dare to compare themselves to uncorrupted [*incontaminatis*] virgins.
>
> Those handmaids [*famulae*] of God, who by barbaric oppression [*oppressione barbarica*] have lost the integrity of their modesty, will be more praiseworthy for their humility [*humilitate*] and shame [*verecundia*], if they dare not compare themselves to undefiled [*incontaminatis*] virgins [*virginibus*]. For although all sin is begotten from the will, and an unwilling mind [*mens invita*] might not be polluted [*pollui*] by the corruption of the flesh [*corruptione carnis*], nevertheless it will be less to their detriment if they should grieve that they have lost even in the body that which they might not have lost in their soul.[28]

This *causa* remarkably demonstrates a medieval distinction between consent of the flesh and consent of the mind. Maidens who survive rape but lose their virginity are still considered pure if they never mentally consented to the rape. Referencing St. Lucy enshrined in canon law that spiritual salvation was available to women who modelled their behaviour on the virgin

---

28 *Decretum*, C. 32, q. 5, cap. 1–4, 14, pp. 1132–33, 1136. Thank you, Jonathan Brent, for helping me with this translation.

martyrs. Through their suffering, women were able to emulate the martyrs in that they too endured violence, but they did not mentally consent and give into the sexual temptation. Although these hypothetical women are considered forever changed and not virginal, they retain, through their suffering, a martyr-like religious status. This mental non-consent to rape allowed medieval women to still be considered victims and worthy of eternal salvation, even if they endured sexual defilement. The survivors of rape are acknowledged in Gratian's *Decretum* as still worthy of God's love. The distinction between bodily and mental consent—as well as the explicit reference to St. Lucy—worked to provide an avenue to sanctity through rape and sexual assault. If suffering rape was an imitation of the virgin martyrs (as Gratian claims), then enduring rape was a means for women to achieve an elevated level of holiness. To achieve this special spiritual praise, the woman must never mentally consent to the rape in order to preserve her innocence of the mind.

Gratian clearly explains that women who survive rape occupy a privileged position of moral superiority. Other notable theologians, such as Thomas Aquinas, also supported this idea that rape was an avenue to spirituality. As Suzanne Edwards argues, this notion of moral elevation through surviving rape is contrary to hagiography where female saints are willing to sacrifice their life to escape rape.[29] That is to say that death is a more attractive option than enduring rape in saints' lives. The logic provided in the hagiography of virgin martyrs, such as St. Lucy, suggests that it is better to be martyred than it is to be raped. According to Edwards, this allows for the space in which rape survivors have endured something that is even more holy than death itself.[30] By losing one's virginity through rape, the woman has endured an event that even the female saints viewed as too great of a sacrifice to make. This was all dependent on the chastity of the mind being preserved, which required that the woman did not mentally consent at any time. However, theologians were hesitant to believe women who claimed mental non-consent, as they thought the weakness of the flesh could overpower the mental non-consent.[31] This binary distinction between the body and mind of rape victims is reminiscent of *Bracton*'s belief that rapists lose control of their rational mind through unrestrained "hot lust," and it is identical to secular lawmakers who also argued that the reluctant but willing

29 Edwards, *The Afterlives of Rape*.

30 Edwards, *The Afterlives of Rape*, 21–23.

31 Edwards, *The Afterlives of Rape*, 25.

accomplice to her own rape was a victim not of her rapist but of the desires of her own body.[32]

Putting that aside, sanctity through rape was further troubled with the mental non-consent of the woman. Although her mental chastity was deemed crucial to Gratian, there was the opposite effect to canonists who viewed the mental non-consent as a reluctance of the woman to endure her suffering. Virgin martyrs endure their suffering willingly and, consequently, a woman who is raped and does not willingly endure it cannot be a martyr, as a true martyr consents to their suffering for the sake of faith.[33] Effectively, a woman cannot accept her rape and consent mentally (to ensure sanctity) because then she loses the chastity of the mind which is so critical to Thomas Aquinas and Gratian, among others. As Edwards notes, this is a no-win situation: if she consents, she is not of pure mind, and if she does not consent, she did not willingly accept her suffering.[34] Despite the paradoxical accounts of rape and divinity, hagiographical texts of threatened rape allow for the figurative space of rape leading to virtue, not shame. The importance here is the repeated emphasis in canon texts—whether through the *Decretum* or *Golden Legend*—that the rape victim's body and mind could act in opposition to one another. The repeated distinction between the bodily consent of the flesh and the mental (non-)consent of the woman clearly demonstrates that medieval scholars were concerned about the consequences of the duality of mental and physical (non-)consent of rape victims.

The cults of the virgin martyrs were intentionally used to appeal to young girls, instilling sexual purity and promoting the ideal virginal state. The young virginal maidens are continually described in sexualized language, but the explicit sexual act—rape—never occurs. The literate and non-literate audience members of female saints' lives were bombarded with not only literary texts of virgin martyrs but also images "on rood screens, stained glass windows, books and paintings," which Kim Phillips states would have inevitably "had a deep effect on their imaginations and perceptions of femininity."[35] It is important to note that saints' lives had a broad impact on social culture, as they were read aloud in church to listening audiences of diverse socio-economic backgrounds. Thus, these texts would pre-

32 For a discussion on *Bracton* see Chapter 1. For a discussion on the reluctant but willing accomplice, see Chapter 4.

33 Edwards, *The Afterlives of Rape*, 28–30.

34 Edwards, *The Afterlives of Rape*, 28.

35 Phillips, "Desiring Virgins," 55.

sumably have been well known to many diverse women and girls as well as lawyers, judges, and jurors working within the king's courts.

What might readers take from these stories? Saints who denied the sexual advances of wicked men and died in defence of their virginity were offering audience members narratives of women's resilience and Christ-like determination. The extremely graphic and sexualized violence against virgin martyrs demonstrate to the audiences of women and girls that death is confirmation of resistance and ultimate bodily autonomy.[36] While hagiography theoretically allowed maidens to choose chastity over marriage, the narratives also demonstrate the very real dangers in asserting bodily autonomy against the desires of men, which could result in extreme violence and death. As part of a cultural tolerance of sexual violence, a woman's refusal of sex is used as justification for male violence.[37] Through their emulation of the virgin martyrs, women were integral in producing the cultural gender norms of femininity as much as men were in producing these texts to begin with. Women were not all passive participants in the patriarchy, but some supported, upheld, and even contributed to it.

The fifth-century teachings of St. Jerome explain how women's virginity was in constant danger of corruption. Jerome warns: "if you walk laden with gold, you must beware of a robber," and "although God can do all things, He cannot raise up a virgin after she has fallen ... He has no power to crown one who has been corrupted."[38] The use of "corruption" is identical to the secular laws and treatises previously discussed, and the multivalent definitions of corruption allow for the secular and sacred interpretations of defilement, pollution, violation, and harm. From the Late Roman period, ecclesiastical authorities warned women that virginity is both the ideal feminine state but also a state that invites sexual corruption and thus one's virginity is something to physically defend. If women cannot properly defend their saintly virginity, Jerome warns them that "it would have been better to have submitted to marriage with a man ... than to fall into the depths of hell while striving to attain the heights [of saints]."[39] The negative attitude towards marriage as the least evil of sexual sins if one must have sex was popular throughout the

36 For a discussion on Middle English hagiography, see Innes-Parker, "Sexual Violence and the Female Reader," 208–14.

37 For more on this concept see Harris, *Obscene Pedagogies*, 135.

38 Schulenburg, "The Heroics of Virginity," 32–33. Schulenburg makes reference to Jerome, *The Letters of St. Jerome*, trans. Charles Christoper Mierow, 135, 138.

39 Schulenburg, "The Heroics of Virginity," 33. Schulenburg makes reference to Jerome, *The Letters of St Jerome*, 138–39.

medieval period and reinforced in secular romance, as virginal maidens save their pure bodies for their husbands. The writings of Jerome—among other so-called Church Fathers—laid the foundation for the later medieval *raptus* laws, in that virginity was worthy of physical protection. In part, this is evident in the harsher punishments for virginal rape as well as the legal expectation that women should defend themselves aggressively against their own rape. The legal expectation of resistance to prove physical non-consent in the secular courts and the conflicting recognition of the possibility of mental non-consent is, therefore, not confined to the secular world, but rather it is reinforced and support by church rhetoric.

The close connection between ecclesiastical doctrine and *raptus* laws is further evident in church teachings of sacrificial mutilation to protect one's chastity and the legal expectation of physical bodily proof of resistance to rape in secular criminal courts. Stories of nuns mutilating their faces to protect their virginity from enemy soldiers appear in chronicles as an unfortunate consequence of war.[40] Here it is important to heed Brenda Silver and Lynn Higgins' call to re-read the rape as rape within narratives, especially in saints' lives, where it is too often displaced in favour of some greater moral truth, such as the religious oppression of Christians. Early Church Fathers once again helped in laying this foundation, as Jerome wrote in his *Commentary on Jonah*: "it is not lawful to commit suicide except when one's chastity is jeopardized."[41] According to Jerome, if a woman cannot maintain physical and mental non-consent, then it is best if she just kills herself. Suicide in defence of virginity was further supported by Ambrose of Milan in his writing *Concerning Virgins*[42] and Augustine of Hippo in *City of God.*

Augustine's *City of God* blurs the distinction between the rape, abduction, and marriage of the Sabine women by the Romans. By referring to *de raptu Sabinarum*, Augustine initially states that "without the consent of [the

---

40 Saunders, *Rape and Ravishment*, 139–41. Saunders makes reference to Roger of Wendover's *Chronica, sive Flores Historiarum*, which recounts the self-mutilation of the nuns of Collingham. See also Wolfthal, *Images of Rape*, 62–75.

41 Schulenburg, "The Heroics of Virginity," 34. Schulenburg makes reference to St. Jerome, *Commentariorum in Jonam Prophetam Liber Unus*, P. L. 25: 1129: "Unde et in persecutionibus non licet propria perire manu, absque eo ubi castitas periclitatur." Available at The Catholic Library Project, "Jerome, *Commentariorum in Jonam Prophetam Liber Unus*," bk. 1, vers. 12. See also Jerome's discussion on suicide in defence of virginity in *Against Jovinianus*, bk 1, chap. 41.

42 Schulenburg, "The Heroics of Virginity," 34. Schulenburg makes reference to St. Ambrose, *Concerning Virgins in St. Ambrose*, eds. Philip Schaff and Henry Wace, chap. 7, pp. 386–87.

women's] parents, but with force [the Sabine women] [are] taken away."[43] Augustine then leaves the figurative space for a just war when "in that case Mars might have helped his son in a struggle to avenge with arms the wrong done to him when alliance in marriage was refused, and to attain in this way the women that he had chosen."[44] Augustine even suggests that, in war, the booty rightfully belonging to the victors can include the women of the conquered land.[45] Furthermore, Augustine discusses the difficulties of proving mental non-consent to rape when, perhaps unwillingly, the woman's body may enjoy the rape:

> But not only what concerns pain [*dolorem*], but also lust [*libidinem*] that can be inflicted on another's body [by force], whatever that deed might have been, although it does not thrust out modesty [*pudicitiam non excutit*] that is to be retained through the most steadfast mind, but [it] thrusts in shame [*incutit pudorem*], shame for fear that [it was done with the will [*voluntate*] of the mind] [*mentis*], which perhaps could not have taken place without some carnal pleasure [*carnis voluptate*].[46]

Augustine implies that most rape victims will feel shame because they will have some physical pleasure from the assault. Yet Augustine is explicit in stating that *si autem animi bonum est* (if, however, goodness is of the soul), then *etiam oppresso corpore non amittitur* (it is not lost even by the oppressed body).[47] This *animi bonum*, good of the soul, appears in opposition to *pudorem*, the shame from the physical pleasure. Augustine concludes that through rape women can become more holy only if their mental state is non-consenting: "nor does the violent lust of another take away the purity of the very body [which] is maintained by the steadfastness of restraining one's passions and desires"[48]

Augustine's writing was extremely controversial to later lawmakers, because in the criminal courts the bodily (non-)consent was considered paramount. Even if the mind did not consent, the woman was still culpable.

---

43 Augustine, *City of God*, bk. 2, chap. 17, pp. 196–97. Translation my own.

44 Augustine, *City of God*, bk. 2, chap. 17, pp. 198–99. Translation by McCracken.

45 Augustine, *City of God*, bk. 2, chap. 17, pp. 198–99: "Aliquo enim fortasse iure bello iniuste negatas iuste victor auferret." Translated by McCracken: "For perhaps some law of war might have justified in taking away women who had been unjustly refused."

46 Augustine, *City of God*, bk. 1, chap. 16, pp. 76–77.

47 Augustine, *City of God*, bk. 1, chap. 18, pp. 80–81.

48 Augustine, *City of God*, bk. 1, chap. 18, pp. 80–81.

Here, however, Augustine was expressing a sort of sympathy for women raped of their virginity and allowing them entrance into the heavenly kingdom so long as they maintained mental non-consent to the rape. Augustine describes the constructed legal identity of the reluctant-but-willing accomplice, for whom the physical pleasure derived from the rape could lead to consent even though they may have initially resisted. This dogma had devastating consequences in the legal trials of rape appeals, where men of law who knew the church teachings viewed women suspiciously as lustful creatures who may have physically enjoyed their rape despite their mental non-consent. Put simply, Augustine demonstrates the belief that there is a duality of mental and physical (non-)consent in rape victims, but the mental non-consent is unknowable to anyone other than the woman herself and the divine.[49]

Concluding Thoughts

Theological debates about the sanctity or elevated holiness of rape survivors provides a nuanced interpretation of the differences between mental and physical (non-)consent which is only hinted at in the secular *raptus* laws. However, this theoretical debate had little impact on the church courts' interpretations of sexual crimes against women, as mental consent was necessary for willingly enduring one's suffering, but the same mental consent also equated corruption of the chastity of the mind. The no-win situation for rape survivors in church courts and doctrine is indicative of medieval England's conflicting societal attitudes towards rape survivors in general. Hagiographic texts, biblical stories, conduct literature, and canon law codes ensured that even though women may be threatened with sexual violence, they were expected to resist while remaining passive and subordinate. The conflicting expectations entangled women in difficult positions, as they brought suits of sexual violence forward. The church's views on women as descendants of Eve ensured that women claiming rape were potentially distrusted as being seductresses. This suggests that medieval English culture retained a distrust of women's rape accusations. In trying to rationalize the thought of women as inherently sexual—due to their anatomy and supported by church doctrine—canonists struggled with the concept of women being victims of sexual crimes. As Ellen Rooney claims, "if all femi-

---

49 This is tied to discussions around the rape of Lucretia. See Piercy, *Resistance to Love*, 12; Schwebel, "Chaucer and the Fantasy of Retroactive Consent," 389.

nine behaviour can be read as seductive, women cannot avoid complicity."[50] Despite this hesitancy to believe rape survivors, some prominent members of the church believed that a woman's mind and body could be in conflict during rape. The contradictory consent models were not confined to canon texts, rather permeating the sacred and secular realms.

50 Rooney, "Criticism and the Subject of Sexual Violence," 1275.

Chapter 3

LAWS IN PRACTICE

THE EYRE COURTS

YOUNG MARGERY LE FEVER was living with her father, Peter, and enjoyed a rather uneventful, even if boring, childhood.[1] However, on the day, Margery was at Alice Marbarne's house, when two men—Thomas de la Forde and Richard, son of Benedict—saw her alone and took this opportunity to rape young Margery, one after the other. Thomas raped Margery first. This was little Margery's first sexual experience. After the assault, Margery alerted the authorities and demanded her day in court. Ten years later, the day finally came. Young Margery described the force that Thomas used to rape her and how he caused her to bleed. The twelve male jurors, all of whom were from the same community as Thomas and Margery, agreed that Thomas did rape Margery. But the jurors told the court that Margery was not a virgin at the time of the rape ten years ago. Perhaps they debated amongst themselves the seriousness of non-virginal rape and whether Margery could prove that she was indeed a virgin back then. In the end, the jurors sent the signal that Margery's (alleged) non-virginal rape wasn't that big of a deal. They ordered Thomas to pay a half mark and ordered Margery to forgive Richard.

Margery's 1274 case is indicative of the continual EC insistence on virginal rape despite the statutory laws' explicit mention of maidens and matrons' rights to legal recourse. Studying the written laws of *raptus* in comparison to the laws in practice allows historians to get a better sense of how they worked in real life situations and to appreciate the complexity of applying case law. Although the laws progressively eclipsed women's place as victims of rape and/or abduction in favour of their male kin, as they increasingly tried to erode women's rights to appeal, women continued to bring appeals forward. The following case studies involve the non-noble (with the exception of Sir Hugh) and allow for the rare opportunity to study the ordinary in what Michael Goodich calls "history from below."[2] Applying a micro-historical approach to demonstrate larger macro processes and legal identities, this chapter aims to highlight the tokens of "proof" required to

---

1 TNA, JUST1/540 m19.

2 Goodich, "Introduction," in *Voices from the Bench*, 1.

make a successful appeal and, in turn, allows us to consider what this tells us about rape and consent in the EC. There are inconsistencies between the laws in theory (as written) and the laws in practice which demonstrate, as Gwen Seabourne states, "a 'realistic' view of law."[3] I am not claiming that this schism between the laws in theory and practice was problematic for medieval criminal courts, but rather that the application of *raptus* laws was broader in interpretation than one may assume if only reading the laws in isolation from case records. The laws, constructed and implemented by men, do not necessarily illuminate the lived realities of women, and thus just studying the written laws without looking at the laws in practice distorts the actual experiences of common medieval people.

The following case records were selected based on access, temporality, and information. I accessed cases through both a research trip to TNA and the online AALT website. I searched for cases that fit within the timeframe of the court of the general eyre based on plea roll survival, dating from approximately 1194 to 1348. Lastly, cases were sorted through the information they provided. I began by looking for *raptus* cases, and then I filtered these cases using the auxiliary words *concubuit* (to lie with sexually),[4] *carniliter* (by physical intercourse, sexually),[5] *virginitatem* (virginity),[6] *deflorare* (to deflower (sexually), ravish),[7] and *sanguinem* (blood),[8] to determine those that were likely rape cases. I started looking for *raptus* cases in the plea rolls from all available extant records on AALT during the reign of King John. I found fifty-three *raptus* cases, and, of them, only five were unambiguous rape cases, characterized by the auxiliary words discussed above. These five cases come from Cornwall and Lancashire. During the reign of Henry III, I searched every available AALT JUST1 record in counties Bedfordshire, Berkshire, Buckinghamshire, Cambridgeshire, Cornwall, Derbyshire, Devon, Dorset, and Durham from 1216 to 1248. This resulted in forty-three *raptus* cases, of which fourteen included the previously mentioned auxiliary words to determine that they were rape cases. For cases under the legal ages of Westminster I and II, I re-examined the cases found by Harold Schneebeck. During Westminster I (1275–1285) Schneebeck claimed to have found thirty-seven rape

3 Seabourne, *Women in the Medieval Common Law*, 6–7.

4 DMLBS, "concumbere," article 1a.

5 DMLBS, "carniliter," article 2a.

6 DMLBS, "virginitas," article 1a.

7 DMLBS, "deflorare," article 1b.

8 DMLBS, "sanguis," article 1a.

cases in the JUST1 records. However, upon a close reading of these cases, Schneebeck translated *raptus* as "rape" without any further consideration, and, as such, I have found that there are only twenty-one unambiguous rape cases during this ten-year period. These cases come from Cornwall, Cumberland, Devon, Dorset, Essex, Hampshire, Kent, Lincolnshire, Nottinghamshire, Sommerset, Sussex, Wiltshire, and Yorkshire. During the age of Westminster II, I searched available JUST1 records from 1285 to 1348 (the date of the last known eyre) in counties covered in the previous legal ages. I found forty-five *raptus* cases resulting in twenty-one rape cases. They come from Bedfordshire, Cumberland, Dorset, Lancashire, London, Norfolk, Suffolk, Sussex, and Yorkshire. In total, I studied 179 *raptus* cases (sixty-six during the legal age of *Glanvill*, thirty-one during *Bracton*, thirty-seven during Westminster I, and forty-five during Westminster II), of which only sixty-one are explicitly rape cases. These cases span the years 1201 to 1330 and come from twenty-two counties in both the northern and southern eyre circuits.

This chapter examines the tokens of proof that were used to substantiate a woman's accusation of rape. What language is included in the appeals and indictments to make a successful case and what inferences can scholars make about contemporaneous understandings of rape and (non-)consent from that language? The individual records of women and young girls who experienced extreme bodily harm and violation allow historians to consider the structural processes of medieval England for determining rape and (non-)consent which sustained a cultural toleration of sexual violence. These records are written by men, consumed by men, and made for the all-male legal profession. But they do represent a reality, a lived experience of trauma which was recorded and which we can revisit. As the elusive Banksy once noted, "they say you die twice. One time when you stop breathing and a second time, a bit later on, when somebody says your name for the last time."[9]

Glanvill-Era Cases, 1201–1227

While *Glanvill* states that *raptus* is the forcible rape of a woman, the plea rolls are sparse, with minimal extra information provided and little use of the previously-mentioned auxiliary words. As such, I begin my analysis with cases that only stated *raptus* in the plea roll, and then I examined the few cases that are unambiguous rape cases. Even though *Glanvill* defines *raptus* as what we now understand to be rape, I leave the translation as *raptus* for

9 "Banksy Quotes," *Urban Artists Association*.

cases that do not include any of the auxiliary words. I translate *raptus* as "rape" only for the cases that do include the use of the auxiliary words which make it clear that rape, not abduction, is the crime under consideration.

Looking at all available JUST1 records on AALT during the legal age of *Glanvill*, I found sixty-six cases of *raptus* dating from 1201 to 1227, which is just seven years after the earliest extant EC plea roll of 1194. As far as the extant records allow us to speculate, these early cases occurred within the first decade of the circuits of the eyre. Of the sixty-six *raptus* cases identified, all of them were brought to court by a woman's appeal; only one was successful in obtaining a conviction, while eleven ended in concord, three resulted in outlawry, two in outright acquittal, and forty-nine in failed appeals. Of the fifty-one cases that resulted in acquittals and failed appeals, forty-one women were deemed culpable for false appeal, equating to 80.39% of all acquittals and failed appeals. Meaning, out of the entire sixty-six *raptus* cases, women were deemed culpable 62.12% of the time. Seven of the sixty-six cases list multiple men as acting in *forcia* and *auxilio*, as accessories to the crime.[10] This indicates that approximately 10.61% of the cases were not lone-*raptus* cases, but rather groups of men were involved and named in the women's appeals.[11]

Three of the seven cases of group *raptus* occur in the Buckinghamshire eyre of 1227.[12] An unmarried woman named Mabel appealed Thomas of *raptus* and named two other men, Walter and Henry, as acting *de forcia*, as accessories to the crime.[13] Mabel did not come to pursue her appeal, but "after Mabel comes and withdraws [her appeal] ... and she herself is in custody, afterwards Thomas comes ... [he is] quit."[14] In another case of group *raptus* Matilda appealed Simon of *raptus* and Alexander of *forcia*.[15] Matilda did not come to pursue her appeal and was placed in mercy. Although in all seven of the group *raptus* cases only one man is accused of *raptus*, we should not read these as lone rapes and/or abductions because other people are accused of aiding in the crime in some capacity. Even though we do not know

10 TNA, JUST1/1 m4d (2 cases); JUST1/479 m8; JUST1/479 m1d; JUST1/54 m15; JUST1/54 m16d; JUST1/54 m18d.

11 The number of cases increases if abduction cases (with no mention of *raptus*) are included. But here, I am only including cases which mention *raptus*.

12 TNA, JUST1/54 m15, m16d, m18d.

13 TNA, JUST1/54 m15. Translations of all cases are my own unless stated otherwise.

14 TNA, JUST1/54 m15: "post venit Mabel et retraxit ... et ispam custodiam post venit Thomas ... quietus."

15 TNA, JUST1/54 m16d.

in what capacity these other individuals acted, we should be cognizant of the fact that they are accused of a crime. These "other people" (in these cases, men) are usually ignored by *raptus* scholars, largely due to the limitation of the archival material. However, we ought to acknowledge the frequency in which *raptus* is happening in groups so that we may better understand group sexual violence in the medieval past.[16]

When looking at rape cases specifically—those that include the previously mentioned auxiliary words or phrases—there are only five cases during this legal age. Three come from the 1201 Cornwall eyre and two from the 1202 Lincolnshire eyre.[17] Malot Crawe appealed Robert, son of Godfried, of rape in 1201.[18] Robert came to defend himself, but the brief (less than two lines long) record plainly states: "it is testified that he thus raped [*rapuit*] her and that she was seen bleeding [*sanguinolenta*]."[19] Despite the physical injury she endured, the jurors concluded that *concordati sunt*, "they are in concord," because "he has taken her as his wife."[20] Here we see *Glanvill*'s marriage clause, which was enacted without the explicit wishes of the parties involved, suggesting that this does not appear to be a pre-arranged elopement. In the same plea roll, there is another rape appeal ending in matrimony: that of Lucy Balland, who appealed Stephen Hokor of having "laid with her with force" and made her bleed.[21] The record states that "they are in concord" through marriage. In the same 1201 Cornwall eyre, Marina appealed Roger de Bond of raping her virginity, "and it was testified that she was covered with blood."[22] Roger defended himself, but the margin inscription *custoditur* implies that he was placed in custody as Marina was not imprisoned for false appeal. Of the three Cornwall rape appeals, all of them mention blood, one mentions virginity, and two ended in marriage, suggesting that rape was at times an acceptable precursor to matrimony.

---

16 For more of my discussion on this topic, see Cooper "'Let's Bring the Boys In'"; Cooper, "Re-Reading Medieval English Cases of *Raptus*."

17 TNA, JUST1/1171 m3 (2 cases), m4; TNA, JUST1/479 m7, m1d.

18 TNA, JUST1/1171 m3; *Select Pleas of the Crown*, vol. 1, p. 3.

19 *Select Pleas of the Crown*, vol. 1, p. 3; TNA, JUST1/1171 m3: "testatum fuit ipse eam ita rapuit et quod visa fuit sanguinolenta."

20 TNA, JUST1/1171 m3: "cepit eam sponsam."

21 TNA, JUST1/1171 m4: "concubuit vi."

22 TNA, JUST1/1171 m3: "Marina ... appellat Roger de Bond de Rapo quod ipse eam pro abstulit virginitatem suam ... testatum est quod ipsa fuit sanguinolenta"; DMLBS, "sanguinolentus," article 1a.

We are not always told the nature of the concord. For example, in the 1202 Lancashire eyre, a young woman named Jueta appealed a man named William of rape, and she was described as bleeding.[23] The record then simply states that Jueta and William are in concord, and William is in mercy. The exact nature of the concord is left unrecorded, as is typical in the plea rolls. The fifth rape case found also ended in concord, as Levina appealed Simon of raping her virginity, but "they are in concord," and Simon was ordered to make payment for the "violation."[24]

These five rape appeals demonstrate that the women's appeals were legal constructions of expected tokens of proof of a crime. They all mention blood and/or virginity. The inclusion of "she was seen bleeding" is the expected evidence of a rape as stated by *Glanvill*, and, consequently, it is likely that these were not the actual words spoken by the women. The inclusion of physical injury subscribes to *Glanvill*'s expectations of what rape should look like. Since not all cases that mention blood include virginity (nor do all virginal rapes mention blood), we can speculate that the blood here is physical injury and not necessarily virginal blood. We can infer from this that appeals without physical injury were not as likely to make it to the EC, which allows us to speculate that blood was indicative of non-consent.

Throughout the *Glanvill* age, women and young girls were captured for false or failed appeal in 62.12% of the *raptus* cases (forty-one out of sixty-six), demonstrating the harsh consequences of having an appeal fail. I have found only one likely conviction during the *Glanvill* age: that of Marina's appeal of virginal rape against Roger, discussed above.[25] This likely conviction of Roger does not prescribe the felony punishments mandated by *Glanvill*. The lack of felony convictions I have found are consistent with John Bellamy's findings: of the thirteen appeals made during the 1221 Gloucestershire eyre, there were zero convictions.[26] The *fama*, or reputation, of both the accused man and the complainant woman likely persuaded the EC, as did the expectations of "what rape should look like." During the *Glanvill* age, when rape was evident by the bleeding body of the woman (as demonstrated by the cases above), the EC opted for concord most of the time.[27] *Glanvill*-era

---

23 TNA, JUST1/479 m1d: "de rapo ... concubuit cum ea ... sanguinolenta."

24 TNA, JUST1/479 m7: "Levina ... appellat Simon ... de rapo ... quod ipse abstulit ei virginitatem suam ... Concordati sunt ... infracta"; DMLBS, "infractus," article 4a.

25 TNA, JUST1/1171 m3.

26 Bellamy, *The Criminal Trial in Later Medieval England*, 178.

27 It is impossible to make any meaningful statistical analysis with only five cases.

plea rolls emphasize the physical injury and bleeding body as the signs of proof that a rape occurred, and that the woman did not consent. Here, the physicality of non-consent was paramount.

Bracton-Era Cases, 1232–1274

Bracton outlines some of the harshest punishments for convicted rapists: the loss of eyes and genital mutilation. Despite these severe punishments, courts continued to prosecute rape by trial jury, meaning that members of the same county of the accused were responsible for determining his guilt. There might have been reluctance among jurors to punish their fellow neighbours with such severe mutilations. Even *Bracton* encourages caution in the application of capital punishment when a felony was committed, stating "punishments are rather to be mitigated than increased." Indeed, corporal punishment was a mitigated sentence compared to capital punishment.[28] Those who were most likely to be convicted of a felony were either caught during the crime, known criminals, or foreigners unknown to the jurors.[29] Since jurors tended to know the accused, it was unlikely that the full punitive measures outlined in *Bracton* would be prescribed to convicted rapists. To date, there is only one single case known during the age of *Bracton* in which the prescribed punishment of facial and genital mutilation was completed. This very obscure case, from 1222, is referenced by *Bracton*. It seems peculiar and suspicious that *Bracton* has recorded this single instance of the punishment, and it should likely not be read at face value.

Frequently appeals would fail if women brought the appeals forward improperly—that is, non-appearance in court, failing to show their wounds to the coroner, or failing to raise the hue and cry immediately after the attack. Rape appeals were weakened by lapsed time before the accusation, as it might have indicated a woman's malicious intent. A victim of rape had to demonstrate physical evidence of non-consent, and if there was an attack on her reputation or moral character, the case could still fail. As with the previous legal age, out-of-court settlements and concord were typical methods

However, of the five rape cases, four ended in concord, two of those explicitly mention marriage. The use of concord for rape cases in the *Glanvill*-age is consistent with *raptus* cases generally: of the sixty-six *raptus* cases found, eleven ended in concord (equating to 16.66% of the cases).

28 *Bracton*, vol. 2, p. 299, l. 16. See Kamali, *Felony and the Guilty Mind in Medieval England*, 274–78.

29 Bellamy, *Crime and Public Order*, 160.

used to settle rape appeals. Of those convicted during *Bracton*'s legal age, my research has found no cases that ended in mutilation. This agrees with other scholars who have yet to find a case beyond *Bracton*'s 1222 reference.

Out of the thirty-one EC *raptus* cases examined here during the age of *Bracton*, there are only fourteen unambiguous rape cases (those that include the auxiliary words mentioned above) and there are zero convictions for the felony of rape (even though under *Bracton* rape was a felony). The numerous procedures involved in making a proper appeal created countless opportunities for the courts and the accused to find fault in the woman's appeal, and thus the appeal would frequently fail.[30] For the *raptus* appeals that did not fail, the courts would seek to settle most often with an amercement. Three of the thirty-one *raptus* cases end in concord, equating to 9.68%. This is below the concord rate in the previous legal age of *Glanvill* (16.66%). The 77.27% acquittal and failed appeal rate during *Glanvill* is similar to the 70.97% acquittal and failed appeal rate during *Bracton*.[31]

Bracton placed such emphasis on the rape of virgins that it also acted as a deterrent to the prosecution of rape of non-virgins. During the 1244 Devon eyre, there was a case where the woman's appeal was dropped because she was a widow and the plea roll states explicitly that "a woman can only appeal about the rape of her virginity and the death of her husband in her arms."[32] This strict interpretation of *Bracton* resulted in the failed appeal of the complainant and the acquittal of the defendant, as the jury found him *non est culpabilis*. The record does not diminish the woman's claim of rape, as it states that "he both seized her" (*cepit eam*) and "he had sexual intercourse [*concubuit*] with her." However, this was deemed irrelevant to the legal prosecution since she was not a virgin, and thus her appeal failed.

Of the explicit rape cases, Margery's case mentioned in the opening of this chapter is exemplary in demonstrating the court's—specifically the trial jurors—unwillingness to send their neighbour—a convicted rapist—to receive mutilation. During the 1274 Middlesex eyre, a young girl named Margery, daughter of Peter le Fever, appealed two men, Thomas de la Forde and Richard son of Benedict "of raping her virginity against the peace."[33]

30 Of the thirty-one *raptus* cases, seventeen (54.84%) resulted in a failed appeal.

31 Of the thirty-one *raptus* cases under *Bracton*'s age, five ended in outright acquittals and seventeen resulted in failed appeals.

32 TNA, JUST1/175 m44d: "appellum de virginitate sua rapta et viro suo in brachia sua occiso."

33 TNA, JUST1/540 m19: "de raptu virginitatis sue contra pacem."

This was a group rape. Margery made the appeal (*Margeria appellat*), stating that ten years prior to the trial, in 1265, "Thomas himself came ... to the house of Alice Marbarne ... and both raped her [Margery] with force and made her bleed."[34] Thomas was also present, as the record states that "the aforementioned Thomas asks the judge about his own appeal." Thomas challenged Margery's appeal, and the twelve jurors stated, "that when the aforementioned Thomas violated her against her will, it was, they said, when she was not a virgin at that time."[35] The jurors' verdict allowed for the prosecution of rape but not the rape of a virgin. The record is vague in stating "afterwards, the aforementioned Thomas satisfied the aforementioned Margery, and he made a fine with the lord King for half a mark."[36] Despite Margery le Fever's failed appeal, there is no record that she was imprisoned for false appeal. The second man accused, Richard, was brought to court for rape, which was *promulgat* (made known), leaving little ambiguity that this was a group rape and that the community perceptions (the court of public opinion) of the event mattered to the judicial rulings. *Bracton* mentions that multiple men can be accused of *forcia*, which *Bracton* states can involve holding the woman down, raping her, or aiding the primary culprit. In most records, we do not get such explicit detail about the nature of the involvement of the other men, but here Margery accused both Richard and Thomas of rape. Thomas is accused of having raped her virginity, while Richard is accused of raping her, presumably after Thomas. However, the record ends with "therefore the woman's peace is granted to him."[37] Margery le Fever's case is exemplary to what I have found with all cases that went to trial during the *Bracton* era: despite being found culpable, rapists were never convicted of felony rape. Rather, these cases are settled through concord or amercement. Critically, this case demonstrates the bodily injury expected of women and how that injury was legally secondary to the loss of virginity. I am not aware of a case where the "legal women" inspected the body for corruption or virginity years after the crime occurred. Speculatively, Margery's *fama*—her presumed sexual reputation—could have been used against her in her appeal. This case demonstrates that jurors would mitigate the felony

34 TNA, JUST1/540 m19: "ipse venit ... ad domum Ahlae Mabarne ... et facit eam sanguineolentam et vi eam rapuit."

35 TNA, JUST1/540 m19: "quod predictus Thomas violavit eam contra voluntatem suam set dicunt quod non fuit virgo tunc temporis."

36 TNA, JUST1/540 m19: "Postea predictus Thomas satisfecit predicte Margerie et finem fecit cum domino Rege per dimidiam marcam."

37 TNA, JUST1/540 m19: "ideo conceditur ei femina pax."

by claiming that the woman was not a virgin, but they would still allow her to appeal the rape of a non-virgin, which was a lesser offence (in this case, treated as a trespass).

The importance placed upon loss of virginity seems to have permeated other felony charges, as it was intentionally included in appeals where the virginal status of the woman did not legally matter. This is evident in an attempted rape of a thirteen-year-old girl, Emma, daughter of Richard Toky, recorded in the Bedfordshire coroners' rolls.[38] On May 24, 1270, Emma was gathering wood when "Walter Gargolf of Stanford came, carrying a bow and a small sheaf of arrows, took hold of Emma and tried to throw her to the ground and deflower her."[39] Emma raised the hue and cry, demonstrating her verbal and mental non-consent. Her father, Richard, came charging over, but "Walter immediately shot an arrow at him, striking him," and Walter ultimately killed Richard. The attempted virginal rape of Emma did not necessarily matter to the legal proceedings of felony homicide, and yet it was included in the coroners' rolls. Presumably, *Bracton*'s indignation of the rape of virgins supported this legal narrative where Walter's murder of Richard was compounded with felonious intent by the attempted deflowerment of Emma.

Bracton's prioritization of virginal rape may have been used by jurors to dismiss charges where loss of virginity could not be proven while also allowing for the mitigated conviction of non-virginal rape. I have found only two convictions where concord is not mentioned. The first comes from the 1248 Berkshire eyre, where Margery claimed that Nicholas, son of Geoffrey de Whatecumber, raped her of her virginity.[40] Despite being placed in *misericordia* (mercy) for her failed appeal, Nicholas was fined for the assault. The second case ending with a conviction is that of Heloise, a wife and thus, presumably, not a virgin.[41] In the 1232 Buckinghamshire eyre, Heloise appealed two men, Hugh and Alexander, who came to her house, where Hugh "with force laid [*concubuit*] with her against the peace,"[42] and Alexander *fuit in forcia*, "was an accessory to the crime." Alexander did not come to court to mount a defence. However, Hugh did attempt to exonerate himself, but the

---

38 TNA, JUST2/1 m1d. Translated from Hunnisett, ed., *Bedfordshire Coroners' Rolls*, vol. 41, pp. 27–28; see Hanawalt, "Whose Story Was This?,"137.

39 Translated by Hunnisett, ed., *Bedfordshire Coroners' Rolls*, vol. 41, pp. 27–28.

40 TNA, JUST1/38 m33: "rapuit ei virginitatem suam contra pacem."

41 TNA, JUST1/62 m5.

42 TNA, JUST1/62 m5: "vi concubuit cum ea contra pacem."

jurors concluded that Hugh "with force had laid with her ... and therefore Hugh is in custody."[43] Notably, this is another group rape case, as Alexander was named as explicitly aiding Hugh in the rape in some capacity. Alexander's involvement must have been culpable enough for him to want to flee the criminal proceedings instead of proving his innocence.

There are two other group rape cases within the same 1232 Buckinghamshire eyre plea roll: those of Cecilia and Julianna.[44] Cecilia appealed two men of raping her virginity, but she retracted her appeal and was deemed culpable for false appeal.[45] Juliana, daughter of William le Hare, also appealed two men, Richard and Stephen, of raping her virginity.[46] As with the case of Cecilia, the plea roll for Juliana names one man (Richard) who is accused of *raptus* and another man (Stephen) who is accused of *forcia*. The case of Juliana is unique in describing how Stephen aided Richard in the rape by stating that "he pulled her into a certain cellar and closed the door on her," at which point Richard presumably raped her.[47] Juliana is then described as a pauper in the plea roll, indicating that she is poor. Richard, the primary offender, fled and was placed in outlawry while Stephen appeared in court and was found not culpable. The jurors concluded that Richard "did not violently rape Juliana of her virginity." Juliana was to be placed in custody for false appeal.

As with the previous legal age, women could be deemed guilty of false appeal. Of the sixty-six *Glanvill*-era *raptus* cases, 62.12% recorded that the woman was to be captured for a failed appeal. During *Bracton,* 38.71% of the thirty-one *raptus* cases indicate that the woman was to be imprisoned for false appeal. The large threat of going to prison for a failed appeal would have inevitably influenced the reluctance of women and girls in bringing rape accusations forward. In the 1238 Devon eyre, a young girl—presumably unmarried based on the inclusion of *filia*—named Agnes appealed a man named Amalric.[48] Agnes claimed that Amalric came to her house at night "and raped her and with force, [he] laid with her, and he raped her

43 TNA, JUST1/62 m5: "vi concubuit cum ea ... et ideo Hugo custoditur."

44 Discussed further in Cooper, "Re-Reading Medieval English Cases of *Raptus*."

45 TNA, JUST1/62 m3d: "abstulit ei virginitatem suam."

46 TNA, JUST1/62 m5d.

47 TNA, JUST1/62 m5d: "traxit eam quoddam cellarium et firmavit hostium super eam." Thank you to Sara Butler for helping me with this translation.

48 TNA, JUST1/174 m40.

virginity."[49] Amalric came and defended himself. We are not told what he stated but simply *ven[it] et defendit totu[m]*—that "he comes and defends all." Whatever he said must have been convincing, as the jury concluded that "he is not culpable, therefore he is quit, and Agnes is committed to Gaol for false appeal, [but] she is a pauper."[50] Perhaps it was Agnes's lack of physical injuries or her reputation that belittled her appeal. It is possible that her pauper status worked against her in court, as Amalric (who is not mentioned as being a pauper) may have had a stronger social network to aid in his acquittal. Like the case of young Juliana above, both Agnes and Juliana allegedly experienced virginal rape by men who may have been above their own socio-economic class, and both young women were deemed culpable for their own failed appeals. The statistics indicate that these experiences were not unique, and it was statistically probable (54.64%) that women would be found guilty of false appeal during *Bracton* and *Glanvill*.[51]

The records only tell us the pauper status of the individual if they were liable to pay a fine, so we cannot know for sure if the acquitted men were paupers since the record did not need to indicate their status. Nonetheless, it is notable how frequently women and girls of pauper status are recorded in the plea rolls as victims of sexual violence. The cases of Agnes v. Amalric and Juliana v. Richard and Stephen demonstrate this, as does the rape case of Matilda, daughter of Robert, who in the 1241 Berkshire eyre appealed William of acting "with force, he laid with her and deflowered her."[52] William defended himself, and the jury concluded that "the aforementioned William is not culpable therefore he himself ... is quit and Matilda is a pauper."[53] Matilda was seized for false appeal, but the record's inclusion of her pauper status is indicative of the fact that she received mercy. In the same 1241 Berkshire eyre, an unmarried woman named Alice made an appeal of virginal rape against Nicholas, who claimed that he did not "deflower her" and

---

49 TNA, JUST1/174 m40: "et ipsam rapuit et vi concubuit cum ea et rapuit ei virginitatem."

50 TNA, JUST1/174 m40: "non est culpabilis ideo quietus et Agnes committitur Gaole pro falso appello pauper est."

51 This represents twelve *Bracton*-era *raptus* cases and forty-one *Glanvill raptus* cases combined where women were captured. Out of the thirty-one *Bracton raptus* cases and the sixty-six *Glanvill raptus* cases (totaling ninety-seven cases), fifty-three women were ordered to be arrested equating to 54.64% of the *raptus* cases.

52 TNA, JUST1/37 m31d: "vi concubuit cum ea defloravit eam."

53 TNA, JUST1/37 m31d: "predictus Williamus non est culpabilis ideo ipse ... quietus et Matilda pauper est."

that they are in concord. The jury concluded that Nicholas "is not culpable," that "they are in concord," and, thus, "he is quit." Alice was to be imprisoned for false appeal, but she was pardoned and in mercy because she was a pauper.[54] Likely, all these women (Agnes, Juliana, Matilda, and Alice) would have experienced additional pressures in court due to their pauper status. *Bracton* was built on a legal tradition, as stated in *Glanvill*, which viewed rape accusations made by women of lower social standing than the accused men as suspicious and perhaps malicious in nature. These cases suggest, as Ruth Mazo Karras argues, that rape was not only a "gender privilege" but also a "class privilege," meaning that sexual violence against women "was an expression of power not just over women but over a subordinate class."[55] Carris Harris's analysis of rape in pastourelles provides further understandings on the "multiple disadvantages" and "structural inequalities" that certain economically and socially disadvantaged women and girls faced when bringing forward accusations of rape by elite-status men.[56] The weaponization of rape as a class and gender privilege could have impacted the criminal courts because these men may have been of higher socio-economic standing than the women and young girls they allegedly raped, which enabled them the privilege of believability in court.

In the 1238 Devon eyre, Margaret, daughter of William de Lawheie, appealed Arnald, the deacon of Soumonton of *rapo*.[57] The record states that Arnald "stole [*abstulit*] her away to his home," but "the jury said he did not rape [*non rapuit*] her and that a long time before he had slept [*concubuit*] with her and that she did not anymore, and that she did not give her consent and so he took her by force [*cepit eam vi*] and slept [*concubuit*] with her." In this case, we can explore multiple axes of privilege and oppression through gender, age disparity, and social class. In Amanda McVitty's study of treason as a gendered crime, she found that male testimony—the public voice of men—held "enormous value as both moral sooth and legal proof" to such a degree that "men's words remained integral to their social embodiment as true men."[58] *Bracton* states that the defendant can simply claim that sexual consent was given and that was (according to the treatise) legitimate

54 TNA, JUST1/37 m34d.

55 Karras, *Doing Unto Others*, 177.

56 Harris, *Obscene Pedagogies*, 108, 118.

57 TNA, JUST1/174 m32d. Thank you Sara Butler for helping with this case translation.

58 McVitty, *Treason and Masculinity in Medieval England*, 12.

grounds for an acquittal. Medieval English criminal courts may have viewed capital punishment as an inappropriate punishment for rape (based on the lack of felony convictions). Additionally, they likely had legitimate grounds to mitigate felony appeals to trespass suits due to insufficient evidence. But there is also the possibility that the criminal courts were founded on the believability of male testimony and the trepidation of female credibility in rape cases where there was minimal bodily injury.

Of the fourteen rape cases found during the *Bracton* age, five resulted in failed appeals,[59] three acquittals,[60] three concords,[61] two convictions,[62] and one was moved to church courts.[63] Of the fourteen appeals, ten of them mention a loss of virginity and just one mentions blood, once again indicating that blood in plea rolls of rape cases likely indicates physical injuries due to resistance and not necessarily a loss of virginity. Overall, both the *Glanvill* and *Bracton* legal ages have spotty records of rape appeals with incomplete information, sparse recording, and few details. All the convictions were mitigated to a trespass. The EC were evidently reluctant to prosecute rape as a felony, as doing so would ensure the convicted man's mutilation. Although the sources explicitly state legitimate excuses for dismissing a case, the implication from these sources makes it appear that the harsh punitive measures prescribed in *Bracton* resulted in jurors' unwillingness to convict.

Westminster I-Era Cases, 1275–1285

Westminster I claims that any woman can appeal *raptus*, including maidens and wives, but when looking at the plea rolls during this legal age, the issue of the woman's virginity repeatedly became the primary focus of rape trials. As the eyre case records will show, despite the higher conviction rates under Westminster I, there was still a strong reluctance to convict a man of raping a virgin through an appeal, as this could lead to the punitive mutilation of the *Bracton* age. Conviction rates depended largely on the severity of the bodily harm, tangible proof of physical resistance and non-consent, the virginal status of the woman, her reputation in general, and the socio-economic status of both the woman and the accused man.

---

59 TNA, JUST1/62 m3, m3d; JUST1/175 m44d; JUST1/540 m18; JUST1/696 m7.

60 TNA, JUST1/62 m5d; JUST1/174 m40; JUST1/37 m31d.

61 TNA, JUST1/540 m19, m22d; JUST1/37 m34d.

62 TNA, JUST1/62 m5; JUST1/38 m33.

63 TNA, JUST1/174 m32d.

Of the twenty-one rape cases during Westminster I, six resulted in failed appeals,[64] six ended in convictions,[65] four in outlawry,[66] three acquittals,[67] and two concords.[68] The rape cases (like the *raptus* cases generally) are relatively evenly split, with ten coming by appeal and eleven by indictment. One of the cases settled by concord was that of Juliana Pekenot, from the 1279 Surrey eyre.[69] This is an interesting case to demonstrate the marriage clause in practice, as the indictment failed because both Juliana and her husband/rapist Elias claimed that they were married prior to the rape. Elias Pekenot de Dontofold raped Juliana, the daughter of Horsesoul, and "he had both laid with her by force and raped her virginity."[70] The record states "after, for that reason, he himself was arrested," the reason seemingly being the loss of virginity. The record continues: "afterwards the aforementioned Elias came and pleads that he promised himself to the aforementioned Juliana before he had laid with her and Juliana came, this same [thing] she testifies, for this reason from here [from now on] they are quit."[71] Because both Juliana and Elias agreed that they were betrothed prior to the loss of virginity, the marriage clause was enacted to save Elias from prosecution and the case was dropped. Evidently, the legal framework situated rape and marriage on the same continuum—the former equating to illicit sex, the latter licit sex. When both the man and woman claimed marriage, there was a hypothetical legal "erasure" of rape. The record reveals that both Elias and Juliana acknowledged the loss of virginity. However, the loss of virginity was now legal because they were betrothed, despite any parental objections there may have been. Juliana may have even felt parental and societal pressure to marry Elias and save her and her family's reputation. The record does not indulge in the nuances of this marital arrangement. Nonetheless, in this

64 TNA, JUST1/112 m13d; JUST1/242 m93d; JUST1/497 m48d; JUST1/789 m29; JUST1/1078 m60; JUST1/1005 m142.

65 TNA, JUST1/186 m39d; JUST1/369 m31, m7d (3 cases); JUST1/759 m28.

66 TNA, JUST1/207 m48 (2 cases); JUST1/789 m11, m21d.

67 TNA, JUST1/133 m25; JUST1/669 m8d; JUST1/789 m3.

68 TNA, JUST1/877 m61d; JUST1/921 m14.

69 TNA, JUST1/877 m61d.

70 TNA, JUST1/877 m61d: "Elyas Pekenot de Dontofold rapuit Julianam filiam Horselsoule et vi concubuit cum ea et rapuit virginitatem suam."

71 TNA, JUST1/877 m61d: "postea venit predictus Elias et dicit quod ipse affedauit predictam Juliam antequam concubuit cum ea et Juliana venit et hoc idem testatur iodeo inde Quieti."

case, we can see how the marriage clause in rape cases both enabled couples to choose their own partner and eliminated any criminal indictments.

The other indictment to be settled out of court was recorded in the 1279 Sussex eyre.[72] The jury presented William Page, who worked as a miller, and alleged that "he raped Alice de Kyngesmannesdouuter with force [he] laid with her and raped [her] of her virginity."[73] The record states that "afterwards, it was testified through the rules of the coroner that the previously mentioned Alice appealed the aforementioned William in the County," but that the appeal was not pursued "and she herself did not come to prosecute her own appeal."[74] The record further states "therefore he [William] was arrested and [many of his people prosecuted with him] in paying the fine."[75] The terms of the *concordati* are not stated. Despite Alice's failed appeal, the king still indicted William, as the eyre roll states "the jurors inquired if he was guilty of the aforementioned deed, they said that he was and that they agreed. Therefore, the aforementioned William was arrested."[76] William ended up fleeing from the indictment and was consequently placed in exigent and outlawed.

The only indictment to be dropped altogether was because the woman's virginity was in question. During the 1285 Essex eyre, the jury presented "Adam de Bassingborn who raped [*rapuit*] Rose, daughter of John Hervy ... with force and against her will."[77] The sheriff then testified that Adam could not be found, at which point the justice asked "if he had raped her of her virginity," and the jurors responded "no, because he often had sexual intercourse with her."[78] There is no indication as to what happened afterwards, but since Adam was not placed in exigent or declared an outlaw, nor was he considered guilty or acquitted, it seems that the indictment was not pur-

---

72 TNA, JUST1/921 m14.

73 TNA, JUST1/921 m14: "Juratorians presentant quod Williamus Page molendinarus ... rapuit Alice de Kyngesmannesdouuter vi concubuit cum ea et rapuit virgintatem suam."

74 TNA, JUST1/921 m14: "postea testatum est per rotolus coronatoris quod predicta Alicia appellavit predictum Willielmum in Comitatu ... et ipsa non venit ad prosequendum appellum suum."

75 TNA, JUST1/921 m14: "ideo capitur et pluris sui de prosequendus in mia [misericordia]."

76 TNA, JUST1/921 m14: "et juratores requisti si culpabilis sit de predicto facto dicunt quod sit et quod concordati sunt. Ideo predictus Willielmus capitur."

77 TNA, JUST1/242 m93d: "vi et contra voluntatem suam."

78 TNA, JUST1/242 m93d: "si rapuit ipsam de virginitatem suam dicunt quod non ... sepius concubuisset cum ea."

sued. Rose's presumed past sexual history with Adam was grounds for the indictment to be dropped regardless of whether she was raped or not. This brief record (just over three lines long) offers an insight into how the sexual reputation of the woman influenced criminal court proceedings. Alleged past consensual sex was legally justifiable grounds to dismiss an alleged rape.

Of the six rape cases ending in conviction, five were secured through indictment and one through an appeal. John Colemen and Robert Edward were indicted at the 1279 Kent eyre for "leading a certain woman" (*quondam mulierem*) into "their boat across the Thames at Gravesend toward Essex."[79] The indictment states that John and Robert "detained her with them for one night and with force they laid with her."[80] The plural use of *concubuerunt* makes it clear that both men were accused of using force to sleep with the unnamed woman, leaving little speculation that this was a group rape. The jurors said that they are culpable and to be arrested. However, after the verdict both men paid a fine of five marks (one mark was approximately thirteen shillings, four pence), and the case was closed. The very next case on the same membrane is the indictment of Cok Benekin who was arrested because "by force he had laid with a certain other woman," not the same unnamed woman in the previous case.[81] The jury found him culpable, but after their verdict, Cok paid twenty shillings (one pound) and was released. Neither of these convictions resulted in the statutory punishment of two-years imprisonment, nor do they prescribe to the felony punitive measures of loss of life and member. Perhaps it is because the women involved were unknown to the jurors. There is also the possibility that forced sexual intercourse coming to court through indictment, regardless of virginal status, was not actually considered a felony under Westminster I. Another indictment case leading to a conviction is that of John Hardying, who seized (*cepit*) Joan, daughter of Bernard de Bydecomb, and "with force [he] laid with her, therefore he is captured."[82] John defended himself, but the jury found him culpable, "therefore he is committed to gaol and have the punishment of the statute."[83] Presumably two years, but we cannot be sure.

---

79 This section of the case only is translated by Schneebeck, "The Law of Felony in Medieval England," 448.

80 TNA, JUST1/369 m7d: "ipsam secum per unam noctem detinuerunt et cum ea vi concubuerunt."

81 TNA, JUST1/369 m7d: "vi concubuisset cum quadam alia muliere."

82 TNA, JUST1/186 m39d: "et vi concubuit cum ea ideo ipse capitur."

83 TNA, JUST1/186 m39d: "Ideo ipse committatur gayole et habeat penam statuti etc."

Westminster I prescribed two-years imprisonment, but the courts interpreted this as a guideline more than a binding punitive measure, as a record of indictment from the 1279 Kent eyre demonstrates. William Attehacche "raped Cecilia, daughter of Gilbert Bradegate, he [William] both laid with her by force and raped her of her virginity." [84] William defended himself, stating that "he did not rape the aforementioned Cecilia." The twelve jurors concluded that "the aforementioned William with force laid with her and against her will he raped her of her virginity."[85] The verdict includes: "therefore he is committed to gaol and in custody for three years as per the statute."[86] Westminster I included a two-year prison sentence and a fine at the king's pleasure, which, if not paid, would increase the prison sentence. The prison sentence could be dropped altogether in favour of amercement.[87] The courts in practice, however, appear to be loosely interpreting the punitive measures by issuing William a three-year prison sentence.

The conviction of William Attehacche was likely aided by Cecilia's loss of virginity. Even though the new statute was applicable to all women—whether maidens or matrons—the *Bracton*-era emphasis on virginity remained prevalent in the social customs of medieval marriage markets and in the assumptions about appropriate feminine sexuality. The influences of social morals onto the legal realm were evident in rape cases where the loss of virginity, such as Cecilia's, led to a conviction, despite the unambiguous indifference written into the statute. The rape of minors and virginal rape were more likely to secure a conviction than non-virginal rape or women of marital age. In the 1280–1281 Hampshire eyre, Walter Peke was accused of having raped Meynda *etatem novem annorum* (when she was only nine years old).[88] The indictment includes a standardized defence from the accused: "Walter came and said that he did not rape the aforementioned Meynda against her will."[89]

84 TNA, JUST1/369 m31: "rapuit Ceciliam, filiam Gilberto de Bradegate et vi concubuit cum ea et rapuit virginitatem suam."

85 TNA, JUST1/369 m31: "predictus Williamus concubuit cum ea et contra volentatem suam rapuit eius virginitatem."

86 TNA, JUST1/369 m31: "ideo committitur gaole et custodiatur per iii: annos per statutum."

87 TNA, JUST1/369 m7d (2 cases); JUST1/ 648 m17.

88 This case is recorded verbatim in two eyre rolls: TNA, JUST1/784 m17d and the JUST1/789 m11. Both are part of the Hampshire eyre circuit. See Crook, *Records of the General Eyre*, 161.

89 TNA, JUST1/784 m17d and JUST1/789 m11: "venit et dicit quod non rapuit predictam Meyndam contra voluntatem suam."

However, the record states that the twelve trial jurors said that Walter "with force raped" Meynda when she was only nine years old, "taking her virginity against her will."[90] The significance of Meynda's loss of virginity and minor age is clear in the repetition of these statements in the relatively short seven-line record. The jurors sentenced Walter to gaol and to "the punishment of the statute, that is to say, two years."[91] The reference to Westminster I reiterates the severity of the crime, as Westminster I explicitly prohibited the rape of minors, regardless of their consent, and Meynda certainly was a minor at the time of the rape. There is one other indictment leading to a conviction which involved the rape of a child. During the 1280 Sommerset eyre, Robert Pertenent was arrested for raping the virginity of Isabella de Mertok.[92] The record states that "the aforementioned Isabella was seen in court, and she is estimated to be about the age of nine years."[93] Robert was returned to gaol "for two years according to the statute." In these two cases, the minority of their age, as well as the loss of virginity, worked to ensure convictions through indictment. It is also clear that, despite the historiographical debate about the meaning of *raptus* in Westminster I, the statute was being applied to rape cases in the EC.

Three appeals of rape went to trial,[94] with two resulting in the acquittal of the accused and the ordered imprisonment of the women, but both women received mercy because of their pauper status.[95] The earliest is recorded in the 1278 Cumberland eyre, where Juliana, daughter of John, appealed Thomas, son of Robert, who "comes wickedly and in felony, and in premeditated assault, and he seized her and laid her on the ground, and with force he laid with her and raped her virginity from her."[96] The plea roll indicates that Juliana believed this was a premeditated assault, which added to the felonious nature of the crime, as Elizabeth Papp Kamali explains

---

90 TNA, JUST1/784 m17d and JUST1/789 m11: "predictus Walter vi rapuit pridictam Meyndam ... de virginitate sua contra voluntatem suam."

91 TNA, JUST1/784 m17d and JUST1/789 m11: "Ideo predictus Walterus committatur Gaole et habeat penam statuti scilicet duos annos."

92 TNA, JUST1/759 m28: "rapuit ... virginitatem."

93 TNA, JUST1/759 m28: "et predicta Isabella visa fuit in curia et estimatur de etate novem annorum."

94 TNA, JUST1/133 m25; JUST1/369 m7d; JUST1/669 m8d.

95 TNA, JUST1/133 m25; JUST1/669 m8d.

96 TNA, JUST1/133 m25: "idem Thomas venit neqitur et in felonia et insultu praemeditare et ipsa cepit et prostravit ad terram et vi concubuit cum ea et rapuit ab ea virginitatem suam."

that medieval English trial jurors considered if the accused demonstrated intention in planning the attack beforehand.[97] Thomas came and defended himself, and the jurors said that "the aforementioned Thomas is hence not culpable therefore he is henceforth quit."[98] The jury concluded that "the aforementioned Juliana is committed to gaol for false appeal," but "she is pardoned because she [is a] pauper."[99]

The second failed appeal, from the 1281 Nottinghamshire eyre, gives more information, as William, son of Hugh de Codington, acted "in felony" when he both "seized" (*cepit*) and "laid with" (*concubuit*) Eden, daughter of Ingraham Frend de Eyleston, and *ipsam fecit sanguinolentam* (made her bleed).[100] The rape and abduction, as well as the inclusion of physical injuries and bodily harm done to Eden, add to the fulfilment of her resistance, proof of her non-consent, and the embodiment of the legal identity of the "true victim." However, William was found not culpable, and Eden was placed in custody *pro falso appello* (for false appeal), but "afterwards she is pardoned for [she is a] pauper." From these trial records, it is apparent that the lack of detail about the rapes, the non-descript physical injuries done to the women (or lack thereof), the absence of deflowerment in the latter case, and their pauper status (despite being a form of mercy) probably worked against their appeals and believability in court. Ironically, their pauper status likely contributed to suspicion about their accusations (as suggested by *Glanvill* and *Bracton*) *and* ensured that they were saved from imprisonment.

Pauper status worked paradoxically as both a credibility disadvantage and a means to obtain mercy. For example, during the 1281 Wiltshire eyre, Matilda la Pyk appealed Adam Poleyn of "raping her virginity and robbery ... [but] she did not come nor pursue her appeal therefore she is captured, and her pledges are in amercement."[101] However, the plea roll states that Matilda could not "find pledges for faith for she [is a] pauper." At this point, Matilda retracts her appeal, and because her and Adam were not in concord, the appeal fails, and Adam is quit. Matilda la Pyk's pauper status was explicitly connected to her inability to secure sureties in court, reinforcing the impor-

97 Kamali, *Felony and the Guilty Mind in Medieval England*, 52.

98 TNA, JUST1/133 m25: "predictus Thomas non est inde culpabilis ideo inde quietus."

99 TNA, JUST1/133 m25: "predicta Juliana committatur gaole pro falso appello, perdonat qua pauper."

100 TNA, JUST1/669 m8d.

101 TNA, JUST1/1005 m142: "de virginitatem sua rapta ... non venit ... ideeo ipsam capitur...in mia [misericordia] ... non invenuit plegios pro fidem pro pauper."

tance of community networks of support in medieval England's criminal courts. While pauper status could save one from imprisonment, it could also indicate a lack of social networks and sureties in court.

On the other hand, a member of the clergy evaded criminal court trials once benefit of the clergy was established. During the 1280–1281 Hampshire eyre, Matilda appealed Ralph, a clergyman, of raping her virginity.[102] The record states that he "struck her down on the ground and with force he laid with her and raped her of her virginity."[103] Matilda did not pursue her appeal and was "committed to gaol for false appeal." The jury said that they suspected Ralph was guilty, and therefore he was handed over to the church courts, even though Matilda's appeal technically failed.

Cases could be quit or mitigated due to technicalities, as is evident in the failed appeal of Eden in the 1281 Lincolnshire eyre.[104] Eden appealed Simon, son of Hugh, of rape. She appeared in court and claimed that "Simon wickedly and in felony came with force and laid with her and raped her of her virginity."[105] Simon was in court and defended himself by stating "she does not say in what year, nor at what time, he himself ought to have committed the aforesaid felony."[106] The jurors concluded that he was not culpable and was quit while Eden "is committed to gaol for false appeal." Even in extreme cases, a technicality could quash an appeal. In the 1279 Yorkshire eyre, Agnes, daughter of John del Hithe, appealed Gilbert, son of William, alleging that "with force he laid with her and took from her, her virginity and made her bleed."[107] She then appealed Gilbert, son of John, of using force. Both Gilberts came to court and noted that Agnes failed to say what hour this alleged rape occurred. Agnes was arrested for false appeal, and the men were acquitted at the king's suit. The reasons for the acquittals seem minor in comparison to the severity of the alleged crimes. Notably, both women (Eden and Agnes) were imprisoned for this technicality in failing to mention the exact year, day, or hour of the rape. Sixteen of the thirty-seven *raptus*

102 TNA, JUST1/789 m29.

103 TNA, JUST1/789 m29: "Et ipsam ad tarram prostravit et cum ipsa vi concubuit et rapuit eius virginitatem."

104 TNA, JUST1/497 m48d.

105 TNA, JUST1/497 m48d: "Pridictus Simmon nequitur et in felonia venit et vi concubuit cum ea et rapuit ab ea virginitatem suam."

106 TNA, JUST1/497 m48d: "non dicit quo anno nec quo hora ipsem debuit predictam feloniam."

107 TNA, JUST1/1078 m60: "vi concubuit cum ea et abstulit ab ea virginitatem suam et fecit eam sanguinolentam."

cases resulted in the women's (and young girls) arrest, equating to 43.24% of the cases. Of the twenty-one Westminster I-era rape cases, eight included the ordered arrest of the women, equating to 38.01%. Despite the higher conviction rates during Westminster I, there was still a serious threat of imprisonment for the women bringing rape appeals forward.

The courts interpreted Westminster I broadly, as seen in the conviction through indictment resulting in three-years of imprisonment. Similarly, the only conviction from an appeal sheds light on the courts' mentality, as the rape of virgins continued to be viewed as a different crime from the rape of non-virgins despite the indifference towards them in the statute. In the 1279 Kent eyre, Emma, daughter of Christine, appealed Hugh, son of Henry de Alkyndoun, of rape.[108] Emma claimed that Hugh "laid with her with force, and raped her of her virginity," but Hugh defended himself, stating that "this is not the manner," or that this is not the way that the rape occurred.[109] The jury found Hugh "culpable" of rape. However, the record also states that "because Emma was not a virgin at the time of the rape, he is therefore placed in prison for two years as the new statute states."[110] The inclusion of her non-virginal status makes no sense, as Westminster I claims that the *ravie* of virgins and non-virgins is treated as equal. The case of Emma indicates that the courts in practice had latitude and continued to interpret the rape of virgins as entirely different—and more severe—than the rape of non-virgins when made through an appeal.

The law in practice was influenced by the social milieu of trial jurors as well as community morals, which idealized the virginal maiden. The case record suggests that Hugh only received imprisonment (as stated in the "new statute") as opposed to mutilation (as in the previous legal age of *Bracton*) because Emma was not a virgin. Clearly, the courts interpreted the rape of virgins as a felony and more serious than the rape of non-virgins, but they were still hesitant to convict men of raping virgins through appeal. Emma's trial record strongly implies that the EC interpreted Westminster I as being applicable to both the appeal of rape of non-virgins and the indictment of the rape of virgins (as with the case of Cecilia above), whereas the *Bracton*-era punitive mutilation could still be prescribed to men convicted of virginal rape through appeal only. This strongly indicates that despite what the stat-

108 TNA, JUST1/369 m7d.

109 TNA, JUST1/369 m7d: "vi concubuit cum ea et rapuit ei virginitatem suam … non est mode."

110 TNA, JUST1/369 m7d: "Emma tunc non fuit virgo Ideo custodiatur in prisona per duos annos secundum novum statutum."

ute of Westminster I claims, the jurors and justices of the eyre continued to interpret the rape of virgins as a felony, which was punishable by mutilation if made by an appeal, whereas indictments were treating it as trespasses, even if the woman lost her virginity.

The case of Agatha de Trebernech highlights the use of the marriage clause under Westminster I. During the 1284 Cornwall eyre, David de Trebernech was indicted after he had been appealed previously by Agatha de Trebernech of raping her virginity, but she subsequently "withdrew her own appeal." [111] Even though Agatha had agreed to marry David (quashing her appeal), David was now "requested" for an indictment. It was concluded that David "had laid with her freely," and this had been against the will of Agatha.[112] Agatha's consent to marry her alleged rapist, David, nullified her appeal, but he was still indicted for a trespass because he laid with her before the marriage took place, and it was believed to have been against her will. This marriage clause may have resulted in "marital misery,"[113] as the marriage appears to have been a means of settlement more than a couple's elopement.

As with the previous legal ages, group sexual violence was a relatively common occurrence during Westminster I, with 18.92% of the *raptus* cases naming multiple offenders. This is higher than the age of *Glanvill* (10.61%) and nearly identical to *Bracton* (16.13%). Group rape—as with lone rape—could be mitigated if the victim was not a virgin. For example, during the 1280–1281 Hampshire eyre, Alice appealed Robert, William, and another Robert of rape and robbery, but she did not pursue her appeal and was arrested.[114] The three men appeared in court and were acquitted of the robbery charge, but "the jurors said that they raped her [Alice] and with force they laid with her, but she was not a virgin," and they were acquitted.[115] The plural *rapuerunt* and *concuberunt* make it clear that all three men were accused of raping Alice. However, her lack of virginity resulted in their acquittal.

---

111 TNA, JUST1/112 m13d: "retraxit se de appello."

112 TNA, JUST1/112 m13d: "concubuit cum ea sponte ... mulieri suo contra voluntatem suam."

113 Butler, *Language of Abuse*, 97.

114 TNA, JUST1/789 m3.

115 TNA, JUST1/789 m3: "non sunt culpabiles de aliqua roberia sed dicunt quod eam rapuerunt et vi cum ea concuberunt sed non fuit virgo."

Regardless of the statute's broad approach to *raptus*, in practice the issue of virginity was clearly still influencing court decisions. Of the twenty-one rape cases, seventeen mention a loss of virginity or inquire about the virginal status of the woman. Cases describe violence, women and girls being thrown to the ground, and bleeding as evidence of their non-consent. The physicality of non-consent and the expectation of physical resistance were used as the tokens of proof to substantiate the accusations of rape, while previous sexual history and non-virginal status were used to belittle rape charges. Despite how the statute was written, when applied to rape cases, the interpretation and implementation was heavily dependent upon contemporaneous morals and social attitudes towards rape victims and female sexuality.

Westminster II-Era Cases, 1285–1330

Even though Westminster II made *raptus* a felony—regardless of whether the trial was initiated through an appeal or an indictment—of the six convictions I found (five indictments and one appeal), none of them resulted in felony punitive measures. There was, as Thomas Green argues, a significant social component to rape trials, in that the sexual deviancy of women was heavily influenced by social norms and the common belief that rape should be dealt with through "informal" community networks rather than the public criminal courts.[116] Successful convictions largely depended on the social and virginal status of the woman. Indictments and appeals were rare unless the woman claimed to have been raped of her virginity. Consequently, the EC during the long legal age of Westminster II were, in practice, reluctant to convict men of felony rape regardless of whether the woman was a virgin or not. The social attitudes towards rape most likely conflicted with the written law, as the lack of felony convictions suggest that jurors did not think the punishment of death fit the crime of rape. Amercements and two-year imprisonment were frequently the choice of penalty, harking back to the earlier punishments of Westminster I.

Of the twenty-one rape cases under study here, seven resulted in acquittals,[117] six in convictions,[118] four failed appeals,[119] three in outlawry,[120]

116 Green, "Societal Concepts of Criminal Liability," 675.

117 TNA, JUST1/137 m7d, m14d; JUST1/213 m34, m49; JUST1/547A m66d; JUST1/579 m13; JUST1/1098 m76/7.

118 TNA, JUST1/18 m4d; JUST1/137 m2, m6, m8, m6d; JUST1/328 m6.

119 TNA, JUST1/413 m1, m13d; JUST1/579 m32d; JUST1/924 m60d.

120 TNA, JUST1/26 m28, m37d; JUST1/833 m33d.

and one was moved to church courts.[121] As with the previous legal age, there is a relatively even split of eleven rape appeals and ten indictments. Four indictment convictions came from the same 1292–1293 Cumberland eyre. The first indictment is of Alan, who "with force he laid with her [Christiana] and took away her virginity and made her bleed."[122] Christiana did not pursue an appeal within the forty days as "sustained by the first statute of the lord king," and even though Westminster I was repealed in 1285—seven years prior to this indictment—the EC referenced the forty-day limitation as still applicable to a woman's appeal of rape. The jury concluded that Alan "is culpable" and is sentenced to "two years in the form of the statute."[123] Christiana is fulfilling all the necessary tokens of victimhood dating back to *Glanvill*: she was a virgin and was seen bleeding because of her rape. Her physical non-consent was evident to the men of law. Although virginity was irrelevant to felony prosecution under Westminster II, the indictment of the rape of a virgin amounted to two years imprisonment, as mandated by the former Statute of Westminster I. It appears that, much like Westminster I, the appeal of virginal rape and the indictment of virginal rape were seen to deduce different punitive measures.

Another failed appeal leading to a successful indictment is that of Juliana, daughter of Hugh Galt, who appealed Robert Crastan of rape and William of force and aid.[124] She did not pursue her appeal, so she was captured, and her father was placed in gaol. Robert defended himself at the king's suit and was found culpable. However, the jurors claimed that the rape occurred in 1279, prior to the implementation of Westminster II, and therefore Robert was sentenced to prison for two years as maintained by the former statute of Westminster I. Robert was able to pay a fine of 5 shillings to ensure his release. The punitive imprisonment of two years and amercement leaves little ambiguity that this indictment was seen as a trespass. Similarly, in the same Cumberland eyre, Alice, daughter of Thomas, appealed John, son of Robert, of rape, as well as three other men of force and aid.[125] Alice did not pursue her appeal and was consequently seized, and her sureties were placed in mercy. At the king's suit, the jury "testify that the aforementioned

121 TNA, JUST1/833 m33d.

122 TNA, JUST1/137 m2: "vi concubuit cum ea et abstultit ab ea virginitatem suam et fecit sanguiolentam."

123 TNA, JUST1/137 m2: "est culpabilis ... duorum annorum in forma statuti."

124 TNA, JUST1/137 m6.

125 TNA, JUST1/137 m8.

John, son of Robert, raped the previously mentioned Alice's virginity with force, and he laid with her with force ... therefore he is arrested."[126] The rape allegedly occurred in 1283, allowing for the application of Westminster I punishments during the legal age of Westminster II. John was to be imprisoned but was able to pay a fine for his release. The emphasis on force and loss of virginity are reminiscent of *Bracton*-era attitudes despite the indifference to deflowerment in Westminster II. Much like today in certain legal jurisdictions (such as Canada or the US), the time of the crime determined the punishment, as the statutory penalties of Westminster I could be applied retroactively during the age of Westminster II. Notably, even these convictions were not prescribed the full punitive measures of Westminster I, as amercement was used to negate imprisonment.

Another conviction through indictment is that of Walter, son of David de Carlaton, Walter, son of Annfeys, Hugh Rast, Adam, son of Thomas, and Simon le Pestiur, who all "seized Emma daughter of John ... and with force they led her away ... and took her to the house of David le Carpentur and the aforementioned Walter [son of David] laid with her with force."[127] The primary offender, Walter, came to the king's suit to defend himself and the jurors said that he was culpable of raping Emma, "but they said that after the fact she consented [*consensit*] and the aforementioned Walter married her."[128] Usually a concord through matrimony quashed any criminal charges, but it was determined that this marriage "was against her will and therefore he is in custody."[129] Walter had to pay a fine of 40*d*. This case demonstrates the fluidity of the criminal courts' application of statutory law. Westminster II clause A2 clearly states that if a man *ravist* any woman (married, lady, damsel, or other) with force—even if she consents afterwards—he was still liable for a felony charge at the king's indictment. But here, Emma's marriage to Walter worked to mitigate the severity of the rape in court, regardless of the statute. Emma's mental and verbal consent to marriage after the rape can be interpreted as coercive consent, as the jurors agreed that Walter did

126 TNA, JUST1/137 m8: "testanter quod predictus Johnes filius Robert rapuit virginitatem vi predicta Alicam et vi cum ea concubuit ... ideo capitur eos."

127 TNA, JUST1/137 m6d: "ceperunt ... Emmam filiam Johnus de Soureby et eam vi abduxerunt ... domum David le Carvpentur et eam ... predictus Walterus vi concubuit cum ipsa. Ideo predicti ... capitur."

128 TNA, JUST1/137 m6d: "sed dicunt quod ipsa ex post facto consensit et predictus Walterus ipsam disponsavit."

129 TNA, JUST1/137 m6d: "Et qua hoc fecit contra voluntatem suam ideo ipse custoditur."

rape Emma prior to her consent to matrimony and that this marriage "was against her will." Regardless, the marriage clause was upheld, an amercement was made, and the crime of rape was settled.

The final conviction through indictment comes from the 1307 Bedfordshire eyre, where William de Drayton was indicted for having "with force oppressed Avis, daughter of John le Chapman, he had laid with her against her will and against the peace."[130] Found guilty, William came and paid the small fine of one-half mark.

The five indictment convictions (those of Alan, Robert, John, Walter, and William) demonstrate that the criminal courts were clearly still interpreting Westminster I trespass punishment as applicable to rape indictments under Westminster II, regardless of the virginal status of the woman. A number of these indictment convictions came by way of abetted appeals, and as was typical of other failed appeals (not just rape), these usually led to indictment convictions of a trespass. Notably, three of the five indictment convictions involved groups of men. These include the cases of Juliana, Alice, and Emma. Of the twenty-one rape cases during Westminster II examined here, five of them involve multiple men accused of aiding the crime in some capacity, equating to 23.81% of the cases. Although such a small case-study pool makes statistics problematic, this hints at the relative frequency at which collective sexual violence was occurring amongst groups of men in high medieval England.

Men who flee from the courts were suspected of culpability and considered outlaws. The failed appeal of Margery, daughter of Andrew del Hyl, against Stephen for raping her virginity demonstrates the likelihood of the accused's outlawry resulting in the woman's release from prison.[131] Margery failed to pursue her appeal in the 1286 Suffolk eyre, and she was arrested. However, at the king's suit, the jurors "said the aforementioned Stephen is culpable," but "he does not come, and he takes himself away ... therefore he is exigent and outlawed." The margin inscription of *cap[itur]* and *in m[isericordia]* for Margery's arrest is crossed out and above it is *ex[igitur] et vtl[agitur]*, indicating that Stephen's outlawry and suspected culpability led to the release of Margery. During the "revival" of the eyre in 1330, there is the indictment of Hugh de Potton, who "feloniously raped Johanna, daughter of Adam Scot, at the age of ten, against her will, and he deflowered

130 TNA, JUST1/18 m4d: "vi oppressit Auicia filia Johannis le Chapman eam concubuit contra voluntatem suam et contra pacem."

131 TNA, JUST1/833 m33d.

her."[132] The courts ordered for his arrest, but the sheriff testified that Hugh could not be found because he fled. The jury likely suspected Hugh was culpable and thus placed him in outlawry to try and force him to answer the charges. Missing defendants were challenging,[133] as were women's appeals that lacked physical injury, abduction, and a loss of virginity. For example, Goditha, daughter of Richard, appealed Henry de Wymerley of violently raping her virginity in the 1292 Lancashire eyre, but the appeal failed because Goditha allegedly gave birth nearly three years prior to the alleged rape, and thus her virginity was already gone.[134]

Appeals that made it to trial did pose significant risks to both the complainant (if her appeal was deemed to be false) and defendant (if convicted). In the 1288 Dorset eyre, Alice, daughter of Michael en la Gardyn de Kniythrerem, appealed Stephen Bernard, who in the middle of the night came to Alice's house and "wickedly seized the aforementioned Alice, and he struck [her] down and with force he laid with the very Alice ... against her will he raped [her] virginity with force."[135] Stephen came and defended himself, claiming that "he did not commit any felony to her," stating that "he did not rape her of her virginity," and that "he laid with her with her consent."[136] Stephen claimed that the sex was "not against her will," and the jury ruled that Alice had done this "with voluntary consent," and Stephen "laid with her and not against her will."[137] The court concluded that "the aforementioned Alice is committed to gaol for false appeal." Of the twenty-one rape cases, women were seized for false or failed appeals 38.01% of the time (eight out of twenty-one). In a "he said/ she said" trial, Alice brought a strong case forward to appeal Stephen. She claimed to have endured a violent attack and a loss of virginity. Presumably, the force used against her resulted in physical proof of non-consent. Yet, Stephen's claim that the sexual intercourse with

132 TNA, JUST1/26 m28: "Felonice rapuit Johaman filia Ade Scot etatus decem annorum contra voluntatem ipsium Johannem et eam defloravit."

133 Sara Butler notes that "nearly 72 percent of criminal perpetrators in medieval England fled; because there were no police forces, they were never tried." See "Getting Medieval on Steven Pinker," 33.

134 TNA, JUST1/413 m1.

135 TNA, JUST1/213 m34: "predictam Alicam nequiter cepit et prostravit et vi concubuit cum ipsa ... contra voluntatem et rapuit ab ea vi virginitatem suam."

136 TNA, JUST1/213 m34: "non aliquam feloniam ei fecit ... nec virginitatem suam rapuit ... concubuit cum ipsa de voluntati."

137 TNA, JUST1/213 m34: "spontanea voluntate ... concubuit cum ipsa et non contra voluntatem suam."

Alice was done under the pretenses of consent must have seemed believable to the jurors. We can speculate that Alice did not have enough bodily injury to prove a violent sexual assault nor to prove her resistance to rape, and, evidently, she was believed to have consented. Here, the alleged mental and verbal consent of Alice, as stated by Stephen, was used to acquit Stephen, regardless of any physical proof of non-consent of Alice. The duality of mental and physical (non-)consent aided in Stephen's acquittal and Alice's imprisonment.

The second appeal that went to trial, also from the 1288 Dorset eyre, is nearly identical: Alice, daughter of William le Brewer, appealed Adam le Traverner of rape.[138] Alice le Brewer accused Adam: "against her will he wickedly and in felony seized and placed her in the house of the Adam in the same village and with force he laid with her and he took away from her, her virginity."[139] The jury ruled that Adam "is not culpable of the aforementioned rape" because "the same Adam had laid with her, with the consent of Alice herself," and therefore it was "not against her will."[140] The record ends with "the aforementioned Alice is being committed to gaol for false appeal." However, "afterwards she is pardoned for ... she is a pauper."[141]

The standardization in record keeping and use of consistent legal terminology in the eyre rolls was formulizing during the age of Westminster II. Both cases from the Dorset eyre include the adverb *nequiter* (wickedly) repeatedly throughout the women's appeals. This reinforced the felonious nature of the crime, as *nequiter* made it clear to the trial jury that the accused were deliberate in their actions.[142] Both appeals include abduction as well as rape (*cepit*), and both include slight variations of the standard phrase *vi concubuit et virginitatem suam contra voluntatem et rapuit* (with force he laid with her and against her will, [he] raped her of her virginity). This nearly identical phrase underlines the continued importance of the loss of virginity and use of force in a rape conviction. The fact that these appeals

138 TNA, JUST1/213 m49.

139 TNA, JUST1/213 m49: "contra voluntatem suam nequiter et in felonia cepit et positam in dimum ipsius Adem in eadem villa et vi cum ipsa concubuit et virginitatem suam ab ea abstulit."

140 TNA, JUST1/213 m49: "non est culpabilis de predicto rapo qua dicunt quod idem Adam de volentate ipsius Aliae concubuit cum ipsa ... non contra voluntatem suam."

141 TNA, JUST1/213 m49: "Et predicta Alice comitatur gaolae pro falso appelo etc. Postea perdonatur pro ... quia pauper."

142 Kamali, *Felony and the Guilty Mind in Medieval England*, 60.

are so similar suggests that they are not the actual words spoken by either woman. The appeals were summarized into the "appropriate" standard, formulaic appeal by the court clerk for the court records. Similarly, both defendants have the same phrases in their defence, stating that the rape was consensual, resulting in both women being sent to prison for false appeal. The pity shown to Alice le Brewer—she was pardoned from imprisonment because she was poor—also highlights the socio-economic class aspect of legal trials. Despite being saved from prison because of her pauper status, there is a strong potential that her pauper status worked against her in the actual court proceedings in her inability to secure a conviction. She may have been viewed negatively by the "good honest" men who made up the trial jury. Poverty was viewed as indicative of poor moral judgement[143] in a similar (but inverted) manner to how beauty was a marker of nobility. Such social attitudes and popular imagination about the woman's moral status and physical appearance interfered with criminal proceedings, as Barbara Hanawalt describes, convictions "depended upon the condition in society of the victimized woman."[144] The conflicting consent models—physical and mental—are evident in the cases of both Alices. Both women claimed to have endured violence and thus physical proof of their non-consent, and both women allegedly gave mental consent. The duality of mental and physical (non-)consent resulted in the acquittals of the accused and the ordered imprisonment of the women.

During the 1292–1293 Cumberland eyre, there is another failed appeal which includes all the standard phrases mentioned above, but it is more explicit in the physical bodily injury that the woman endured. Juliana de Burtholm appealed David de Kingeschalesof, allegeding that "in premeditated assault he seized her, and he struck her down on the ground, and with force he laid with her and took away her virginity, and he made her bleed."[145] Once more, the conflation of abduction and rape is identical to the two appeals of the Alices above, as is the loss of virginity. Juliana's physically injury—presumably occurring when she was forcefully struck to the ground—is indicative of her resistance and non-consent. David defended himself by claiming that "the previously mentioned Julian is the wife of Walter," and she did not say this in her appeal, and she failed to mention exactly where

143 Kane, *Popular Memory and Gender in Medieval England*, 62.

144 Hanawalt, *Crime and Conflict*, 105.

145 TNA, JUST1/137 m14d: "in assaltu praemeditato cepit eam et prostravit ad terram et vi cum ea concubuit et abstulit ab ea virginitatem suam et eam fecit sanguinolentam."

she was bleeding. This suggests that "blood" was not obviously related to a loss of virginity, but rather some other physical injury occurred because of physical resistance to the rape. The emphasis on virginity, bodily injury, and her husband, Walter, is counter to the Statute of Westminster II's claim of maidens and wives' right to appeal. Despite her physical bodily proof of non-consent, David eventually put himself before the jury, who found him "in no way culpable." Once again, the status of "victim" went from the woman to the accused, as the courts ruled that "the previously mentioned Juliana is committed to Gaol for false appeal." In theory, Juliana fulfilled all the criteria for the legal identity of the "true victim": she was both seized and raped, she lost her virginity, and she had physical bodily proof of her resistance. Even with all the boxes ticked, Juliana could not secure a conviction and was herself imprisoned. Westminster II's stated capital punishment via appeals may have continued to contribute to the reluctance of trial jurors to convict men of rape despite the victim's fulfilment of the legal criteria of the crime.

A fourth rape appeal that went to trial comes from the 1287 Hertfordshire eyre.[146] Agnes, daughter of John de Enovere, appealed Hugh, son of Thomas le Tenur, "of rape and robbery having broken the peace of the lord king." Agnes told the jurors that she lived with her father, John, and when Hugh "discovered her in a certain field called Wylleber in the village of Hitchen and with force, and against the peace of the lord King, he raped her of her virginity."[147] Hugh was present and pleaded his defence in court. Throughout the trial it was revealed that Hugh "seized her and [she] having been bruised, he carried [her] and with force he wished to lay with her."[148] The plea roll states in detail the violent beating that Hugh gave Agnes in the attempt to rape her, as Hugh "squeezed her so violently that blood flowed from the middle of her face and nose."[149] It was recorded that Agnes was a child at the time of the attack in 1283—*minoris etatis*, or "of minor age"—as "at that time she was not yet seven years old."[150] The jury found that Hugh

146 TNA, JUST1/328 m6.

147 TNA, JUST1/328 m6: "invenit ipsam Agnes in quodam campo qui vocatur Wyllober in villa de Huthe et vi et contra pacem domino Regis rapuit virginitatem suam."

148 TNA, JUST1/328 m6: "ipsam cepit et adtritam provexit et vi cum ipsa concubuisset voluit."

149 TNA, JUST1/328 m6: "et ipsam ita vehementer strinxit quod sanguis per medium os et nares ipsius Agnetis."

150 TNA, JUST1/328 m6: "Agnes eo quod non extitit tunc temporis etatis septem annorum."

"was not himself able to rape her of her virginity, but he let himself in as far as he was able and treated her worthlessly."[151] The jurors concluded that Hugh was to be placed in custody until he made satisfaction (*satisfecit*), or payment, to the king and to Agnes. The jurors downgraded the entire felony to a trespass because the attempted rape of Agnes did not result in a loss of virginity. Even though in the attempt to rape a child Hugh violently assaulted Agnes, the courts deemed the actions a non-felony. The courts seemly placed high value on full penetration and completed rape, even in the case of minors. In the attempt to stop the rape, young Agnes fought off Hugh's violent attack, and thus, like virgin martyrs, this young girl preserved her virginity at the expense of her physical body. Agnes's physical proof of non-consent was evident through her extreme bodily injuries. Agnes's injuries ensured her victim status, but the preservation of her virginity worked against her in the criminal courts, as a violent assault of a minor was not considered a felony. The preservation of her virginity was considered more important than the bodily harm done to her—much like virgin saints or romance heroines.

One exemplary case of failure due to a technicality is that of Joan, daughter of Eustace le Seler of London, recorded in the 1321 London eyre roll among many other manuscripts.[152] This case was recorded in England's highest court rolls, the King's Bench Rex rolls.[153] According to Barbara Hanwalt, the 1321 London eyre roll was "entered in a jail delivery session held in 1321 and records an appeal she [Joan] made to the coroner on 6 February 1321, almost a year after the event."[154] The appeal made to the coroner states that Joan "makes her own appeal towards Raymond de Lymogus of rape."[155] The record uniquely but critically states that the appeal is *in hec*

151 TNA, JUST1/328 m6: "virginitatem ipsius rapere non potuit set in quantum potuit se inde intromisit et ipsam viliter tractavit."

152 TNA, JUST1/547A m66d; London, BL, MS Harley 453, fol. 34; London, BL, MS Addit. 25029, fol. 106v; Cambridge, Harvard Law School Library, MS Dunn 41, fol. 66r; Cambridge, Harvard Law School Library, MS Dunn 51, fol. 86v; Dublin, Trinity College Dublin, MS E. 5. 11, p. 162; Cambridge, Cambridge University Library, MS Gg. vi. 7, fol. 113v; London, BL, MS Harley 1807, fol. 387v; London, BL, MS Harley 5146, fol. 95f; Cambridge, Cambridge Pembroke College, MS 271, fol. 77v; Oxford, Bodleian Library, MS Rawl. D. 506, fol. 5v; Oxford, Bodleian Library, MS Tanner 450, fol. 378r. See Barabara Hanawalt's article devoted to this case, "Whose Story Was This?," 124–41.

153 TNA, KB 27/240 m104d, Rex 1; KB 27/242, m1 and m154.

154 Hanawalt, "Whose Story Was This?," 128–29.

155 TNA, JUST1/547A m66d: "fecit appellum suum versus Reyuumdumn de Lymogos de Raptus."

verba (in these words), meaning in her exact words. This is important to the later acquittal of Raymond which was obtained due to a technicality. Joan le Seler claimed that Raymond raped her with an emphasis on her physical body (*corps*), and that he committed a felony by raping her "against her will and against the peace."[156] The use of *corps* and *volunte* ensures that this was against Joan's mental and physical consent. According to Joan, Raymond raped her of her virginity when she was only twelve years old. This was not only against the peace of the king but also "Raymond's actions went against her own dignity."[157] The record states *Et hoc optulit prout*—that this was exactly the appeal that Joan presented. Raymond appeared in court, and "he defended elegantly the whole of the rape and felony."[158] The record repeatedly states that these were the exact words spoken by Joan—"and in this way she tells her own appeal to the crown Justice."[159] This is important to the failure of the appeal, as Joan was now deemed an accessory to the crime of rape because she changed the previously mentioned day in question from what she stated in her appeal to the coroner.[160] Since Joan mixed up the exact day that the rape occurred, *non posset bis esse rapta de una et eadem virginitatem* (she is not able to be raped twice of one and her same virginity). The misremembering of dates made "Joan not able to proclaim this"—that is that Raymond raped her of her virginity when she was twelve years old. Raymond was released "without day," but Joan, however, was placed in custody "for her previously mentioned false appeal."[161] She was going to be sent to the gaol, but "she is pardoned because she is below [legal] age."[162] Raymond was later indicted at the king's suit, where, under the confirmation of the seal, the jurors acquitted him. The indictment record states that "at the suit of the king of rape and felonies the aforementioned Raymond is ascertained of the previously mentioned [crimes]," and he was acquitted.[163] This ends

---

156 TNA, JUST1/547A m66d: "eu conutre sa volunte et en countre la pees."

157 TNA, JUST1/547A m66d: "et dignitatem suam."

158 TNA, JUST1/547A m66d: "mundus defendit ominem raptum et feloniam"; Lewis and Short, *A Latin Dictionary*, "Mundus, a, um, adj." article 1.

159 TNA, JUST1/547A m66d: "Et modo in appello suo quod narrat coram Justic[iam]."

160 TNA, JUST1/547A m66d: "se forciam raptam per predicem diem ... variatonem."

161 TNA, JUST1/547A m66d: "pro falso appello suo predicto custodiatur."

162 TNA, JUST1/547A m66d: "set pardonatur quia infra eatatem."

163 TNA, JUST1/547A m66d: "predicto compertum est quod idem Reymunndus ad sectam Regis de raptu et felonia predictus."

the plea roll of Joan's alleged rape, her failed appeal, and the indictment of Raymond. The technicality seems minor to the overall crime of a rape of a minor. The record explicitly calls Joan an accomplice to her own rape (*forciam*), thus labelling her, at the age of twelve, with the legal identity of the blame-worthy and culpable woman.

The same case, recorded in the Rex rolls of the King's Bench, is much more detailed. Joan made her appeal, stating "he himself [Raymond] [came] to the house of the previously mentioned Eustace, with force and arms, and against the will of Joan he seized her, the same Joan, by her own left hand."[164] The inclusion of force and arms (*vi et armis*) is, by the mid-fourteenth century, a standard phrase in trial documents of *raptus*, but it nevertheless adds more detail to the abduction than what is recorded in the plea roll. The Rex roll continues: "he abducted [her] indeed into the room of the Raymond ... and in that very place he threw away her [Joan] to the ground, and against her will he feloniously laid [with her]."[165] The physical force Raymond used to dominate Joan is highlighted in her appeal to ensure that she fulfils the identity of the "true victim" by resisting the attack. The record indulges in graphic detail that "he completely raped [her] of her virginity against the peace."[166] According to the Rex roll, Raymond appeared in court "and pleaded that he is a clergyman and that he is not able to be governed [judged] thenceforth without his own people" about this matter.[167] Raymond was attempting to claim benefit of the clergy in an effort to escape secular courts in favour of ecclesiastical courts. Although Raymond was denied clerical status and was indicted, he was ultimately acquitted at the king's suit.[168] Raymond was proclaimed a *liber*—a "free man"—and Joan was ordered to pay back any damages that he incurred because of her appeal.[169] This is an extraordinary case including the rape, abduction, and loss of virginity of a

164 TNA, KB 27/240 m104d Rex 1: "domini predicti Eustastini vi et armis et contra volentatem ipsius Johanne cepit ipsam Johaniam per manum suam sinisteram."

165 TNA, KB 27/240 m104d Rex 1: "abduxit namque ad cameram ipsius Reymondi ... et ipsam ibidem ad terram projecit et secum contra volentatem suam concubuit felonice."

166 TNA, KB 27/240 m104d Rex 1: "et ipsam de virginitate sua penitus rapuit contra pacem."

167 TNA, KB 27/240 m104d Rex 1: "et dicit quod clericus est quod non potest inde sine ordinariis suis."

168 TNA, KB 27/240 m104d Rex 1: "Raymundus in nullo est calpabilis de raptu et felonia predictus."

169 TNA, KB 27/240 m104d Rex 1: "predicta Johanna sufficiat ad dampna."

minor as well as the accused man claiming clerical status, resulting in the young girl sentenced to prison but saved by her minority age. Finally, she was forced to compensate the defendant for damages.

The case of Sir Hugh, from the 1293–1294 Yorkshire and Northumberland eyre, demonstrates the EC reluctance to grant men the benefit of the clergy.[170] Hugh, son of Henry, was indicted for the rape of a young girl (*rapuit quamdam puellam*),[171] named specifically in the eyre roll as Matilda, daughter of Ingrede.[172] The record states that Hugh was in the village of Ingelton "with two of his servants" (*garcionibus*), named Henry Dent and Thomas son of William, when "Hugh saw the aforementioned Matilda standing in the door of the aforementioned Ingrede's house," and he told his servants, Henry and Thomas, "to seize and lead away Matilda to his manor house." The plea roll states that "against Matilda's will they seized her and dragged her by the arms outside her mother's house and they led her to the manor-house of Hugh himself, in the same town."[173] Presumably Ingrede was aware of the attack against her daughter, as "immediately she raised the hue and cry before them." Hugh allegedly "detained her [Matilda] and laid with her, but they [the jurors] said that Matilda first assented to the will of Hugh himself, before he had laid with her."[174] Despite Matilda's alleged consent after the abduction, but before the rape, Hugh was still placed in custody because "he seized and led her away against her will." The temporality and duality of (non-)consent is important here. Matilda's initial physical non-consent is evident by the inclusion of *traxerunt* (they dragged her). Matilda's subsequent verbal and mental agreement—her *assensit* to the will of Hugh—are carefully described as not agreeing with her own will but with his *voluntati*. This can thus be interpreted as indicative of Matilda's initial physical non-consent and subsequent coercive mental consent as an act of survival.

---

170 TNA, JUST1/1098 m76/77; London, LI, MS Misc. 87, fols. 35–43; London, BL, MS Addit. 31826, fols. 206v–207r; transcribed by Horwood, ed., *Year Books of the Reign of Edward the First*, 529–32.

171 Horwood, ed., *Year Books of the Reign of Edward the First*, 529.

172 TNA, JUST1/1098 m76/77. The following transcription is taken from both TNA, JUST1/1098 m76/77 and BL, MS Addit. 31826, fols. 206v–207r.

173 TNA, JUST1/1098 m76/77: "Matillidem ceperunt contra voluntatem suam et traxerunt per brachia extra domum matris sue et eam duxerunt usque manerium ipsius Hugonis in eadem villata."

174 TNA, JUST1/1098 m76/77: "Et predictus Hugo eam ibidem detinuit et concubuit cum ea set dicunt quod predicta Matillida assensit prius voluntati ipsius Hugonis antequam concubuit cum ea."

In the eyre plea roll, Hugh was fined and released, but in the *Year Book* and British Library manuscript, there is much more detail, as Hugh was accused to have "knew her carnally against her will."[175] Hugh was denied counsel, and he allegedly said to the justice, "Lord, I ask you, am I able to have counsel lest I will be seized in the court of the King for lack of counsel."[176] After he is refused counsel, Hugh claimed: "I am a clergyman and I ought not to respond without my ordinary." The justice responded: "we declare, that you dismiss the privilege of the clergy, because you [Hugh] are bigamous, because you gather together in matrimony with a widow and when you will respond that you gathered together with her, she was indeed a virgin."[177] Hugh responded that "she herself was a virgin when I betrothed her." The justice claimed "that this immediately ought to be known," and that "twelve honourable men who lead in virtue of the oath" must determine "if she was a widow when Sir Hugh came together with her."[178] Hugh objected to the trial jurors *per illos sum accusatus* (for those same men accused me)—that is the trial jurors were the same men as the presenting jurors. Hugh also claimed, "that I am a knight and thus I ought not to be judged unless it be my own peers," meaning other knights.[179] The actions taken by Hugh show a high level of legal awareness and knowledge of the right to a fair trial jury that is made up of peers and individuals who were not on the presenting jury. The justice calls in knights (*nominabantur milites*), but Hugh does not plead (*non consentio*), at which point the justice warned him, "if you wish to refute the common law, you will bring unto yourself thence ordained penalty, that is to say, 'one day you will eat and another day you will drink; and the day which you will drink you will not eat and vice versa.'"[180] Hugh once again refuses the trial jurors, as they are the same men who accused him of rape.

175 Horwood, ed., *Year Books of the Reign of Edward the First*, 529; BL, MS Addit. 31826, fols. 206v–207r: "et eam congnovit carnaliter contra suam voluntatem."

176 BL, MS Addit. 31826, fols. 206v–207r: "sed non quod consules eum ... Domine, rogo vos quod possum habere consilium ne subripiar in curia Regis pro defectu consilii."

177 BL, MS Addit. 31826, fols. 206v–207r: "ego sum clericus, et non debeo respondere sine ordinariis meis ... nos dicimus quod vos amisistis privilegium clericale, eo quod estis bigamus, quia matrimonium contraxistis cum vidua, et respondebis utrum quando contraxistis cum ea fuit virgo vel."

178 BL, MS Addit. 31826, fols. 206v–207r: "honeravit duodecim qui dixerunt in virtute sacramenti ... ispsa fuit vidua quando dominus Hugo contraxit cum ea."

179 BL, MS Addit. 31826, fols. 206v–207r: "ego sum miles, et non debeo judicari nisi per meos pares."

180 BL, MS Addit. 31826, fols. 206v–207r: "si vos velitis legem comunem refutare,

He then asks that the charges be read out to him, but the justice refuses to read the charge to him and says that if he wishes to have some of the trial jurors removed, he is certainly entitled to that right. But the justice tells Hugh: "if you know why they ought to be removed, you say [these reasons] by voice, or in writing."[181] This is troubling for Hugh, and the judge refuses to read out the charges to him, claiming that he ought to read them himself. Hugh admits, "I do not know how to read, [and] I beg for my own counsel" (*nescio legere peto consilium meum*). The justice says that Hugh ought to be able to read if he is a member of the clergy, and again Hugh states: "I do not know how to read."[182] The justice exclaims: "how is this, when you have wished to be aided by the benefit of the clergy, and yet in this manner you do not know how to read your own charges."[183] The record claims that Hugh stood there quietly, not responding (*setit in pace quasi confusus*), and the justice felt bad for his confusion (*non sitis stupefacti*) and thus allowed a member of the court to read the charges of rape to Hugh, and he claimed that "he did not rape" her. The twelve jurors stated that it was not Hugh himself, but rather the "men of lord Hugh that raped her with force."[184] The justice asks for clarification, to ensure that the men were not acting with Hugh's consent.[185] The jurors responded no, Hugh's consent was not given, and the justice asked to confirm if the men *cognoerunt ne eam carnilitar* (knew the woman carnally), and the jurors responded that this was true. This was clearly a group rape, as the plural *homines* (men) is used. The servants of Hugh "knew her carnally."[186] In the end, the court ruled that Hugh was to be acquitted of all charges.

---

vos portabitis peonam inde ordinatam, scilicet, 'uno die manducabitis et alio die bibebitis; et die quo bibitis non manducabitis, et e contra'."

181 BL, MS Addit. 31826, fols. 206v–207r: "si sciatis aliquod dicere quare removeri debent, dicatis unica voce sive in scripto."

182 BL, MS Addit. 31826, fols. 206v–207r: "non, quia debent proponi per os vestrum ... ego nescio legere."

183 BL, MS Addit. 31826, fols. 206v–207r: "Quomodo est hoc, quod vos voluistis juvasse vos per privilegium clericale, et modo nescitis legere calumpnias vestras."

184 BL, MS Addit. 31826, fols. 206v–207r: "nos dicimus quod ipsa rapiebatur vi per homines domini Hugonis."

185 BL, MS Addit. 31826, fols. 206v–207r: "fuit ne Hugo consentiens ad factum vel non."

186 For another case of a servant accused of *raptus*, see TNA, JUST1/579 m32d. For a discussion on male-bonding through rape see Armstrong-Partida, "Precarious Manhood," 125–75; Hanawalt, "Women Before the Law," 185; Hanawalt, *Crime and Conflict*, 109; Rossiaud, *Medieval Prostitution*, 20–22.

The case of Sir Hugh is remarkable for numerous reasons, including his elite status and the legal right to be tried by one's peers. As a knight, Hugh refused to be tried by an ordinary jury, so the justice agreed and brought in other knights to sit on the jury. This legal right adds to the social and community implications of criminal trials. The social attitudes and community beliefs were influencing the courts' rulings, as one had the right to be tried by one's social equivalents. Status, socio-economic class, and community morals were intrinsically connected to the application of the laws. The high degree of legal knowledge in non-legal professionals (such as Hugh) is evident from this case record, as the demand for a fair trial was repeatedly requested.[187] This illuminates a growing legal awareness among the laity and perhaps a shared knowledge amongst men on how to avoid a rape appeal. The actions of Hugh's men did not make him accountable for their felonies. As for Sir Hugh's men, the charges were dropped, and I have not been able to find indictments for them to see if they were ever convicted of rape. The duality of mental and physical (non-)consent was described as working at different times in this case. Matilda initially resisted the rape, provided physical proof of non-consent, and then likely felt intimidated into acquiescing, as the records alleges that she then agreed, thus providing mental consent.

Within the *Year Book of the Kent Eyre of 1313–1314* is the exceptional case of Alice who appealed John of raping her virginity.[188] John defended himself unsuccessfully and was found guilty of felony rape. The record states that under the statute of Westminster II, Alice was given the opportunity to "tear out John's eyes and cut off his testicles, as he was a married man."[189] The record ends with the statement that if John was single, then "the judgment would have been that he should marry her or suffer that penance."[190] This case is significant in that the record is regurgitating earlier *Bracton*-era punishment during the legal age of Westminster II. Even though this case is an outlier, it demonstrates the EC continued interpretation of physical mutilation as punishment, which could be negated by the woman's hand in

187 This was not necessarily unique. See Neville, "Common Knowledge of the Common Law in Later Medieval England," 461–78.

188 Maitland, Harcourt, and Bolland, eds., *Year Books of Edward II*, 134–35. I have personally consulted both the British Library and Lincoln's Inn Library *Year Books* and compared it with the Maitland et al. transcription. BL, MS Addit. 32086, fols. 65v–66r; London, LI, MS *Year Book of the Time of Edward 1*, fol. 46r.

189 *Year Books of Edward II*, 134–35: "qe le fait fust fait auaunt le statut ... il eust este agarde de ele eust creue les oyls Johan e cope ses botons pour ceo qil fust marie."

190 *Year Books of Edward II*, 134–35: "mes si ele fust seingle le juggement serreyt qil la esposast ou qil eust cele penaunce."

marriage. This unique case implies that the criminal courts viewed rape as a crime of bodily urges, as the "hot lust" of men—which was initiated by sights of beautiful women—led to rape. The assumed corporality of the crime lay with both the rapist and the victim.

Concluding Thoughts

Out of the 179 *raptus* cases, and when only looking at the sixty-one rape cases, I have found fifteen failed appeals, fifteen convictions, thirteen acquittals, nine concords, seven outlawries, and two that were moved to church courts. Of the sixty-one rape cases, 40.98% of women and girls were to be imprisoned *pro false appello*, although not all of them had to serve time.[191] There are zero felony convictions. However, it is important to acknowledge how even in failed appeals there may have been victories for the wronged woman through the securing of settlements. In rape accusations with little bodily injury, jurors were warned that the accusations could be made in malice, and, as such, any doubt in the accusations aided in the accused's release. Overall, these rape cases suggest a reluctance to convict men of felony rape—perhaps because they were indeed innocent, but also because of the severity of the punishment, with the worst being physical mutilation and execution. The case studies illuminate the numerous socio-cultural conditions that influenced the proceedings, such as the physical proof of resistance to the alleged rape and the schism between the statutes' indifferences to virginity and the EC persistence on a loss of virginity to secure a trespass conviction.

Bleeding, bruising, loss of virginity, and physical force are repeatedly emphasized in the plea rolls, indicating that the woman was indeed victimized. The inclusion of physical force and blood was more than legal rhetoric; it was signifying that this was indeed a crime against the woman's will, as she tried to physically resist the rape, and she can "prove" it by her bodily injury. Importantly, several of the cases examined throughout this chapter show a recognition of the duality of mental and physical (non-)consent and an attempt to harmonize these conflicting consent models into a clear verdict for each case. While the trial records hint at the two models of (non-) consent, contemporaneous medical texts discuss the consent of the flesh of rape victims explicitly.

---

191 This number represents a total of twenty-five (out of sixty-one) women: nine from *Bracton*; eight from Westminster I; eight from Westminster II. When looking at the 179 *raptus* cases, this figure increases to eight-five women equating 47.48% of *raptus* cases: *Glanvill* (41), *Bracton* (12), Westminster I (16), Westminster II (16).

Chapter 4

CONSENT OF THE FLESH

THE CULTURAL BELIEF in the duality of mental and physical (non-)consent was upheld by contemporaneous medical understandings of human anatomy and the assumed necessary conditions for procreation to occur. This chapter provides analyses of medical texts and their endorsement of the conflicting consent models by looking at the consequences of pregnancy from rape. This chapter demonstrates how the previously discussed laws, legal treatises, trial records, and ecclesiastical texts are congruent with the medical and legal assumptions of a woman's consent of the flesh. Through an examination of the two-seed theory of conception and its assumed justification of bodily consent, I will offer three legal identities of women appealing rape that medieval English culture constructed.

Two-Seed Theory of Conception

The two-seed theory of conception—a pre-modern medical model of procreation—had profound implications for medieval understandings and interpretations of the duality of mental and physical (non-)consent. Largely attributed to Hippocrates, the two-seed theory of conception requires that both the male and female produce a seed for procreation, and this was one of two theories of conception that medieval Europe inherited from Antiquity. Aristotle advocated for the one-seed model in which only the male produces a seed, and the female provides the "environment" (womb) for procreation. Despite conflicting ideas between Hippocrates and Aristotle, by the Middle Ages the Hippocratic model, endorsed by Galen, was gaining in popularity.[1] The late-thirteenth century text *De secretis mulierum* explains that doctors endorse the two-seed theory of conception, while noting that a man ought to seduce a woman "to arouse the woman's appetite for coitus so the male and female seed will run together in the womb at the same time" in order for conception to occur.[2] This medical model of conception was supported by William of Conches, tutor to English king Henry II, who wrote in his *Dragmaticon Philosophiae*:

1 Histed, "Medieval Rape," 746–47.

2 Lemay, *Women's Secrets*, 63–65, 114–15.

> Conception from one seed is not possible: For unless the sperm of the man and woman meet, the woman does not conceive. Therefore prostitutes, who only have coitus for money, having no pleasure there, they emit nothing, nor do they beget [a child].[3]

Undoubtedly, the lack of safe and available contraceptives resulted in female sex workers experiencing unplanned pregnancies.[4] Unfortunately, prevailing medical theory worked against medieval female sex workers as the proof of their pleasure (and thus their physical consent) was evident from their pregnancy. William continues with the two-seed theory, stating:

> It comes to mind for me that recently you have said, without the female seed nothing can be conceived; but this is not truthful. We see, for instance, in raped women [*raptas*], crying out in protest [*reclamantes*] and deploring [*plorantes*] having suffered violence [*violentiam passas*], to have conceived. From whence it appears that none of those women in that trouble held pleasure. But without pleasure [*sine delectatione*] the seed [*sperma*] is not able to be emitted [*non potest emitti*]. Even though of rape it is at first displeasing [*Etsi raptis in principio opus displicet*], in the end, however, it is pleasing to the frailty of the flesh [*ex carnis fragilitate placet*]. Therefore, there are in a human being two wills [*duae voluntates*], the rational [*ratiocinatiu*] and the natural [*naturalis*], which are thought to be incompatible in us [*repugnare sentimus*]: for what is often displeasing [*displicet*] to the rational mind [*rationi*] is pleasing to the flesh [*placet carni*]. Therefore, even though there is no will of reason [*non est voluntas rationis*] in a raped woman [*rapta*], there is pleasure of the flesh [*delectatio carnis*]. And why do you doubt there to be the sperm of the mother in conception, when you see sons begotten similar to [their] mothers and who are assembled in their weakness.[5]

William of Conches provides the twelfth-century philosophical understanding of mental and physical (non-)consent as being incompatible in a way that is remarkably similar to the ecclesiastical debates about rape and sanctity. Indeed, even the phrase "pleasure of the flesh" is identical to the lines spoken by St. Lucy in Jacobus's *Golden Legend*.[6] Scientific and religious thought were intricately interwoven in the Middle Ages, as is emphasized by the

---

3 William of Conches, *Dragmaticon Philosophiae*, bk. 6, chap. 8, §. 6, p. 208. I have compared this transcription to London, BL, Addit. 18210, fols. 55r–76v. Translations are my own.

4 This is not to say that contraceptives were not known in the Middle Ages. See Riddle, *Contraception and Abortion from the Ancient World to the Renaissance.*

5 Conches, *Dragmaticon Philosophiae*, bk. 6, chap. 8, §. 9–10, pp. 209–10.

6 See Chapter 2.

medical and theological belief that the female body is inherently more sexual than the male's and thus prone to temptation and giving into bodily urges. William touches on the difficulties concerning conception and pleasure specifically regarding sex workers and rape victims. The fact that pregnancies from rape occurred was a direct challenge to the contemporaneous medical theory that conception cannot occur without pleasure. To harmonize theory and fact, William of Conches influentially claims that rape survivors who conceived must have experienced pleasure. However, he is clear that in all instances—and despite how much displeasure it is to the mind—the body will only conceive if the body gets pleasure from the sexual act.

This acknowledgment of the mental non-consent of female sex workers and rape survivors—placed in contrast with the physical consent of the flesh resulting in pregnancy—is grounded in the medieval medical understanding of anatomy. Despite the "misogynistic view" of conception,[7] the two-seed theory of conception was logical from a rudimentary understanding of human anatomy which was founded on the "one-sex model." The one-sex model was not universally accepted, and references to it in common law are rare.[8] There were various competing models of anatomy throughout the Middle Ages, including the two-sex and three-sex conceptualization. Nonetheless, the one-sex model supported the belief in the two-seed theory of conception, which undermined women's abilities to appeal rape when procreation occurred. According to this view, during sexual arousal, men produce semen which is necessary for conception, and the female anatomy was assumed to be an inverted but rather similar version of the male body. Figures 1 and 2 below visually demonstrate this assumed "inversion" of the female sex organs. Both images come from medical treatises, composed ca. 1292, which are now bound together in a single manuscript.[9]

When comparing the two images of female and male genitalia—as understood from the era of the Second Statute of Westminster II—the penile shaft in Figure 2 is inverted but rather similar to the vaginal canal in Figure 1, and indeed the inscription reads *hec est via veretri* (this is the way of the penis).[10] The binary anatomy of males and females was believed to have been a hierarchal pair: the female body was considered by Aristotle, Galen and those

---

7 Dunn, *Stolen Women*, 53.

8 Seabourne, *Women in the Medieval Common Law*, 15–16.

9 Oxford, Bodleian Library, MS Ashmole 399, fols. 13v, 24v.

10 DMLBS, "veratrum," article 1a. For more on the gendered history of medieval medicine, see Green, *Making Women's Medicine Masculine*.

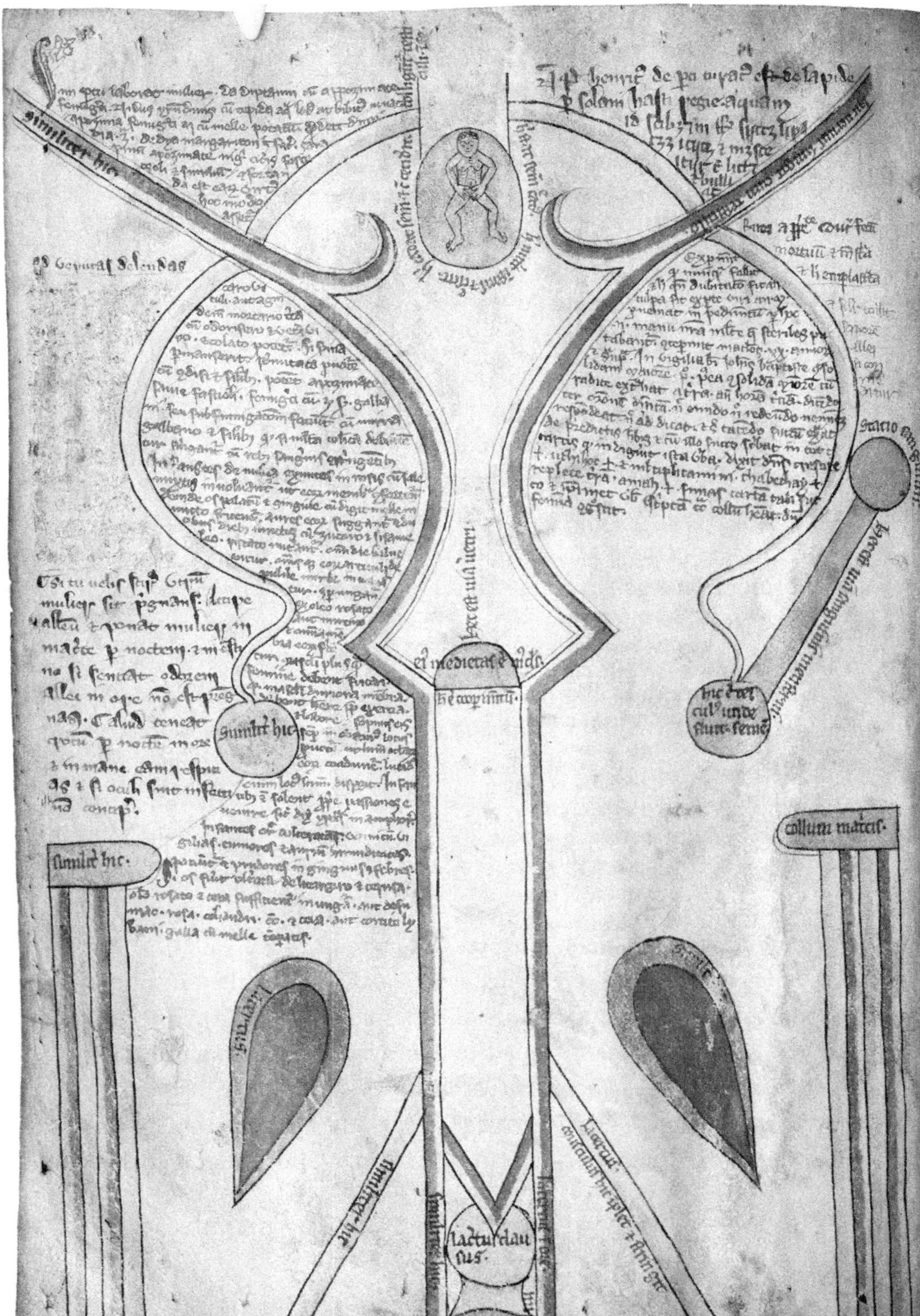

Figure 1. *Anatomy of Female Genitalia*. Oxford, Bodleian Library, MS Ashmole 399, fol. 13v. © Bodleian Libraries, University of Oxford.

Figure 2. *Anatomy of Male Genitalia*. Oxford, Bodleian Library, MS Ashmole 399, fol. 24v. © Bodleian Libraries, University of Oxford.

after them to be a "less perfect" version of the male body.[11] Thus, the idea was that men visibly produce a seed during sexual arousal and that women, with their inverted male anatomy, must also produce a less visible seed when aroused.

In the mid-thirteenth century, the notable scholar Thomas Aquinas argued that sexual desire was a sickness and a disease that compromised a man's reason. Here again the incompatibility of the rational mind and the pleasure of the flesh is reiterated. However, Galen—whose medical teachings of humoral theory were widely practiced throughout Europe—argued that sexual release was necessary for the health of the human. Humoral theory claimed that the balance between blood, black bile, yellow bile, and phlegm in the human body was necessary for healthy living. These humors were supplemented by the qualities of being hot, cold, dry, or moist. Sexual pleasure released bodily fluids, much like the common practice of bloodlettings. In this way, the rational mind stayed rational through sexual release. That is, the pleasure of the flesh aided in ensuring rationality, so instead of being incompatible, they were necessarily and mutually working for the harmony of the mind and body. This was, in part, the rationale for regulated brothels in urban centres. The assumed cold and wet nature of females assured that the female body craved the hot male sperm, and, consequently, Galen's medical theory supported ecclesiastical doctrine which considered females inherently more lustful than males. The congruency between medical knowledge, scientific logic, and theology worked to ensure that women who appealed rape were generally treated with suspicion.

Galenic theory influenced medical thought for centuries, as is evident in Lanfranc of Milan's thirteenth-century treatise *Science of Cirurgie*.[12] Lanfranc was a popular surgeon in Paris, and his treatise influenced the medical field in Europe, having a particularly large influence in England and France. Lanfranc endorsed the "one-sex model," claiming that the womb is an inverted penis, the ovaries are inverted testicles, and that both male and female bodies produce sperm during arousal which is necessary for procreation. In Middle English manuscripts, Lanfranc's theory of conception is explained:

> I will discuss the gestation of [an] embryo, that is to say, how a child is begot in the mother's womb. Galen and Avicenna say that of both the sperms of man and woman—working [*wirchynge*] and being acted upon together [*sof-*

11 Cadden, *Meanings of Sex Difference in the Middle Ages*, 21–23, 33–38.

12 London, BL, MS Addit. 12056, fols. 31r–43r (ca. 1420); Oxford, Bodleian Library, MS Ashmole 1396 (ca. 1380).

> *ferynge togedires*], so that each of them work in and are worked upon by the other—[the] embryo is begot ... so that both the sperms of man and woman make the gestation of embryo.[13]

Lanfranc's inclusion of eleventh-century Islamic scholar Ibn Sina, latinized as Avicenna, shows the wide scope (both temporally and spatially) of the acceptance of the two-seed theory of conception. In his *Canon*, Ibn Sina describes the male genitalia as "complete" and the female genitalia as a smaller, less developed form of the male's,[14] which suggests that learned men in the Muslim and Christian worlds restated the two-seed theory of conception as fact for centuries. This medical model of conception laid the foundation for the contemporaneous belief of the duality of mental and physical (non-)consent

Conception as Bodily Consent

Despite the theologians' nuanced interpretations of physical and mental (non-)consent to rape, the medieval EC consistently viewed women who endured rape as being either culpable or victimized. Looking at the treatises of *Glanvill* and *Bracton*, it is evident that men of law viewed rape victims in binaries: "true victims" could evoke sympathy from the courts, whereas "false victims" were viewed suspiciously by these powerful judicial men. These two identities were created and maintained throughout all five legal ages of *raptus* laws, from *Glanvill* to the Statute of Rapes, and, as we have seen, the EC upheld them in their rulings and sentencings. Believability of survivors resulting in convictions was seemingly dependent on women who endured the most brutal of attacks and who put up the greatest resistance as proven by bodily injury. I classify these individuals as representative of the "true victims" of rape. However, the schism between the consent of the flesh and the consent of the mind, as well as the belief that the mind and body could operate independently of one another, opened the figurative space for a third legal identity to emerge. When the female body *does things* that the female mind does not agree with, the courts viewed these unfortunate women in non-binary terms.

---

13 Fleischhacker, ed., *Lanfrank's Science of Cirurgie Part 1*, 21–22. Middle English text from London, BL, MS Addit. 12056, fols. 38v–39r. Translation is my own.

14 Jacquart and Thomasset, *Sexuality and Medicine in the Middle Ages*, 36–37. Jacquart and Thomasset make reference to Avicenna, *Canon,* trans. Gerard of Cremona, bk. 3, fen. 20, 1, chap. 1.

Although not explicitly stated in the secular laws, there was a third legal identity which held real legal repercussions. Within the binary of the "true versus false victim," the third identity that a woman could occupy is that of the reluctant, but willing, accomplice to her own rape. The phrase "reluctant, but willing, accomplice" is inspired by James Brundage, who states that canon law viewed a woman who did not put up enough resistance to her rape as "an accomplice, even if a reluctant one."[15] However, I argue that this concept more accurately describes how the courts viewed women who became pregnant because of their rape. Eyre rolls indicate that women and girls who did not resist their rape well enough were more than accomplices. They were culpable and could be sent to prison for false appeal. The third identity was constructed by the EC in practice and supported by medical assumptions of conception, despite the laws not mentioning it explicitly. That is, a woman who conceived because of her rape was considered neither entirely a true victim, nor entirely a scheming malicious woman. The polarity of mental and physical (non-)consent was considered by the courts to be apparent in these pregnant rape victims despite the written statutes' indifferences towards pregnancy through rape. With this in-between, middle category, the spectrum of legal identities that raped women could embody in the criminal courts of medieval England is complete.

The consequences of pregnancy from rape were not drawn from the legal statutes themselves but from various treatises by medical and legal professionals. Throughout the twelfth and thirteenth centuries, numerous authors of legal treatises wrote about the legal implications of pregnancy from rape, basing their beliefs on the accepted medical view of conception at that time. The late thirteenth-century legal treatise known as *Britton*[16] was extremely popular in medieval English legal circles. The treatise claims to have been commissioned by King Edward I, and it is the first legal treatise in England not to be composed in the language of the church (Latin) but rather the language of the royal court (French). *Britton*'s novel inclusion of conception through rape is not evident in the contemporaneous Statutes of Westminster I or II. The treatise states explicitly what happens if a woman who is also pregnant appeals a man of rape:

---

15 Brundage, *Law, Sex and Christian Society*, 107.

16 An early manuscript of *Britton* (ca. 1305) is held at the British Library (BL, MS Harley 324, fol. 54). I have consulted this manuscript in person and compared it to the text edited and translated by Francis Morgan Nichols below.

> With regard to an appeal of rape [*apel de rap*], our pleasure is, that every woman, whether virgin [*pucele*] or not, shall have a right to sue vengeance for the felony by appeal in the county court within forty days, but after that time she shall lose her suit; in which case, if the defendant confesses the fact, but says that the woman at the same time conceived by him, and can prove it, then our will is, that it be adjudged no felony, because no woman can conceive [*conceyvre*] if she does not consent [*assente*].[17]

Britton leaves nothing ambiguous about the legal implications of pregnancy from rape by clearly equating pregnancy to the woman's physical consent. Conception, according to *Britton*, automatically eliminated any possibility of a felony charge for rape, as conception legally implied consent of the flesh. This notion was further supported by the anonymously authored treatise *Mirror of Justices* (ca. 1290s), which states that a woman's consent is evident by either a resulting pregnancy—"that she conceived a child by him at the same hour" as the rape—or by lack of signs of violence—such as "no torn clothes, bloodshed, hue and cry, or other evidence of violence."[18] Critically, the connection between physical bodily proof and non-consent is made explicit and the association with pregnancy as part of this bodily proof of consent is mentioned. *Mirror of Justices* claims that a woman lacking those markers of resistance or who is pregnant must have consented to the attack. This notion was reiterated in *Fleta* (ca. 1290), another popular treatise, which states *si autem conceperit hora in appello contenta* (if however, she conceived during the hour [the time of the crime] in which she is appealed) the appeal is dropped, because *eo quod sine assensu concipere non potuit* (she is not able to conceive without assenting).[19] It is worth noting here that the text uses *assensu* (assent) and not *consensu* (consent) DMLBS defines *assensus* as denoting "agreement" or "complicity, [or] abetment," and *consensus* as "consent [or] agreement."[20] Despite the potential late fourteenth-century usage of "consent" to include acquiescence and silence, the two terms were

---

17 Nichols ed. and trans., *Britton*, vol. 1, chap. 24, par. 4, p. 114. Translation by Nichols.

18 Whittaker, ed. and trans, *The Mirror of Justices*, chap. 21, p. 103. The French transcription and translation are available in Whittaker's edited text. See also Kelly, "Statute of Rapes and Alleged Ravishers of Wives," 385.

19 Seldon, ed., *Fleta*, bk. 1, chap. 35, p. 54. I have compared Seldon's transcription to London, BL, Cotton MS Julius B VIII, fol. 24r. Translation is my own.

20 DMLBS, "assensus," articles 1a, 1b; "consensus," article 1a. In the verbal form: "assentarie," can mean "to flatter" (article 1a) or "to assent" (1b); "consentare" primarily means "to approve" (article 1a).

"near-synonyms."[21] As the laws and case studies suggest, the courts relied on determining non-consent through physical proof and a failure to raise the hue and cry. In modern understandings (such as in the US and Canada), consent involves both assent—that is agreement—and that assent must be given without "incapacity, deception, or coercion."[22] In this modern usage, assent can involve agreement to coitus as a form of acquiescance, as doing so may be the safer option. However, this is not considered freely given consent. In this modern context, assent does not mean consent "if the victim did not operate under sufficient freedom, capacity, and knowledge."[23] In this reading, *Fleta*'s use of *assensu* could suggest that a woman's assent to coitus was given (irrespective of circumstances) and made evident by the pregnancy. The corporality of assent legally outweighed any notions of mental non-consent to rape which could result in the dismissal of rape appeals.

The distinction between physical and mental (non-)consent, as previously discussed in Gratian's *Decretum*, is entirely neglected in the treatises of *Britton* and *Mirror of Justices*. Unlike Gratian, these two legal texts show no concern for the woman's mental non-consent. They use the lack of physical injury as proof of culpability, and, in turn, such lack of physical injury becomes justification for the acquittal of the accused rapist. The congruency of opinion between three contemporaneous, popular, and influential legal treatises—*Britton*, *Mirror of Justices*, and *Fleta*—suggests that, despite the statutory laws of Westminster I and II not including conception as equivalent to consent, lawyers and judges were certainly discussing the possibility amongst themselves. The courts viewed the reluctant but willing accomplice scathingly, as is evident from the highly influential (in that it was copied down in various *Year Books*) case of Joan of Kent.[24]

I have found no records of pregnant women appealing rape in the EC plea rolls themselves. However, the *Year Book* from the 1312–1313 Kent eyre does include a failed appeal of a pregnant rape victim named Joan and

21 As in Wyclif's discussion on consent to sin: "Oo maner of consent is, whanne a man is stille and telliþ not" (ca. 1385). See *Oxford English Dictionary*, "consent, n.," article 3a. See also Somerset, "Consent/Assent," 27, 31.

22 Ferzan and Westen, "How to Think (Like a Lawyer) About Rape," 763–65.

23 Ferzan and Westen, "How to Think (Like a Lawyer) About Rape," 765.

24 Horwood, ed., *Year Book of King Edward I*, 520–21; Maitland, Harcourt, and Bolland, eds., *Year Books of Edward II*, 111; Schneebeck, "The Law of Felony in Medieval England," 469–70. I have compared these transcriptions to London, BL, MS Addit. 32086, fol. 67r.

the subsequent indictment of the accused. The various records[25] state that Joan appealed a man by the name of W. of rape, but her appeal failed due to technicalities.[26] Because Joan did not specify the exact time and date of the rape, Joan was to be imprisoned for false appeal and W. was acquitted at her appeal.[27] However, W. was still indicted at the king's suit, at which time he was "put in irons."[28] There, W. was indicted for *ravistes la pucelage Johane* (raping the virginity of Joan). The records state that Joan was thirty years old at the time of the indictment and was "carrying a child in her arms."[29] The judge asked Joan who the father of the child was, and she confessed that it was W., the very man she was appealing of rape. The judge stated that "this was a wonderful thing,"[30] since "a child could not be begotten unless both were consenting parties."[31] Despite the fact that the prevailing Statute of Westminster II made no mention of the implications of pregnancy from rape, it appears that the courts were entrenched in the contemporaneous medical belief of the two-seed theory of conception as purported by William of Conches, Lanfranc of Milan, and the treaties *Britton*, *Mirror of Justices*, *Fleta*, and *De secretis mulierum*. This medical belief had profound influence on the courts' interpretations of culpability in rape cases, as is evident in this case, since W. stated that he could not be "guilty of rape or of any other felony." The jurors agreed that W. was not culpable and ultimately acquitted him of all charges. Even though conception being equivalent to bodily con-

25 The case of Joan is recorded in three manuscripts: Oxford, Bodleian Library, MS Tanner 13, fols. 415–85; London, BL, MS Addit. 32086, fol. 67r; London, LI, MS Year Books, Edward I, A., fols. 35v–36r. I have personally studied both BL, MS Addit. 32086 and LI, MS Year Books, Edward I, A. and compared them to the transcriptions in both *Year Books*. They are all consistent in meaning but vary in spelling. All transcriptions are taken from LI, MS Year Books, Edward I, A., fols. 35–36, unless stated otherwise.

26 LI, MS Year Books, Edward I: "e demaunda de lappelour desicom ele en contant ne fit nul mencion de rap en contant, pur quei il demaunda jugement de son mavey conte."

27 LI, MS Year Books, Edward I: "si agarde la court qe Joan aille a la prisone pur son maveys counte ... W. quite de son appel quaunt a sa seute."

28 LI, MS Year Books, Edward I: "et respoigne a la seute le Roy vicomte mettez en fers."

29 LI, MS Year Books, Edward I: "si est ele de trent anz et porte un enfant parentre ses braz."

30 This dialogue is not included in Lincoln's Inn MS, but does appear in BL, MS Addit. 32086, fol. 67: "dit fust qe cest mervueille ... qe un enfant ne purr amie ester engendere sanz volunte de une part e dautre."

31 LI, MS Year Books, Edward I; BL, MS Addit. 32086, fol. 67: "engendere sanz la volunte de deux."

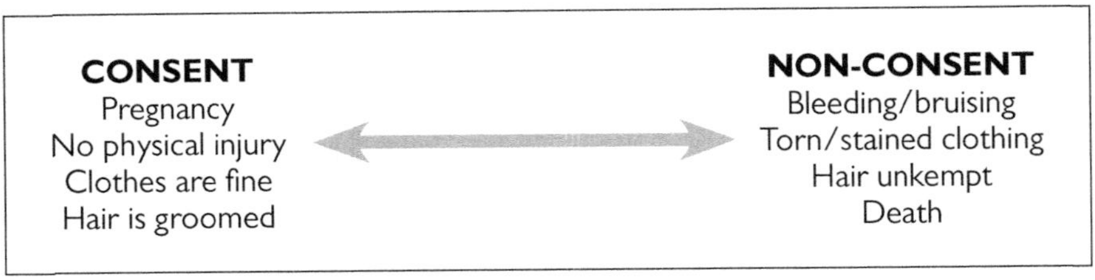

Diagram 1. The Physicality of (Non-)Consent.

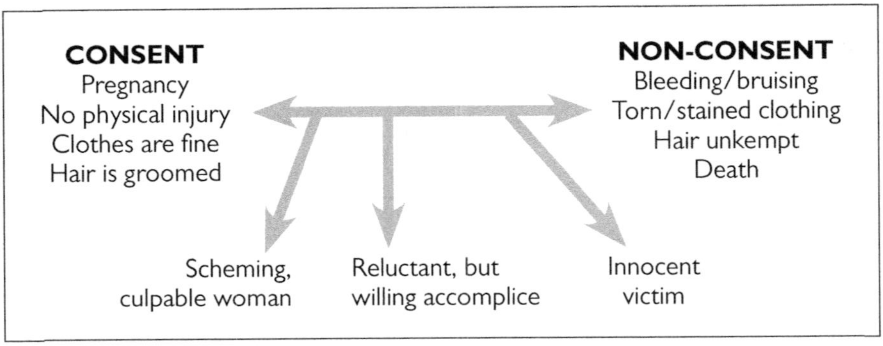

Diagram 2. The Spectrum of Constructed Legal Identities.

sent was not legally binding in medieval England's *raptus* laws themselves, it evidently had legal impact. The courts constructed the legal framework which determined that Joan may have not mentally consented to the sexual intercourse but, regardless, her body consented, which was evident (to the courts) by her pregnancy.[32] Joan was the reluctant but ultimately willing accomplice to her own rape, and therefore W. was not culpable.

The treatises (*Britton*, *Mirror of Justices*, and *Fleta*), as well as the secular laws, ensured that the burden of proof of non-consent laid exclusively with the woman and was only verified through the inspection of her body. Diagram 1 illustrates the physicality of (non-)consent using the prescribed visual proof which was required. The tokens of proof are gathered from EC records, legal treatises, manuscript illuminations, conduct literature, romance narratives, and statutory laws. Diagram 2 includes my proposed

32 Sara Butler discusses a case from 1465 Lancashire where Elizabeth Venor was raped and impregnated by John Worth. Elizabeth appealed John stating "'... that her flesh was in a manner agreed,' but 'in her soul she never assented, that is, in all her entire will in her soul, so that she was not at ease.'" Butler, *Divorce in Medieval England*, 61. See also Histed's retelling of Lady Isobel Butler's 1436 rape and pregnancy by William Pulle in "Medieval Rape," 743–55.

spectrum of legal identities superimposed on the previous diagram of physical bodily proof of (non-)consent.

An individual's identity is a construction both in the (subconscious) performance and in the language used to describe them. Of course, these proposed identities were not necessarily how the women viewed themselves. Rather, women appealing rape in medieval English criminal courts were socially and linguistically prescribed certain "identities" which were interwoven with cultural notions of rape and (non-)consent. The bodily proof of (non-)consent to rape worked to create the legally constructed identities of women who went to court, and, consequently, their identity (and legal ruling) depended upon the degree of physical proof of the crime. The physicality of (non-)consent and the resulting legal identities are continually reinforced in the actual court documents, hagiography, and, as will be discussed in the following two chapters, secular romance narratives. The case of Joan from Kent shows the devastating repercussions for women who conceived during rape, as her case was automatically thrown out. Although Hiram Kümper correctly warns scholars that "the idea of pregnancy as generally obviating rape charges should not too readily be applied to the whole medieval period,"[33] the case of Joan demonstrates how the EC could—and at times did—interpret conception as consent of the flesh.

The nuanced interpretations of mental non-consent, as proposed in Augustine's *City of God*, are entirely neglected here, where the proof of rape was interpreted by an examination of the woman's physical body. It is important to note the devastating repercussions that such a literal body of proof had. If a woman consented to the rape in fear of her life and was thus compliant to the demands of the rapist because she had no physical injury, then she could be deemed culpable for her own rape in the king's courts. However, cases involving coercive consent or other non-violent means to ensure submission seem to have been easier to secure a conviction in civil—not felony—suits. This is highlighted by the 1292 Hereford case of Isabella Plomet. Isabella won a civil conviction against her dentist, Ralph de Worgan, for drugging and raping her.[34] Civil suit courts, like the ecclesiastical texts previously discussed, offer complex understandings of mental non-consent that appear more "modern" than those of *Glanvill* or Westminster II. Nonetheless, in the criminal courts of the eyre, the physicality of (non-)consent was king.

33 Kümper, "Learned Men and Skilful Matrons," 108.

34 This case was discovered by Seabourne, "Drugs, Deceit and Damage in Thirteenth-century Herefordshire," 255–76; see also, Harris, "Medieval Histories of Intoxication and Consent," 109–34.

The visible proof of the crime was used to determine innocence or guilt of the woman. A true victim had to have physical injury. A reluctant but willing accomplice may have had mental non-consent, but her body consented which was evident by pregnancy. Lastly, the laws constructed the identity of the culpable woman who had no physical injuries to show as proof of the rape. Although the secular laws made no explicit mention of resistance, the implication of physical injury suggests a struggle between the individuals involved, and such struggle would not have likely occurred unless the woman was reluctant to comply with the assault. Thus, even though the laws only state physical injury, we can logically conclude that such injury was the consequence of resistance to the rape, as it denotes a physical altercation of some sort. This legal necessity of physical injury to ensure believability in court worked to sustain the burden of a body of proof that lay entirely on the woman. This body of proof in court was also extended beyond physical injury to include the pregnant body.

Bodily Victimization

The inclusion of both male and female sperm for the gestation of the embryo was largely assumed as biological fact, although Aristotelian theory was still debated. This medieval medical thought was supplemented with ideas from leading scholars that lust and coitus were simultaneously sinful and necessary. Consequently, medical texts state that men needed sexual release for their health. This was further compounded with the common societal belief that sex work was "a necessary evil"[35] in medieval Europe to allow men sexual release or else they would become overwhelmed with their "hot lust," as purported in *Bracton*. According to Ruth Mazo Karras, sex work was "a necessary outlet for masculine sex drives which, unrelieved would undermine the social order."[36] The *Bracton*-era belief in over-active male libido was grounded in contemporaneous societal, medical, and scientific beliefs about male sexuality. Karras states that "people believed that pressure builds up and has to be released through a safety valve (marriage or prostitution), or eventually the dam will burst and men will commit seduction, rape, adultery, and sodomy."[37] This implicitly suggests that medieval Europeans believed that every man was a potential rapist if they did not have an "outlet"; that

35 Turner, "The Leper and the Prostitute," 129.

36 Karras, *Common Women*, 5–7, 114–15.

37 Karras, *Common Women*, 6, 20.

is to say, all men were potential rapists if they did not have easy access to a woman's body through marriage or a sex worker. Consequently, sex work was regulated in urban centres and considered necessary to protect both women and men from rape. To protect their daughters and wives and maintain social order against rape, men of law regulated brothels and did not punish the men who visited them. However, sex workers were traditionally blamed for seducing men into sexual temptation even though they were reluctantly deemed necessary for maintaining the greater social order.[38]

This medieval medical belief in uncontrollable male sexuality, which necessitated the toleration of sex workers, ensures that men were the victims of their own bodies in a way that is remarkably similar to the legal identity of the rape victim who conceives. As previously discussed, *Bracton* is heavily entrenched in and further promoted this notion of excessive and dangerous male sexual urges. There is a medical and legal precedence to the belief that all men are potential rapists, but it is within the power of "good" men to control these sexual impulses. If a man is unable to manage his lust, he will rape. The loss of control of one's lust is equivalent to the loss of control of one's own reason. The rapists are, in this sense, more monstrous than human, much like a "wildman" attacking a lady.[39] As Augustine notes in *City of God*, monsters and monstrous humans are the opposite of an *animal rationale mortale* (a rational and mortal creature).[40] Here, the notions of rapists and wild beasts, or monsters, become conflated, as both are not in control of their own impulses.[41]

The body's ability to not only be the site of victimization for women (in the case of rape) but also be the cause of victimization (in the case of sexual urges) for both men and women was not treated equally. Medical thought victimized both men and women who were unable to control their sexual desires. However, men were largely pitied for their bodily victimization, and, as such, the women who were sex workers were condemned but not the men who used their services.[42] Whereas the male body was viewed as needing moderate sexual release, the secular and ecclesiastical courts criminalized these very same sexual urges in women and rendered them inherently

38 Karras, *Common Women*, 48, 133.

39 As depicted in the fourteenth-century Taymouth Hours book cover image.

40 Augustine, *City of God*, ed. Henderson, bk. 16, chap. 8. See also, Verner, *The Epistemology of the Monstrous in the Middle Ages*, 2–4.

41 Further explored in *Sir Gowther* in Chapter 6.

42 Karras, *Common Women*, 20.

sinful. Gratian's *Decretum* describes sexual temptation as a form of sickness and claims that only weak individuals succumb to their lust.[43] Further, Gratian contributed to the popular belief that women were inherently more likely to fall victim to their sexual urges due to their lack of reason and willpower.[44] While both the male and female body could betray the reason of the mind, the societal tolerance for men's sexual freedom was not equally extended to women, and, moreover, it was legislated against.

The one-sex model of anatomy ensured that it was widely believed amongst scholars that the female seed was only released during sexual pleasure. Critically, this was not solely a medical belief, but it was also highly supported by theologians, who were men of authority in both ecclesiastical and secular courts. This effectively perpetuated the belief that a truly innocent rape victim could not become pregnant from the rape. William of Conches admits that even though the woman's mind may not consent, her body—the desire of her flesh—could consent. This is where the legal identity of the reluctant but willing accomplice is fully formed, given that the courts view these pregnant victims as willing in their flesh despite their potential mental non-consent. Here, the mental non-consent is deemed irrelevant to the treatises, as they relied on the physical bodily consent in rape cases resulting in pregnancy.

In all, we see a cultural discourse that debated the possibility of mental and physical (non-)consent. Throughout the three previous chapters we have seen how the secular laws hint at the conflicting consent models, the ecclesiastical texts explicitly discuss the possibility of mental and physical (non-)consent, and how several EC trial records recognize the conflict of physical non-consent and mental consent. This short yet critical chapter has provided further, evidential proof of the medieval English belief that the consent of the flesh as evidenced by pregnancy could overpower mental non-consent of rape victims. This cultural conceptualization of rape, resistance, and mental and physical (non-)consent is further discussed in the popular literary genre of romance. As will be shown in the following two chapters, the popular entertainment of MER reiterates these same arguments in nearly identical fashion to the legal, medical, and ecclesiastical texts.

---

43 *Decretum*, C. 25, q. 1.

44 *Decretum*, C. 27, q. 1, cap. 4.

Chapter 5

ABDUCTION AND MALICIOUS RAPE ACCUSATIONS IN ROMANCE

DURING A RAINY day in the English countryside, a young woman of about thirteen or fourteen years old seeks indoor entertainment. Tired of practicing her embroidery, she asks her friends if they would like to read a romance. Excited by the thought of simple—if somewhat illicit—pleasure-reading and discussion, which was permitted by her mother before, the young ladies eagerly agree. Going to her father's sizable book collection, she skims past a dozen or so devotional texts, and she looks for an English romance, as the girl's Latin was not particularly strong. She grabs a book off the shelf and joins her friends in a communal reading session. Each woman in the group takes turns reading passages aloud from the romance while the others listen. The reader begins: "listen lords, gentile and noble, I will tell you of Sir Degare." As the story continues, the young ladies listen collectively to the description of the handsome fairy knight approaching a lost princess in the woods. Will he help her find her way home, perhaps with a battle against a giant like Bevis of Hampton did against Acapart? Will he ask to joust against her father and win her hand in marriage, proving his knightly valour like Guy of Warwick and Clarice? Or will he take her away to fairyland, like the fairy king did to Orfeo's wife Heurodis? They listen to the words the fairy knight speaks, his courtly language, and his declaration of love for the princess. The reader continues: "he seized her at once, and did his will as he desired, and bereft her of her maidenhood." The ladies stop to discuss what they just read. The young women talk about how the princess could not escape and how she was left to "weep and cry." What does an imagined woman reader take away from such scenes of sexual violence in romance? The audiences of listening and reading women would have likely been able to connect to this scene of sexual violence, either through their own personal experiences or through the experiences of people they knew.

Rape is commonly threatened and occasionally completed in romance literature. The following two chapters will discuss scenes of rape (threatened or actualized) in MER narratives and analyze how they reinforce the constructed legal identities, how they perpetuate the actual legal requirement of resistance to rape, how they didactically disseminate legal requirements of proof of rape, and how they debate the duality of physical and mental (non-)consent of rape victims. As will become more evident in the following discussion, romance is reflecting a reality but does not necessarily intend to be realistic.

Sir Orfeo[1]

Orfeo, a king in England, is the titular character of this romance, but it is his queen, Heurodis, that this analysis will primarily focus on. She is described as "the fairest lady," both loving and good, and her physical beauty is so great that no man can accurately describe her.[2] We are told that the queen takes maidens with her to "play" in the orchard, at which point Heurodis and her ladies go "to see the spring flowers" and "to hear the birds sing. / They sat themselves down all three / Under a fair grafted tree."[3] Heurodis sleeps in the orchard without the disruption of her ladies until midday—a signpost to the audience that a supernatural encounter is likely approaching. When Heurodis awakes "she cried, and loathsome [*lothli*] outcry made; / She rubbed [*froted*] her hand and her feet, / And scratched her face – it bled profusely– / Her rich robe she tore all to pieces / And was driven [*reveyd*] out of her wit."[4]

Lothli implies being fearful or terrified, and so Heurodis, in this state of frenzy, is first and foremost described as fearful.[5] The description of her physical self-mutilation is graphic, or as James Wade claims, "disturbing,"[6] as *froten* describes the action of crushing, grinding, or scratching.[7] She is physically harming herself, crushing and grinding her feet and hands, as a type of coping-mechanism for the utter fear. At this point, Heurodis is nonverbal, having not said a single word of direct speech. The self-mutilation continues, as she rips at her face to such a degree that she begins to bleed abundantly. We later learn that Heurodis was sent into a state of madness because she

1 The earliest extant Middle English manuscript comes from the Auchinleck manuscript (ca. 1330): Edinburgh, National Library of Scotland, MS Advocates 19. 2. 1. Translations of the MER texts discussed here are my own, often adapted from the TEAMS sources cited.

2 "Sir Orfeo," ll. 53–56.

3 "Sir Orfeo," ll. 67–70.

4 "Sir Orfeo," ll. 78–82.

5 MED, "Lothli (adj.)."

6 Wade, *Fairies in Medieval Romance*, 77.

7 MED, "Froten (v.)."

was visited by a fairy king in the orchard. Heurodis later explains her self-mutilation as a state of panic and horror at what occurred in the orchard:

> There came to me two fair knights / Well armed all quite properly, / And bade me come in haste / And speak to their lord the king. / And I answered with words bold, / I dare not, nor did I want to; ... / Then came their king, as quickly, / With a hundred knights and more, / And damsels a hundred also ... / And as soon as he to me came, / Whether I wished or not, he took me, / And made me with him ride / Upon a palfrey by his side; / And brought me to his palace ... / And afterwards brought me back home / Into our own orchard, / And said to me this afterward,/ "Look, dame, tomorrow that you be / Right here under this grafted tree, / And then you shall with us go / And live with us evermore. / And if you make a hindrance for us, / Wherever you be, you will be fetched, / And torn apart all limbs / That nothing shall help you; / And though you are so torn, / Yet you will be carried with us.[8]

Heurodis's verbal and mental non-consent is explicit, at which point the knights leave on horseback. When the fairy king approaches Heurodis, she states, "whether I wished or not, he took me."[9] Heurodis describes her first abduction as leaving to fairyland by force, in that the fairy king "*made* [her] with him ride" and "*brought* [her] to his palace" and "*showed* [her] castles and towers."[10] In fairyland, Heurodis is entirely isolated, she is away from the known courtly world, and she is the object of his actions.

Once Heurodis is "brought" back to the human world, the fairy king threatens her. She can return to the same tree tomorrow and come with him to live in fairyland forever, or she can try to resist, but this will inevitably fail. Not only will the fairy king find her "wherever [she] be," but he also threatens her with extreme bodily harm. The threat of violence against Heurodis if she attempts to resist her abduction is shockingly graphic and entirely against the expected seduction of a courtly suitor. There is no mention of love or lust. Why the fairy king is insistent on taking Heurodis is left entirely unmentioned. The use of the word *totoren* is critical, as it means "to destroy ... to rip up (one's garments) in a frenzy of emotion or madness; ... strip away (flesh); [or] to lacerate (skin, someone's body, part of the body) savagely."[11] The fairy king's threat is an act of brutality, yet the double meaning of madness or frenzy plays on the queen's state of insanity. In this sense

8 "Sir Orfeo," ll. 135–74.

9 "Sir Orfeo," l. 154.

10 "Sir Orfeo," ll. 155, 157, 159.

11 MED, "Toteren v." article 2.

of the word, the fairy king fulfills his threat by throwing the queen into such a state of madness that she rips up her own garments. To end his threat, the fairy king claims that there is nothing she can do to stop the abduction. Even if she is murdered in the process, they will still take her away. Heurodis ends her only direct speech in the entire narrative with this looming threat of abduction, mutilation, and death.

With this knowledge, we can now re-assess the earlier episode of her self-mutilation. Heurodis's graphic scratching of her face, hands, and feet is reminiscent of the hagiographical debate about suicide and the acceptable means of avoiding rape previously discussed. Patricia Skinner notes that "the sight of a mutilated female face could engender horror and shock in the medieval viewer."[12] The facial mutilation may be referencing the *Bracton*-era notion that men rape women because of their beauty, and it is perhaps implying that mutilation can protect against rape. This was the alleged course of action taken at Coldingham Priory in 870. According to thirteenth-century chronicler Matthew Paris, upon hearing that Norsemen were coming, Abbess Ebba instructed the holy women to cut their noses and lips off their faces with a razor to prevent their rapes.[13] Emulating the virgin martyrs, the women of Coldingham supposedly opted for self-mutilation to defend themselves from rape, torture, and murder. However, the raiders were repulsed at the sight of the mutilated women and decided to "burn down the convent with the nuns inside it."[14] There is a strong correlation here with *Bracton*'s punitive blinding and facial disfigurement. The fact that the mutilation saved the nuns of Coldingham from rape and thus preserved their virginity demonstrates the legal belief, as implied in *Bracton*, that men rape because the women are physically attractive. The uncontrollable passion to rape, as detailed in *Bracton*, was assumed to disappear at the sight of disfigured women. This legendary story, along with the similar *vita* of St. Brigit of Ireland, would have been well known to the medieval audiences of the twelfth to the fourteenth century.

Once we know why Heurodis is so terrified, her state of madness seems more planned. The legal requirement of proof of rape included blood, bruising, and torn or stained clothing. It is significant that Heurodis, in her state of madness, rips her clothes into pieces and causes herself to bleed profusely,

12 Skinner, "Marking the Face, Curing the Soul?," 187.

13 Farmer, "Ebbe the Younger,"; Matthew Paris, *Chronica majora*, ed. H. R. Luard, vol. 1, pp. 391–92.

14 Horner, "Spiritual Truth and Sexual Violence," 671.

suggesting that she may have stained her clothes. These physical markers are all working to ensure that she appears to be a victim of *raptus* according to the legal requirements of women under *Glanvilll*, *Bracton*, and the Statutes of Westminster I and II. Heurodis has the legally necessary physical proof of a crime. Even though these physical injuries are self-inflicted, they act as visible markers of her victimization. The romance appears to be demonstrating her legal identity as a true victim, as she is described specifically as "*reveyd*," or ravished, and James Wade identifies this as a "kind of psychological ravishing."[15]

The next day, Orfeo is determined to protect his beloved wife, so he sends Heurodis into the orchard with the protection of "ten hundred knights ... / Each armed, strong and fierce."[16] Using his queen as bait to conquer the fairy king, Orfeo orders his men to use their shields as a barrier to surround Heurodis. The valiant knights state that they are willing to die to protect their queen, but all human attempts of resistance to the supernatural prove futile: "but yet amidst them straightaway / The queen was snatched away, / With enchantment taken. / Men never knew where she was gone."[17] Orfeo is distraught that Heurodis is taken, and he appoints his high steward to run his kingdom while he himself retreats into the wilderness.[18] The author uses the word *lore* to describe Orfeo's loss.[19] *Lore* is defined primarily as "a loss of thing, property or money," thus suggesting that the abduction was equally a crime against Orfeo for his loss of property.[20] Like Sir Thomas West and the Statute of Rapes, which claims that men are the true victims of *raptus*, Orfeo's loss is representative of this legal claim. The abduction of Orfeo's wife is a crime against him, and this is reflective of the claims of husbands, fathers, and legal male guardians under the *raptus* laws of Westminster II and culminating in the Statute of Rapes. Even though Heurodis is the character who was violently threatened and abducted, the remainder of the romance focuses exclusively on Orfeo's journey: his decision to leave his kingdom and his time in the wilderness. Heurodis's ravishment initiates the plot, but she is silenced and excluded from the narrative until Orfeo finds her. Her fears, mental trauma, and abduction are a plot device to demon-

15 Wade, *Fairies in Medieval Romance*, 77.

16 "Sir Orfeo," ll. 181–85.

17 "Sir Orfeo," ll. 191–94.

18 "Sir Orfeo," ll. 205–12.

19 "Sir Orfeo," l. 209.

20 MED, "Lore n." article 1.

strate the courtly and heroic behaviour of Orfeo. This is reiterated again at the end of the romance, when Orfeo claims that he "had suffered very long ago."[21] Orfeo is claiming the victim status much like how the law treated men as victims in the Statute of Rapes.

While in the wilderness, we are told of Orfeo's great distress and the loss of his kingdom. The romance is illustrating the severe consequences men face after women's abductions. Even though Orfeo's loss is self-imposed, it nonetheless expresses the common fears and anxieties amongst noblemen (as suggest by Thomas West's petitions) that the ravishment of their daughters and wives would lessen their patrimony.[22] When Orfeo finally sees Heurodis, he follows her back to fairyland, which is described as a place of great luxury. But the fairy palace is also a palace of the dead and the mad. The severity of the fairy king's threat is confirmed, as individuals are described as severely wounded and decapitated; some have limbs torn off, some are perpetually suffocating or drowning, and "some lay mad."[23] Fairyland is both beautiful and horrific. The juxtaposition of beauty and the grotesque in fairyland echoes the cultural coupling of rape as an act of lustful admiration as well as violence. Both fairyland and the medieval societal opinion about why rape occurs occupy the same figurative, conflicting, space. That is, the beauty of fairyland turns at once into a horrifying reality in the same way that the beauty of the maiden (according to *Bracton*) leads to the horrific crime of rape. The juxtaposition of fairyland mirrors the contemporaneous popular opinions of rape culture in England: what is initially beautiful and admirable can suddenly turn violent and horrific.

The romance ends with the traditional happy ending expected of the genre. Heurodis leaves fairyland with Orfeo, the loyalty of the steward is tested, and all is restored in the end. The ravisher in *Sir Orfeo* faces no legal repercussions; there are no trials, no criminal allegations, and the ravisher king does not repent for his actions. Perhaps this is hinting at the fact that the laws themselves (as written) claim that ravishers walk around unpunished.[24] As the metaphorical representations of men are displayed in romance as fairies and fiends, it is apparent that romance is representing the lived real-

---

21 "Sir Orfeo," l. 559.

22 Oren Falk argues that Heurodis becomes "unfit to bear the son of Orfeo," suggesting that due to her ravishment, Orfeo never recovers his patrimony from the steward. See, Falk, "The Son of Orfeo," 260–61.

23 "Sir Orfeo," ll. 391–94.

24 See the opening line of the Statute of Rapes discussed in Chapter 1.

ity of a lack of legal accountability for men who rape and abduct women. This displacement of man as fairy allows for this difficult topic to become more approachable.

Overall, Heurodis's abduction and non-consent to leave are likely intentionally ambiguous to inspire discussions. While her verbal and mental non-consent is explicit, it proved futile, as it did not stop her ravishment. The romance plays with the ambiguity of masculine brutality and chivalry by mirroring the two kings, Orfeo and the fairy king, while simultaneously playing with audience expectations of consent and resistance: Did Heurodis agree to leave? What was the enchantment she was under? What about the threat of violence? The narrative of *Sir Orfeo* offers the opportunity for conversations and debates about violence against women as well as the realities of rejecting a violent suitor with verbal and mental non-consent. Still, it ultimately upholds normative assumptions about the man's victim status in relation to a wife or daughter's ravishment and the necessity of resistance to prove non-consent.

Amis and Amiloun[25]

The narrative of *Amis and Amiloun* focuses primarily on the loyalty and affection between the two titular male characters. The theme of brotherhood and honouring pledges is paramount in this romance. Amis and Amiloun are conceived on the same night, born on the same day, both are the son of a baron in Lombardy, they look identical, and they are both dubbed knights at the standard age of fifteen. The pledge of brotherhood between Amis and Amiloun, which is so central to the romance narrative, is not of concern here. Rather, it is the persistent attempts of the duke's daughter, Belisaunt, to seduce Amis that is the focus of the present analysis.

We are first introduced to Belisaunt after Amiloun leaves the duke's house to claim his own inheritance, at which point the duke's evil steward unsuccessfully tries to persuade Amis to swear an oath of fidelity with him. The duke's fifteen-year-old daughter, Belisaunt, is repeatedly referred to as a "lovely maiden," indicating her young virginal status. She asks her ladies "who was considered the doughtiest knight, / And most splendid in each a sight."[26] The ladies tell Belisaunt that Amis is the best "prize," and, upon hear-

25 Extant in four Middle English manuscripts, including Edinburgh, National Library of Scotland, MS Advocates 19. 2. 1 (Auchinleck MS); London, BL, MS Egerton 2862; London, BL, MS Harley 2386; Oxford, Bodleian Library, MS Bodleian 21900.

26 "Amis and Amiloun," ll. 451–52.

ing that, "her love was all alight."[27] Belisaunt quickly becomes lovesick for Amis. As she watches him ride, she "thought her heart would break in two."[28]

In traditional romance fashion, Belisaunt becomes extremely infatuated with Amis as soon as she lays eyes on him. Unlike the other romances discussed in this book, here it is the woman who occupies the role of the persistent wooer. Adhering to cultural expressions of femininity, Belisaunt does not approach Amis at first, but rather she watches him from a distance and waits for him to notice her. However, Belisaunt's attempts to conform to gender expectations cause her severe emotional distress, as she cries in sorrow because Amis does not notice her. To explain why Belisaunt is unable to speak to Amis, we must contextualize the narrative within the period's expected gender roles of heterosexual courtship. Belisaunt is representative of the cultural norms expected of ladies and the troubles of feminine wooing in a culture that idealizes feminine passivity.

Eventually, Belisaunt refuses the expected feminine passivity of ladies and becomes the active pursuer of Amis. While her father the duke is out hunting, Amis enters the garden and listens to the birds under a tree. The romance trope of gardens as magical places has been acknowledged by scholars,[29] as has the literary trope of supernatural beings transforming into birds and seducing humans.[30] However, the frequency of birds singing as a prelude to rape or seduction scenes has yet to be fully discussed. Here, Amis is listening to the birds before he is approached by Belisaunt. Moreover, Belisaunt's mother tells her to get out of bed "and go play in the garden / ... There you may hear the birds sing."[31] Playing in the garden is really playing the game of courtly love and seduction. Belisaunt's mother specifically references the birds as the incentive to go out to the garden, and the birds are the specific reason given as to why Amis is also in the garden. Similarly, Heurodis (in *Sir Orfeo*) listens to the birds in the garden before her abduction. Elizabeth Eva Leach argues that birds can signal sexualized rhetoric in medieval literature, such as the sexual connotation of the nightingale and the cuckoo

27 "Amis and Amiloun," l. 473.

28 "Amis and Amiloun," l. 476.

29 McAvoy, *The Enclosed Garden and the Medieval Religious Imaginary*, 16–17; Saunders, *Rape and Ravishment*, 224; Stevens, *Medieval Romance*, 157.

30 Wicher, "Geoffrey Chaucer's *The Merchant's Tale*, Giovanni Boccaccio's *The Tale of the Enchanted Pear-Tree*, and *Sir Orfeo* Viewed as Eroticized Versions of the Folktales about Supernatural Wives," 44.

31 "Amis and Amiloun," ll. 524–26.

bird's association with a cuckold husband.[32] Leach's analysis of the mythical hybrid sirens (half bird, half nude woman) offers further opportunity to explore the relationship between birds and sexuality in medieval thought.[33] The connections between adultery and the cuckoo, shapeshifters seducing as birds, sexualized sirens, and lustful nightingales suggests that there is a connection between birds and sexuality. The romances under investigation here use bird songs to signal a coming rape and/or abduction either actualized or threatened. Perhaps the sounds of birds indicate a state of isolation outdoors, whether that be the woods in *Sir Degare*, the outdoors of the palace gardens in *Sir Orfeo*, or the orchard in *Amis and Amiloun*.

Reminiscent of the abduction in *Sir Orfeo*, Belisaunt enters the orchard, where she finds Amis alone under a tree listening to the birds. As she approaches Amis, he recognizes how beautiful she is and greets her. The nature of his greeting is left ambiguous, as it is Belisaunt who is given direct speech:

> And [she] said in her courtly love talk, / "Sir knight, on you my heart is brought, / You to love is all my thought/ Both by night and day; / That unless you will be my beloved, / Certainly, my heart will break in three, / No longer I may live ..."[34]

Belisaunt's courtly language in conjunction with her eventual rape threat indicates that the courtly suitor can quickly turn aggressive. This also serves to demonstrate that rape culture is part of the courtly world, embedded *within* courtly culture and not outside of it. The medieval audiences would have undoubtedly recognized Belisaunt's transgression of gender and social norms. Amis explicitly rejects Belisaunt's seduction because of her superior social status, because it would be an offence against his lord—her father—the duke. Amis specifically states that their union would be "much un-right,"[35] because she is a rich female heiress while he is a landless knight. This is reflective of the fears of lawmakers regarding *raptus* claims between individuals of unequal social classes. Amis warns Belisaunt that if they engage in this "game" of courtly love and they are discovered, "we should lose / and for that sin, / Wrath of God thereto. / And if I did my lord this dishonour, / Than were I an evil traitor."[36] In describing their love as sinful, the romance hints

32 Leach, *Sung Birds*, 240–41.

33 Leach, *Sung Birds*, 263.

34 "Amis and Amiloun," ll. 570–77

35 "Amis and Amiloun," l. 598.

36 "Amis and Amiloun," ll. 605–8.

at the social class disparity and Belisaunt's usurpation of feminine passivity, but it also foreshadows the future malicious rape accusations. Amis's use of legal terminology is poignant. Their love is not only sinful in the eyes of God, but, according to Amis, it is also wrong in the secular laws of the realm, as he would be committing petty treason against his superior lord, making him a traitor.

Rejected, Belisaunt becomes angry and accuses Amis of preaching to her on some unfounded higher moral ground. She then threatens Amis with a malicious accusation of rape:

> "Unless if you will grant me my thought, / My love shall be dearly paid for / With pains hard and strong; / My kerchief and my clothes immediately / I will tear every one / And say with great wrong, / With strength you have violated me; / You shall be arrested according to the laws of the land / And condemned high to hang!"[37]

This angry threat of fictitious rape is playing into the overt fears of lawmakers who worried about the downfall of good, honest men due to false rape accusations made by jealous and spiteful women, as suggested in *Glanvill* and culminating in the Statute of Rapes. Belisaunt's threat is extremely specific, as she is referencing the necessary physical evidence of rape. She claims that she will rip her clothing, which is one of the prescribed signs of physical proof of non-consent in both *Glanvill* and *Bracton*. The MED defines *todrawe*—with specific reference to this romance—as "(a) to rip off (flesh, a part of the body); (b) tear out (hair) ... (d) to cause affliction; injure; harm; ... oppress."[38] These actions are almost identical to the secular legal expectations of physical proof of non-consent of rape victims. That is, to have a man oppress a woman to such a degree that it causes her bodily injury, whether that be torn clothing, bleeding injuries, or bruising. This long lineage of physical proof of non-consent was clearly upheld in popular imagination. Belisaunt is keenly aware that her words alone will not ensure a conviction, and physical proof of non-consent to the alleged rape is required. As previously discussed, medieval English *raptus* laws explicitly discuss the fear of women accusing men of rape or of women eloping and using *raptus* as a legal loophole. Here, the fictional Belisaunt is stating the real legal expectations of

37 "Amis and Amiloun," ll. 628–36: "Bot yif thou wilt graunt me mi thought,/ Mi love schal be ful dere abought/ With pines hard and strong;/ Mi kerchef and mi clothes anon/ Y schal torende doun ichon/ And say with michel wrong,/ With strengthe thou hast me todrawe;/ Ytake thou schalt be londes law/ And dempt heighe to hong!"

38 MED, "Todrauen v."

women who accuse men of rape (physical injury as proof of non-consent) while also reflecting the greater fear about women who lie about rape.

Belisaunt's reference to the "laws of the land" and the punishment for convicted rapists (hanging) is striking. Corinne Saunders notes that the inclusion of rape laws in Belisaunt's speech implies that even in the courtly idealized world of romance, there is a need for legal protection against rape and punishment for the rapist, as these laws have a "role in ordering the chivalric world."[39] Belisaunt is sure that she can secure a legal conviction if she tears her clothes and claims rape by the knight. In a sense, Belisaunt is the "perfect rape victim": she is a noble, beautiful, fifteen-years-old virgin, and there are witnesses (her ladies and her mother) to confirm that Belisaunt and Amis were alone in the garden together. In contrast, the accused rapist, Amis, is a landless knight who lives in the household of Belisaunt's father. These factors all work to Belisaunt's advantage and to the advantage of real women appealing rape in the real criminal courts. Belisaunt is not threatening a romance vendetta by her father or seeking personal revenge. Rather, she is referencing the secular laws of the land and the legal implications for convicted rapists.

Amis is shocked by the malicious threat that Belisaunt will accuse him of rape. He stands silently and "disliked it greatly in his heart."[40] He is aware of the severity of her accusations, as he thinks "with her speech she will have me killed."[41] It is her words he fears. Her accusations can cause him to hang. This is the opposite of the explicit fears in *Sir Degare* (discussed in the following chapter), as the princess in that romance fears the male's actions. Here, the knight fears the woman's verbal threats. These are the two driving factors of medieval England's secular *raptus* laws. Both the real actions of men (rape) and the fictitious accusations of women (false accusations) are at the forefront of *raptus* laws from the age of *Glanvill* to the Statute of Rapes. The secular *raptus* laws continually sought to protect vulnerable women from real rape while simultaneously expressing the fear of women's false rape accusations against good men. The duality of the laws—to protect good women from bad men and good men from bad women—is emphasized here in *Amis and Amiloun*.

For fear of his life, Amis consents to Belisaunt's demands, but they are suspected of "great love" by the wicked steward, and thus there is the inten-

---

39 Saunders, *Rape and Ravishment*, 197; Saunders, "A Matter of Consent," 113.

40 "Amis and Amiloun," ll. 637–38.

41 "Amis and Amiloun," l. 641.

tional blurring of lust, seduction, threatened rape, and now love.[42] Amis claims that he wants to marry Belisaunt, which sets up the common narrative arc of lust, seduction, (threatened) rape, and matrimony. Amis states, however, that it is not proper for him, of such lowly status, to marry her. Belisaunt is plotting her marriage with a social inferior in a way that is reminiscent of (although not the same as) Eleanor West's fictitious abduction, discussed earlier. Since Belisaunt and Amis "played in word and deed" and "he won her maidenhead,"[43] there is the very real legal settlement of marriage that Belisaunt and Amis (as both single individuals) could claim. The noble game of courtly love is woven throughout the romance: Amis and Belisaunt *played* together, and Amis *won* her virginity. The romance's continual reference to the game of courtly seduction—in which rape plays a part—is important to take note of, as threatened rape is within the rules of this game of seduction.[44]

When the steward tells the duke about Amis and Belisaunt's secret love, he states, "in your court you have a thief."[45] Amis stole her maidenhood, which effectively takes away the duke's profit from her marriage market value. The duke, as Belisaunt's father, is now the victim of his daughter's malicious rape accusations and scheming. Legal jargon is repeatedly stated in this romance: Amis is called a traitor and sinful, accused of having committed a felony crime, threatened with hanging as capital punishment, and, finally, the crime of theft is stated.[46] The steward tells the duke that Amis "is a traitor strong, / when he with treason and with wrong / your daughter he lain with!"[47] The steward's explicit legal terminology and the continued legal references throughout the romance suggest that there is a sub-context of legal knowledge in *Amis and Amiloun*. The real legal implications of one's actions are influencing the structure of the romance and the audiences' reactions to the romance. Statutory law protected fathers from ravished daughters and the law protected the rights of women to claim marriage through *raptus*. Here we see the intersection of later *raptus* laws which were designed to protect both wronged fathers and raped and/or abducted daughters.

---

42 "Amis and Amiloun," ll. 700–4.

43 "Amis and Amiloun," ll. 767–68.

44 Such language is repeated in ll. 468, 524, 540, 570, 601, 722, 764. It is also noteworthy that Belisaunt initiates the game, but Amis (as the man) is said to have won.

45 "Amis and Amiloun," l. 787.

46 "Amis and Amiloun," ll. 216, 307, 389, 605, 608, 635–36, 787, 790–91, 798, 800–801, 822, 824, 827, 834, 839–40, 960, 1082, 1084.

47 "Amis and Amiloun," ll. 790–92.

The duke, as the victim of his daughter's stolen virginity, claims that he has a great shame, and, like Sir Thomas West in real life, it is the father who has been harmed. The steward tells the duke that Amis must suffer capital punishment for the crime of treason, for he has "forlain that may."[48] This is critical to the legal context, as Amis is not accused of raping Belisaunt, but he *is* accused of sleeping with her consensually and taking her virginity, which is a crime against the father who owned her marriage rights. Belisaunt's verbal and mental consent to coitus—like Eleanor West's consensual abduction—was deemed irrelevant to the crime, because it happened without the permission of their fathers. Moreover, the fictional Belisaunt and the actual Eleanor both engaged in a consensual relationship with a social inferior who was well known to their father, thus making it easier to name the offenders in the legal appeals.

The duke demands retribution, and Amis pleads for a trial by combat. Although this is an outdated form of a judicial trial for rape by the fourteenth century, it is nonetheless important that the romance depicts a real legal consequence.[49] Even though it is implied that the trial by combat is to denounce the accusations correctly made by the steward, those accusations are grounded in the truth that Amis took Belisaunt's virginity without her father's consent. The Statute of Rapes claims that men who are suspected of *raptus* cannot engage in a trial by combat with the woman's father, for fear that the young man would unjustly defeat the old father. So, there were real legal concerns about such practices. Further legal realities are described in the plight of Amis to find guarantors, which leads the people of court to argue for his imprisonment.[50] The reality of the law is being illustrated. Without guarantors, Amis should be placed in custody to ensure that he does not try to flee before he faces judgement.

The remainder of the narrative is focused on the reunion and suffering between Amis and Amiloun. Since Amis knows that divine judgement will ensure that he does not win the trial by combat, he seeks Amiloun's help to fight on his behalf. Having won the trial by combat, the duke allows Amis to marry his daughter. Through this matrimony, Amis inherits the title, lands, and wealth of the duke because Belisaunt is the transmitter of this prop-

48 "Amis and Amiloun," l. 801.

49 Despite the lack of trial by combat in fourteenth-century England, the king of France sanctioned a legal duel over a rape accusation in 1386 (just four years after duels between older fathers and younger alleged "ravisher" were outlawed in the 1382 Statute of Rapes). See Jager, *The Last Duel.*

50 "Amis and Amiloun," ll. 869–70.

erty. The romance continues with Amiloun's plight of leprosy and the sacrifice that both Amis and Amiloun make to save each other. Despite the initial threat of rape and the sham of a trial, the narrative arc of Belisaunt ends in matrimony. This is, of course, typical of romance, but it is also representative of the realities of rape trials. Even fictitious claims of rape and/or abduction could, and did, end in marriage between the rapist/lover and the victim/eloper. *Amis and Amiloun*'s moral lessons are ambiguous, as the malicious accusations of rape—which initially condemns Belisaunt—are transformed into an expression of love. Belisaunt transitions from a wicked suitor to a good wife by the end of the romance.

Amis and Amiloun continually reiterates the duplicity of *raptus* law's intentions, in that they ought to protect women from bad men who rape as well as protect good men from bad women who maliciously—or, as in the case of Eleanor West, fictitiously—claim rape and/or abduction. This duality is often in conflict with each other, and *Amis and Amiloun* plays with this tension. Belisaunt's threat of a rape accusation is intended to force Amis to consent to her seduction. This eventually leads to consensual sex and mutual love between Amis and Belisaunt, and thus the threatened rape claim is unsurprisingly turned into a loving embrace and happy matrimony. This mirrors the legal realities of women and men who were single and either claimed the marriage clause of *raptus* laws or used it as a means of concord. Here, however, the marriage clause does not appear to be a viable option, as Belisaunt's father seeks retribution. Because Amiloun won the trial by combat, Amis is immorally vindicated (since he did not actually fight) against the accurate charges the steward accused him of. On this narrative level, the marriage between Amis and Belisaunt is both unimpeded (due to the divine judgement of the trial) and immoral (because Amis was indeed guilty and never fought). This reading of the legality of the marriage as a consequence of the sham trial suggests that the marriage clause of *raptus* laws was a point of debate and contention among contemporaneous audiences. Indeed, the fourteenth-century case of Eleanor West encourages such a reading. It would have been simpler for Belisaunt and Amis to claim the legal loophole of the marriage clause, but that does not necessarily subdue the father's wrath, and herein lies the mirroring to Sir Thomas West's complaints. Overall, there is a subtext of legal knowledge in *Amis and Amiloun* which is brought up continually throughout the narrative. The duplicity of rape laws, the legalities of rape claims, and the stealing of a noble-daughter's virginity are explicitly discussed in this romance which offered medieval audiences a platform to debate these pressing social issues.

Chapter 6

RAPE IN ROMANCE

Sir Degare[1]

Sir Degare includes a graphic rape scene that leads to the conception of the protagonist, Degare. The following close reading will demonstrate that the nameless raped princess fulfills the constructed legal identity of the reluctant but willing accomplice, and I argue that with this legal identity, the contemporaneous medieval audiences would have read her pregnancy as consent of the flesh and her marriage to the rapist fairy knight as a natural and relatable ending for a rape survivor.

Sir Degare is a traditional narrative based on a knight's identity quest. The romance begins with a strong warrior king in Brittany. However, the king's major flaw is his inability to produce a male heir, as he only has a daughter. We are first introduced to the princess as a virgin "maidenchild," and because the absent queen-mother died in childbirth, the king is very protective of his daughter. This has led many scholars to note the threat of incest, as the king's fondness for his daughter exceeds the cultural norms of acceptable paternal affection.[2] When the princess becomes of marital age, numerous suitors seek her hand in marriage, but the king refuses to let her marry any man unless he can unsaddle him in a tournament. This is prefaced by the fact that the king has never lost a single foot out of a stirrup. Unsurprisingly, the nameless princess remains unwed.

On the annual feast day to commemorate the late queen's death, the king, princess, and their courtly entourage ride into a forest where an abbey is located. The princess is riding with two maidens when she tells them to stop because she needs to go to the bathroom.[3] The ladies dismount in the forest and are separated from the knightly entourage surrounding the king.

1 Composed between 1330–1340, it is also contained in Edinburgh, National Library of Scotland, MS Advocates 19. 2. 1 (Auchinleck MS).

2 Archibald, *Incest and the Medieval Imagination*, 163; Ashton, *Medieval English Romance in Context*, 70–72, 95–96; Florschuetz, *Marking Maternity in Middle English Romance*, 13; Saunders, *Rape and Ravishment*, 215.

3 "Sir Degare," ll. 48–54.

Their isolation from civilization and the protection of court is accentuated, as "the woods were rough and thick."[4] The two maidens and the princess end up in an extremely dense forest and come into "a land" unlike where they were from.[5] When the princess and her ladies realize that they are lost, they cried out hoping that the court entourage will hear them, but "no man" heard them.[6]

The romance continues with the supernatural theme that is initiated with the thick forest, as we are told that the weather is hot, and it is just before noon. So, the ladies decide to lie down under a chestnut tree. As previously discussed in *Sir Orfeo*, these are common literary motifs suggesting a supernatural encounter: mid-day is a typical time for fairy interactions, forests usually lead to otherworlds, going to sleep often initiates a dream-like state of supernatural qualities, and chestnut trees are symbolic of chastity. This is especially important, since the princess's virginity is about to be stolen. The two accompanying ladies fall asleep under the chestnut tree and remain chaste, but the princess does not. Her isolation is emphasized, as she is separated from not only her known world of Brittany but also from her courtly entourage and from her sleeping ladies. Her vulnerability to rape is explicit because of her isolation.

The princess is intrigued by her strange surroundings. She picks flowers, listens to the "song of wild fowl," and travels further into the woods where she is lost and even more alone, as we are told that she does not know where she is and she does not know the way back to her ladies.[7] Here, we have the first direct speech of the princess where she states: "'alas!' she said, 'that I was born! / Now I know that I am lost! / Wild beasts will eat me / Before any man shall find me!'"[8] The princess is explicitly fearful of being overtaken and consumed by wild beasts, but little does she know that it is the approaching fairy knight who will consume her.

Just when the princess is in utter fear of attack by wild beasts, she sees a stranger approach her. The stranger is described in traditional courtly context:

> Toward her came a knight / Gentle, young and handsome man; / A robe of scarlet he had upon; / His face was fair, his body in everyway; / Of courte-

4 "Sir Degare," ll. 55–61.

5 "Sir Degare," ll. 62–65.

6 "Sir Degare," ll. 66–70.

7 "Sir Degare," ll. 77–84.

8 "Sir Degare," ll. 85–88.

> ous manner; / Well-shaped legs, foot, and hand: / There was none in all the King's land / More attractive man than was he.[9]

The stranger is described first as a knight, placing him within the courtly world. The knight appears to come out of nowhere, emerging from within the deep woods, and approaching the princess. The familiar signals of the courtly and knightly identity of the fairy work to place the context of rape on the fringe of a real courtly world. The fairy knight does not follow the norms of courtly seduction even though he is evidently not ignorant of the courtly world, and yet he is seemingly beyond the rules of court, in what Helen Cooper calls the realm of "somewhere else."[10] After his physical description, the knight is given eleven lines of speech:

> Damsel, welcome you are! / Be afraid of no man: / I am here a fairy knight; / My kind is armed [by] nature, / On horse to ride with shield and spear; / Therefore afraid be thou not: / I have nothing brought but my sword. / I have loved you for many years, / And now we are both here by ourselves, / You must become my lover before you go, / Whether you like it or not.[11]

Fear is repeatedly mentioned in this scene, as the princess fears an attack by wild beasts and the fairy knight tells her not to be afraid of him. The fairy knight claims that he has been watching the princess for "many years" and that he loves her. Here, the scene for a heterosexual encounter is set: the knight approaches the princess, he states that he has loved her for years, and now they find themselves alone together. The threat of rape becomes ever more apparent, as the knight claims that she will become his *lemman* (his lover) whether she likes it or not, proving that her consent to sexual intercourse is irrelevant.[12] The rape is explicit:

> Then nothing could she do / But weep and cry and would flee; / And he began to seize her, / And did his will as he desired. / And bereft her of her maidenhood, / And soon afterwards he stood up.[13]

---

9 "Sir Degare," ll. 90–97.

10 Cooper, *The English Romance in Time*, 179.

11 "Sir Degare," ll. 98–108: "Damaisele, welcome mote thou be!/ Be thou afered of none wihghte:/ Iich am comen here a fairi knyghte;/ Mi kynde is armes for to were,/ On horse to ride with scheld and spere;/ Forthi afered be thou nowt:/ I ne have nowt but mi swerd ibrout./ Iich have iloved the mani a yer,/ And now we beth us selve her,/ Thou best mi lemman ar thou go,/ Wether the liketh wel or wo."

12 The literary construction of "whether she wishes it or not" is nearly identical to that in *Sir Orfeo*. See Chapter 5.

13 "Sir Degare," ll. 109–14: "Tho nothing ne coude do she/ But wep and criede and

The text unambiguously tells the audience that there was nothing that the princess could do to stop the rape. The knight's actions are described as simultaneously being an act of desirous love and extreme violence. The narrative places seduction and rape on the same continuum. The difference between the two is depicted as a sliding scale, which is based on the amount of pressure and force used to persuade the reluctant lady. Her verbal and mental non-consent are explicit, and, like actual legal documents, the violence inflicted upon the princess is obscured and stated rather vaguely while working to demonstrate her physical non-consent. The vulnerability of the woman to the desires of the "noble" and "gentle" knight are foregrounded by her weeping, which is a unique line for romance in that it shares the princess's internal fear of knowing that she is about to be raped. The internal state of her mental non-consent is made explicit to the audience while the romance acknowledges that she "would flee" if she could, but there is nothing she can do to escape. The knight is described as forcefully seizing the princess and doing his "will" and "desires" as he rapes her of her virginity.

The seizure of her maidenhood is something to mourn, as the term *binam* signifies loss—implying the taking away of something or the ruining of someone's reputation, both of which can be implied in this context.[14] The knight's dominant position is evident by the term *torforen*, as he both stands up spatially in front of the princess and he physically dominates her. After the rape, the fairy knight speaks to the princess and yet again addresses her as his *lemman*:

> "Lover," he said, "gentle and free," / I know that you shall be with child; / For sure I know it will be a boy; / Forth my sword you shall have, / And when he is of age / That he may protect himself, / Give him the sword, and bid him to attempt / To seek his father in each land. / The sword is good and fitting: / Indeed, as I fought with a giant, / I broke the point of its head; / And soon thereafter he was dead. / I took it [the point of the sword] out and have it here, / Ready in my purse. / Yet sometime may come / That my son meet with me: / By my sword I may know him. / Have a good day! I must go."[15]

This long, eighteen-line, direct speech from the fairy knight reiterates that the rape was an action of passion and love, according to the rapist himself. Margaret Robson suggests that the phallic symbol of the sword, with its

wolde fle;/ And he anon gan hire at holde,/ And dide his wille, what he wolde./ He binam hire here maidenhod,/ And seththen up toforen hire stod."

14 MED, "bininem v.," article 3a.

15 "Sir Degare," ll. 115–32.

missing tip, could reflect a "displaced version of castration for the rapist."[16] Although the notion of the tip-less sword representing *Bracton*-era punitive castration for men convicted of raping virgins is an enticing symbolism, it is ultimately unlikely due to the princess's consent of the flesh nullifying a conviction of rape in the criminal courts. The fairy knight's spatial mobility is implied when he says that their son "seek his father in each land." The fairy knight does not intend to stay in one place, but rather moves throughout human lands and is capable of being anywhere. This encourages the understanding that the threat of rape looms everywhere, both in the courtly world and on the fringes of court, as in this context. Despite the fairy knight's direct speech, the princess remains silent except for her cries. This could imply that in her crying out, the princess raised the hue and cry to try and alert others even though it was ultimately futile. In the twenty-line exchange between the fairy and the princess, all direct speech is spoken by the knight, and of these twenty lines, two of them are devoted to telling the princess explicitly not to fear him. As the knight disappears back into the woods, the princess's silence speaks volumes to her victimization and trauma. The princess's explicit fear of wild beasts in the forest is both rational and foreshadowing her future encounter with the fairy knight. The conflation here of the metaphorical representation of a human man (knight) and an "other" (fairy) raping on the fringes of the courtly world (the forest) displays an anxiety about the failure of masculine gender identity expression in men who rape.

As far as the narrative allows us to speculate, the rapist leaves the scene of the crime without consequence. This is the exact opposite of the princess. She fears incestuous accusations will be made against her and her father, and she fears for her own reputation with the loss of her virginity. Consequently, she is forced to abandon her child. Once Degare is born, the princess leaves the narrative until the end (as does the fairy knight), and the story focuses on the development of Degare. This displacement emphasizes the literary erasure of rape by decentring the narrative away from the fairy knight and princess and focusing instead on Degare, who is ironically the product of rape. The minimal narrative insight into the princess's emotions reveals a transition from fear and shame to eventual love and reunion.

After the rape, the princess is in tears and physically hurt: "utterly weeping she took the sword, / And came home sorely sighing."[17] Here we can read

16 Robson, "How's Your father?," 89.

17 "Sir Degare," ll. 134–35: "al wepende the swerd she nam / And com hom sore sikend."

a survivor-narrative, as the text stresses "the harms of sexual assault," and we can speculate that intended audiences would have recognized the violence of this scene.[18] The rape is explicit; it is not a joke, and it is not trivialized by the narrator. The fairy knight forcibly seized her virginity, which denotes the felony rape of a virgin—the most serious form of rape under England's *raptus* laws. But there are also the real legal and medical implications of her pregnancy, which imply her physical consent to the rape. When considering the medieval medical theory of two-seed conception, the romance narrative implies that the princess's body enjoyed the rape which led to her pregnancy. Medieval audiences would have likely been aware of the legal implications of pregnancy from rape, but it is probable that they would not have questioned that the coitus was non-consensual sex, as is evident from the forceful language and her weeping. The rape scene implies that physical force and violence were used to overwhelm the princess, hinting at the legal necessity—as stated in the laws and treaties repeatedly—of the woman having been *vi oppressam*.

However, the contemporaneous legal, theological, and medical context of this romance ensures that the princess was a reluctant but ultimately willing accomplice to her own rape, since she did not give mental consent, but the weakness of her flesh consented. This is critical to the medieval audiences' potential interpretation of the rape scene. Her pregnancy ensures her consent of the flesh both within the reality of the romance itself and in the very real legal discourse informing the construction of the narrative and audiences' expectations. Critically, the remainder of the romance works to erase the rape and turn it into consensual coitus between lovers, as this unites the already given consent of the flesh with the consent of the mind and ensures a happy ending in matrimony. Because the princess conceives the protagonist hero from the rape, the brutality and the significance of the crime is deflated, as the audience is encouraged to no longer condemn but rather applaud the birth of Degare.

Back at court, we are once again reminded of the trauma that the princess lives with: "His daughter sickened and sorrowed greatly; / Her womb grew more and more; / Meanwhile she tried to hide her suffering. / On a day, as she sat weeping, / One of her maidens perceived it."[19] The contrast between the "glad" and "joyful" men and the sorrowed, sickened, and weeping lady implies that rape and pregnancy have lasting consequences for the princess

---

18 Baechle, Harris, and Strakhov, "Reassessing the Pastourelle," 26.

19 "Sir Degare," ll. 156–60.

while the men are blissfully unscathed and unaware. This also works to isolate the princess as a rape survivor within her own courtly world, as she hides away from everyone else at court. The physical suffering of hiding her pregnancy represents the embarrassment and shame which many women who endure rape unfortunately feel. It is striking that no man at court recognizes the princess's anguish, but it is another woman, her maiden, who picks up on the emotional suffering of her lady. There is a suggestion that rape as a threat applicable to all women (in a medieval English legal context) can bring women across social classes together in support of one another. The maiden asks the princess why she is crying, to which the princess replies:

> A! Gentle maiden, chosen one, / Help me, otherwise I am lost [*forloren*]! / I have ever been gentle and kind [*meke and milde*]: / Indeed, now I am with a living child! / If any man should perceive it, / Men would say by sty and path / That my father the King begat it / And I was never intimate with [a] man! / And if he learns of it himself, / Such grief shall him strike / That never happy shall he be, / For all his joy is in me," / And told her all together there, / How it was begotten and where.[20]

Her self-identification as *forloren*, or "lost," could be hinting at her son Degare—meaning "almost lost"—but alternative meanings of *forloren* have much more serious implications. The term is associated with disgrace and ruin to one's honour. This is a closer reading to the dishonour placed on women who conceive from rape, since they were viewed as weak for succumbing to their assumed sexual desires. The dishonour from her loss of virginity was compounded by the potential rumours of incest. The princess exclaims that she has never been intimate with a man, and this figurative detachment from the real-world occurrence of knights that rape enables a safe distance for contemporaneous audiences to critique real societal problems, as some knights do rape. Moreover, the traditional feminine attributes of being meek and mild are the exact same words used in the First Statute of Westminster (1275), further reiterating a legal influence within the construct of the romance narrative.

After disclosing how she became pregnant, the maiden creates the plan to hide the pregnancy and get rid of the child. Once the baby boy is born, the princess places four pounds of gold and ten pounds of silver in his cradle along with a pair of gloves which will be used as an identity token for her son to find her. The princess is now a consensual lover with the fairy rapist knight, as we are told: "And then she took a pair of gloves / That her lover

---

20 "Sir Degare," ll. 163–76.

sent her from fairy land."[21] The princess's change of emotion from fear to love towards the fairy rapist may seem jarring to modern audiences. However, it is working to unite the duality of consent of the flesh and consent of the mind. In case the medical and legal implications of pregnancy implying the princess's consent of the flesh were too subtle, the romance ensures that her consent after the fact is now explicit, as the princess and fairy knight have mutually referred to one another as lovers. The literary erasure of the rape is happening quickly and subtly within these two lines. The entire expunging of the rape occurs with the narrative exit of the princess altogether, right up to her eventual reunion and marriage with the fairy knight at the end of the romance.

The narrative shifts focus away from the princess and onto the boy, who is eventually named Degare. After twenty years, Degare beings his identity quest, entering a joust against the king of Brittany. Unsurprisingly, Degare unsaddles the previously undefeated king. Unbeknown to anyone but the audience, the prize is his very own mother's hand in marriage. Despite the fact that the princess's father is consenting to allow his daughter to marry the unknown jousting victor, her non-consent to the marriage is suggested: "Then was the damsel sorry, / For she knew: / That he should her spouse be / To a knight that she never had seen."[22] Despite her lack of freely given consent, the princess is brought to the church and the wedding ceremony occurs "under holy sacrament."[23] Even though the church demanded freely given consent to form a valid marriage, this ideal was not always realized, especially for the high nobility and royalty. The princess's dread, sorrow, and lack of consent is a retelling of real lived experiences of some women who had a significant lack of choice in marriage arrangements.

After the wedding feast, Degare and the princess retire to the bedchamber to consummate the marriage when Degare remembers the gloves that were left to him. The princess, immediately recognizing the gloves, confesses to her father that she is not a virgin, as "twenty winters" ago she had "lost" her maidenhood "in a forest."[24] There is no mention of rape or lack of consent to the sexual encounter as she describes it. Once Degare sets off to find his father, he enters an "ancient forest" where "he was begotten some

21 "Sir Degare," ll. 194–95.

22 "Sir Degare," ll. 585–88.

23 "Sir Degare," ll. 610–12.

24 "Sir Degare," ll. 681–89.

while [ago]."[25] Returning to the forest where his mother was raped, the narrative eclipses the brutality of the violent scene with the focus now placed on the conception of the hero. The method of conception, however, is not the intended focus. The text now mirrors the fear of wild beasts in the forest, which the princess experienced earlier. We are told that "No domesticated beasts he found / But many wild beasts he saw / And birds singing high."[26] The parallels in Degare's experience in the forest and his mother's just before she was raped are striking: there are no domesticated animals in sight, but only wild beasts which was the princess's greatest fear prior to her rape; both the princess and Degare are listening to the birds before the fairy knight approaches. There is the intentional duplication of sensory experiences between mother and son, but the stark difference is that Degare is intentionally seeking his father, whereas the princess was the unassuming victim of the fairy rapist.

Degare eventually meets a "doughty knight," which can mean brave, worthy, honourable, noble, gracious, or handsome.[27] Describing the fairy rapist in such courtly language works to illuminate the potential violent methods of seduction utilized by courtly knights. Upon recognizing his father, Degare tells his father that his mother "is in great mourning," and he convinces his father to reunite with his mother: "As soon as the lady saw the knight, / Wondrously well she knew the knight; / Immediately she changed her colour right away."[28] This is their first reunion since the rape twenty years ago. The family reunion is complete with Degare and the princess obtaining a divorce and her subsequent marriage to the fairy knight. This completes the narrative arc for the nameless princess, as her rape is turned into consensual sex between a husband and wife. The marriage clause in *raptus* laws is enacted to transform rape so that, as stated by Frances Ferguson, "marriage is a misunderstanding corrected, or rape rightly understood."[29] Marriage acts in both law and romance as a legal erasure to rape, and because the princess already gave consent of her flesh, the marriage ensures that the rape has been transformed into consensual coitus between spouses.

Fourteenth-century audiences would have likely recognized that the rape was turned into consensual sex with the conception of Degare. The

25 "Sir Degare," ll. 728–29.

26 "Sir Degare," ll. 732–34.

27 "Sir Degare," l. 994; MED, "doughti adj. & n."

28 Sir Degare," ll. 1079–81.

29 Ferguson, "Rape and the Rise of the Novel," 92.

eventual harmony between the princess's initial consent of the flesh (by her pregnancy) and her mental consent later are representative of a legal and medical reality. The rape is not a wish fulfilment on the part of the princess, as has been suggested by Gail Ashton and others, simply because she consents to the marriage later.[30] It is not the fulfilment of a sexual fantasy in an attempt to escape her overbearing father,[31] nor is it entirely correct that the romance is simply stating that marriage is the expected outcome "even in the rape case of *Sir Degare*."[32] The transformation of the rapist fairy knight turned courtly lover, husband, and father, is fulfilling the ideal outcome of the marriage clause in rape laws and EC cases, specifically when both complainant and defendant are single and a child has been conceived. This is the most logical "happy ending" from a contemporaneous legal perspective. Just as the court records depict matrimony as a form of settlement between rapist and survivor, here in *Sir Degare* it acts as a justification to the premarital rape. As stated by Ferguson, "rape simply ceases to exist because it has been, by definition, absorbed into marriage."[33] This is a legal reality that is being mirrored in *Sir Degare*. The fairy knight was initially depicted as a usurper of social order by raping the princess, but he is now a narrative tool to uphold social order through marriage.

The legal and medical contexts which are influencing the construction of the narrative and the audience's expectations must be recognized to understand the princess's eventual marriage to her rapist. The legal implications of her physical consent—given by her body through conception—nullifies any legal claims of rape and places her in the legal identity of the reluctant but, nonetheless, willing accomplice. Therefore, without any legal crime, the romance genre requires a happy ending. This necessarily demands the princess's eventual mental consent and her marriage to the rapist. This may even be suggestive to young women, assuring them that they too can have a "happy ending" in matrimony even if they are raped out of wedlock.

Marriage between rapist and survivor legally nullifies any rape appeals by the woman in medieval English laws. With *Sir Degare*, the graphic rape is almost immediately conflated with expressions of love, the immediate consent of the flesh of the princess, followed by the consent of the mind, and the eventual marital reunion of the rapist and survivor. The romance is illus-

---

30 Ashton, *Medieval English Romance in Context*, 96.

31 Robson, "How's Your Father?," 86.

32 Cooper, *The English Romance in Time*, 256.

33 Ferguson, "Rape and the Rise of the Novel," 92.

trating the legal realities of women who conceive from rape and have little choice but to marry the men that raped them. The literal erasure of the rape is perpetuated throughout the narrative with the conflation of rape and love. She is his lover, and he becomes hers. This, according to Corinne Saunders, suggests that medieval audiences debated the "impossibilities and doubts surrounding the actuality of rape" in the real world.[34]

The marriage between the rapist and the princess legally transforms rape after the fact, turning it into consensual sex while the resulting pregnancy medically and legally drives home the point that this was always consensual coitus. Importantly, legal realities intrude yet again into the narrative, as we are told that the reason for the divorce between Degare and his mother was because the marriage was within the prohibited degrees.[35] Here, the romance is seeking legal realism in what makes a valid marriage. Audience members are being encouraged to recognize the invalidity of the incestuous marriage while simultaneously being encouraged to acknowledge the validity of the marriage between rapist and survivor. Importantly, audiences are presented with the conflicting consent models and the possibility of the consent of the flesh overpowering mental non-consent of rape survivors.

Sir Gowther[36]

This is a narrative of repentance. Gowther was born as a demon child and throughout his youth he commits various crimes, including the rape and murder of a convent of nuns, until he finally realizes the severity of his actions and embarks on a journey of repentance and chivalry. Rape plays a very crucial role in Gowther's penitential quest. The narrative opens with a prayer for God to protect the audience against "the fowle fende."[37] *Fiends* refers to those possessing various demonic qualities, which includes fallen angels or demons who can cause madness in mortals.[38] The text explains that fiends once had the ability to trick noblewomen into sex because they disguised themselves to look like their husbands, suggesting that they may

34 Saunders, *Rape and Ravishment*, 218.

35 "Sir Degare," l. 1093.

36 Extant in two manuscripts (London, BL, MS Royal 17. B. 43; Edinburgh, National Library of Scotland, MS Advocates 19. 3. 1) both dating from the fifteenth century and both likely originating from the North Midlands of England.

37 "Sir Gowther," l. 4.

38 MED, "Fend (n.)."

represent sexual dangers unique (legally speaking) to women who are seemingly easily tricked into sex. These sexual tricksters "caused ladies so great woe" because "that fiend lay with women so near / And made them with child."[39] The legal realism—the statement that only women are victims of rape, whether it be by men (in the real world) or by fiends (in the literary reality of *Sir Gowther*)—further demonstrates the vulnerability of women to sexual assault. The class element must also be noted, as the opening lines state that ladies are tricked by fiends, and thus there is an inherent social class issue because the fiends do not trick peasant women into sex. Presumably, if anything is learned from the pastourelle genre, peasant women are viewed as sexually available and do not need the "refinement" of tricking them into sex.[40]

Gowther is first introduced as a "great demon," and we are told that he gave his mother much sorrow because of his "wild deeds."[41] *Wylde* is defined as "lacking in restraint," "out of one's mind," "perverse, wicked," "wanton; also, lusty," "without civilization," "savage," or "beastly."[42] Gowther's *wylde* nature ensures that he is the opposite of courtly: he is impulse driven, cruel, lacks reason, and has strong sexual urges. Gowther's *wylde* characteristics are emblematic of medieval popular opinions about men who rape; that is, men are overcome with sexual urges, and they lack the discipline to control those sexual impulses. The legally required physical proof of resistance to rape necessarily required physical bodily harm, which in turn requires some form of brutality to produce visible proof of non-consent. There is thus a close connection between the legal requirement of physical injury and the presumed *wylde* and violent nature of men who rape. Here, the romance is making the connection between rapists and *wylde* behaviour by referring to Gowther as such. This notion will become clearer throughout the romance, as it plays with the fine line between a chivalrous knight and a rapist knight, between courtly and wild, between rational and irrational, and between man and monster.

The romance continues with the introduction of the duke and duchess of Austria who remain childless after ten years of marriage. The romance makes it clear that both are to blame for the lack of conception, as the duke

39 "Sir Gowther," ll. 11, 14–15.

40 See Baechle, Harris, and Strakhov, "Reassessing the Pastourelle," 23–25.

41 "Sir Gowther," ll. 22–24: "with his warcus wylde."

42 MED, "Wild(e (adj.)," articles 1a–d.

cannot beget a child nor can the duchess carry a child.[43] However, it is important to remember the legal context. Impotence was grounds for an annulment, and this was particularly damaging for women whose future marriage prospects could suffer because of their presumed inability to conceive. This helps to explain the desperation of the duchess. The legal realism intrudes into the fictional narrative when the duke exclaims to his wife: "'I believe you to be somewhat barren, / It is good that we separate; / I do but waste my time on you, / Heirless much our lands be'; / For weeping he cannot cease."[44] The fictional duke is living in the legal reality of the listening and reading audiences as he explains how a lack of conception is grounds for separation in the fictional world, much like the real lived world.[45] The fact that the duke is emotional exposes the complexities of medieval marriages and the importance for the woman to produce an heir for both her own security and for continuity of the male's dynastic line. The duke does not want to separate, but, for the sake of his patrimony, he must. These emotions are speaking to a reality that imitates the lived experiences of the medieval past.

The duchess is distraught from the news that she will be left alone unless she can conceive, and she repeatedly prays to God and the Virgin Mary to bless her with a child. The desperation for conception and the impending separation from her husband foregrounds the following scene:

> In her orchard upon a day / She met a man, then truth to say, / That of her love besought, / As like her lord as he might be; / He laid her down under a tree / With her his will he wrought. / When he had his will all done / As a shaggy fiend he leapt up quickly. / And stood and her beheld; / He said "I have begotten a child on you / That in his youth full wild shall be, / And weapons mightily wield." / She blessed herself and from him ran, / Into her chamber fast she went, / That was so firmly built.[46]

Reminiscent of the rape scene in *Sir Degare*, the duchess is alone in an orchard. Like forests, orchards are typical places where supernatural encounters occur, and both *Sir Gowther* and *Sir Degare* imply that women who are alone are vulnerable to sexual predators.[47] The approaching being

43 "Sir Gowther," l. 53.

44 "Sir Gowther," ll. 56–60.

45 For a discussion on impotence as grounds for divorce in medieval England see Butler, *Divorce in Medieval England*, 30–31.

46 "Sir Gowther," ll. 67–81.

47 Harris also notes the physical environment as isolating women leading to rape in *Obscene Pedagogies*, 117.

is first described as a man like the fairy knight in *Sir Degare*. We are then told that the approaching man looks like her husband, the duke, and that he initiates the physical exchange by laying her down under a tree. The inclusion of a tree is also a typical romance trope in scenes of rape and abduction, as we have seen with the chestnut tree in *Sir Degare* and in *Sir Orfeo*. The man is the subject of the actions while the duchess is the grammatical object of his actions: *he* laid her down; *he* did *his* will to her; *he* finished *his* desires. There is no mention of her desires, her will, her consent; rather, she is the object of his sexual pleasure, and she is the recipient of his actions. Only after coitus is completed does the man transform into a shaggy fiend. The active position of the masculine is highlighted by his direct speech and the duchess's passivity is reinforced by her silence. Her silence, much like the princess in *Sir Degare*, is a marker of her victimization and trauma. We can interpret her silence as failing to verbally cry out and express mental non-consent through her failure to raise the hue and cry. However, I argue that silence is a form of acquiescing, and silence is itself indicative of non-consent. Silence is a real biological trauma response to rape.[48]

Here, the issue of consent is complex. Did she consent because she thought it was her husband, or did she consent out of desperation to conceive an heir. Alternatively, was this rape because she did not explicitly consent to coitus with the fiend? These are questions which scholars have debated for decades.[49] However, scholars have not yet fully acknowledged the legal realities informing the text. Spouses were required by ecclesiastical law to remain sexually available to one another. The fact that the fiend approached her in the disguise of her husband ensures that the duchess's consent to coitus with her apparent husband was necessarily (legally speaking) required of her. The audience would have expected a wife to willingly accept her husband's sexual advances, as this was part of the legal requirement of medieval marriages. Here, the wife's consent can be assumed even though it was not explicitly given because of the conjugal debt. However, the fact that the man was not actually her husband, and she was ultimately deceived and impregnated, places the duchess within the legal identity of the reluctant but willing accomplice to her own rape. If the coitus was

---

48 For a discussion on the act of freezing and silence as a form of non-consent and a biological reaction to trauma, see de Heer and Jones, "Tonic Immobility as Defensive Trauma Response to Rape," 1–29. See also Galliano et al., "Victim Reactions During Rape/Sexual Assault," 109–14.

49 Cohen, *Of Giants*, 127; Saunders, *Rape and Ravishment*, 224–25; Sylvester, *Medieval Romance and the Construction of Heterosexuality*, 57–60.

completed under the false pretenses that it was her husband, can this be interpreted as falsely assumed consent and ultimately rape? From a modern perspective, yes, but the issue is more complex to medieval minds. The text seems to superficially suggest that, legally speaking, it is not considered rape. However, there is an alternative reading that implies that this could be defined as medieval rape in which the duchess is an unfortunate accomplice. She was expected to consent to her husband because of the conjugal debt, and the fiend took advantage of this legal loophole to create an ambiguous situation in which her consent was not explicit nor was his true identity known to her. Here, the non-consent of the duchess is problematic in a social understanding but not a legal one. The marital debt ensured *legally* that her explicit verbal and mental consent to coitus with her husband was not required, but the social commentary and debate about the realities of marital rape are open for discussion with this passage. Even though marital rape was a non-existent crime in medieval England, we can logically assume that it was a reality for some women. Clearly, marital rape was a social issue (despite not being a legal one at this time), and the potential for it to be debated here in *Sir Gowther* was likely not lost on medieval audiences.

The differentiation in treatment between the duchess's two sexual scenes (one with the fiend and the other with her real husband) is striking and seemingly reinforces that this was indeed rape. The fiend is described as doing his will and pleasure to her. This is in opposition to the description of coitus between the duchess and her husband, in which they "make love" together.[50] The literary treatment of and distinction between sexual intercourse with the fiend and the husband is highly suggestive that the former was non-consensual and thus (from a social perspective) was rape. However, the duchess cannot be a truly innocent victim because of the disguise of the fiend, but neither is she the culpable, scheming women. Consequently, the duchess fulfills the legal identity of the accomplice to her own rape. This is further reinforced to medieval audiences by her resulting pregnancy. Like the princess in *Sir Degare*, the fact that the duchess conceived from the coitus proved (legally and medically) that she had given physical, bodily consent to the fiend.

The similarities between the princess in *Sir Degare* and the duchess in *Sir Gowther* are notable: both characters are unnamed, both are alone in the outdoors when they are raped by supernatural beings, both women are silent throughout the sexual encounter, and both rape scenes highlight

50 "Sir Gowther," l. 90.

the ambiguity between consensual coitus and rape through the conception of the male protagonist. Importantly, both rapists (fairy knight and fiend) express notions of love and admiration for their victims. Once again, lust, seduction, and rape are placed on the same continuum in the chivalric world of medieval England. Masculine aggression was a normalized—although condemnable—display of love.

Once Gowther is born, it is apparent that he has supernatural qualities, as he grows much quicker than a normal infant and is described as "fierce and violent."[51] Gowther suckles nine wet-nurses to death, leaving his mother no choice but to nurse him herself. On her attempt to breastfeed Gowther, he bites off her nipple. His consumption of the female body as an infant foreshadows his physical domination of the female body when he later rapes the nuns. Gowther's biting off of his mother's nipple is reminiscent of the mutilated female body in hagiography and the princess's fears of wild beasts in *Sir Degare*. The male consumption of the female body is a trend in these romances which is associated with beast-like—or monstrous—rapists.

Gowther is repeatedly described as *wylde*. Gowther is a hybrid, part mortal and part demonic. Wild nature and humanity are one in the same in Gowther; he is both a knight and a duke as well as a rapist and a murderer. His uncontrollable sexual urges combined with his physical strength and aggression make Gowther a fearful hybrid. When Gowther preys on women—specifically holy women and virgins—he is not only committing an egregious felony according to contemporaneous statutory laws, but he is also breaking the social code of appropriate, chivalrous, masculine behaviour. While committing these crimes, Gowther is a dubbed knight, and thus we can read his behaviour as an *exemplum* of a criminal knight committing rape much like the fairy rapist knight in *Sir Degare*. This disassociation from humanity—Gowther is both diabolical and a mortal—allows for the literary distance to debate and discuss the crimes he commits as a knight in the courtly world. Gowther (like Degare's fairy father) is both within the courtly context familiar to the contemporaneous audiences and outside of that familiarity because of his supernatural qualities.

Gowther is out hunting when he comes upon a convent. When the prioress and the nuns come out to meet him "they were full [of] fear of his body."[52] The nuns' explicit fear, caused by the sight of Gowther's physical body, is followed by their rape and murder:

---

51 "Sir Gowther," l. 108.

52 "Sir Gowther," l. 187.

> For he and his men both lay with them- / The truth why should I hide? / And then he enclosed them in their church / And burned them up, thus did he work; / Then went his name full wild.[53]

As argued by Amy Vines, the depiction of romance heroes who rape "proves [that] rape is a fundamental aspect of masculine chivalric identity."[54] Vines poignantly states that the hero who rapes is depicted as a man in a frenzied, irrational state, and the scenes are "seen as problematic moments of weakness to be overcome" by learning courtly behaviour.[55] This argument is supported by the fact that physical prowess and heterosexual desires are the hallmarks of a chivalric knight and the assumed ingredients of a rapist in contemporaneous medieval thought. Gowther, as a dubbed knight, represents "the impulses of reckless physical self-assertion which are hidden in all of us, but are normally kept under control."[56] Like men who rape because of irrational lust at the sight of a maiden's beauty (as suggested by *Bracton*), Gowther too is depicted as beyond rational control of his actions because of the sinfulness he inherited from his biological father.

The scene depicts felony rape and murder of nuns, and, according to Westminster II, this is a serious crime punishable by death. The romance also states that Gowther's companions had sex with the nuns, suggesting that it was (according to modern understandings) group rape. Pre-Norman England experienced numerous Danish raids on female religious houses—to such a degree that the forty-one female houses were depleted to just nine by 1066.[57] In ca. 871, Danish raiders burned the nuns to death at the notable Barking Abbey, much like the fictional Gowther after he rapes the nuns.[58] Male violence against religious women was evidently a real problem for early medieval English society. Religious houses were isolated along the English coastline, which allowed for raiders to frequently attack these secluded women. Consequently, the real rape, torture, and murder of nuns in the earlier medieval English past provides contextual information as to why later medieval audiences found stories of sexualized violence against holy women entertaining—even titillating, eliciting both shock and excitement.

---

53 "Sir Gowther," ll. 189–92.

54 Vines, "Invisible Woman," 162.

55 Vines, "Invisible Woman," 162.

56 Bernheimer, *Wild Men in the Middle Ages*, 3.

57 Horner, "Spiritual Truth and Sexual Violence," 658–60.

58 For a translation of Goscelin of Saint-Bertin's account of the Danish raids, see Morton and Wogan-Browne, *Guidance for Women*, 148.

The rape of the nuns is the second rape scene out of four in this romance. The first is the fiend raping the duchess, the third is Gowther raping maidens, and the fourth is Gowther raping married women. We are told that after the rape and murder of the nuns, Gowther then attacks virginal maidens, and, by raping them of their virginity, he ruins their marriage prospects. This too is a crime according to every *raptus* law, from *Glanvill* to the Statute of Rapes. Clearly, Gowther is a serial rapist. The "maidens' marriage would he spoil" further suggests that the consequences of rape are disproportionately devastating to the women, as Gowther never faces any legal repercussions.[59] The legal reality is intruding into the romance, as the narrative implies that the consequences of rape are much more disastrous for women. The rape of wives "against their will" is theoretically felony rape, but as we have seen with the EC in practice, this was not of major criminal legal concern. It is unquestionable that the rape and murder of the nuns is the most heinous crime that Gowther commits, as he is subsequently described as "full wild." The severity of this crime is further reflected in the fact that it receives the most detail (line length) out of all the various crimes he commits. This scene of rape is entirely omitted from the British Library's manuscript version of *Sir Gowther*, suggesting that it was too heinous of a crime to laugh about, especially for a more courtly (less popular) audience. This story pushed the boundaries of acceptable social commentary. Indeed, such romanceswere "danger recreations" of real societal concerns.[60]

The romance excuses Gowther's serial rapist behaviour because of his fiend-like nature. Gowther as a monster commits many crimes, including rape, and it is through the control of his bodily impulses that he is transformed into a secular, saint-like figure. The masculine body is thus susceptible to performing both monstrous and saintly acts, and it is up to the will and reason of the individual to choose the right path. This is reminiscent of medieval medical beliefs that men who do not have easy access to women's bodies for sexual release will rape. Gowther's sexual crimes are representative of the potential sexual crimes of every man, as man is susceptible to the sins of flesh and sexual pleasure. Thus, the fiend-hybrid qualities of Gowther can be interpreted as symbolic of the contemporaneous assumption that all men are capable of rape if they do not have "appropriate" access to women's bodies and control over their libido. All men, it suggests, can become "full wild."

---

59 "Sir Gowther," ll. 196–97.

60 McDonald, "A Polemic Introduction," 16–17.

Despite the severe crimes committed by Gowther, he repents for his actions. His penance includes living in silence and isolation and living with dogs under the emperor's table. The three-day battle between the sultan and the emperor is the final penance required of Gowther, and he miraculously receives the symbols of knighthood. After defeating threatening Saracens, he is transformed into a rational, chivalric knight. The happy ending required of romance is in full form in *Sir Gowther*: he is given a new patrilineage so that he is no longer of demonic origin, he marries the emperor's daughter, and, consequently, he inherits the Holy Roman Empire. To compensate for raping and murdering the convent of nuns, Gowther builds an abbey.[61] While this certainly exemplifies atonement, there are no legal repercussions for the rape and murder of the nuns, and the narrative ensures that the crimes committed against them were ultimately used as narrative building blocks to Gowther's true chivalric identity. By building an abbey, *Sir Gowther* implies that rapists can atone for their actions and no criminal legal punishments are needed to restore justice. Consequently, rape is used as a measurement of the lack of nobility in Gowther, but the audiences are expected to excuse his rapist tendencies because of his demonic hybrid nature. The monstrosity of Gowther provides the fictional screen necessary to create space to debate and discuss the failure of chivalry, the misbehaviour of knights, and the crimes of rape against all women in society. This is critical, as the Statute of Westminster II and the Statute of Rapes claim to protect all women from rape, including wives, widows, virgins and nuns, and it is beyond coincidence that Gowther explicitly rapes all the classes of women described in the statutory laws.

Sir Gowther confronts societal issues and popular anxieties about knights who rape, the crimes of youthful men, and the violence and destruction that they can perpetuate. Despite what the laws state in writing, trial records demonstrate that it was the rape of virgins which garnered the greatest legal retribution. This legal reality intrudes into the fictional narrative, as it is Gowther's rape of the chaste nuns and the virginal maidens which are described as the most condemnable. As suggested by Jeffrey Jerome Cohen, Gowther is a "monstrous hero"; he can be interpreted as representative of medieval social concerns about masculine violence, while the "fragility" existing between Gowther's monstrosity and his knightly identity is a reminder that knights are capable of monstrous crimes.[62] The message

---

61 "Sir Gowther," l. 699.

62 Cohen, *Of Giants*, 77, 81.

to young men in the audience could be inspiring: if Gowther is capable of redemption, so too will the sins of reckless youth be forgiven if they repent. The narrative implications for young women are not as hopeful. The failure of chivalry was an ever-present concern, and *Sir Gowther* demonstrates that failure of masculinity. Overall, *Sir Gowther* highlights many social concerns about rape and women's sexuality, including debates about marital rape and the conjugal debt, the consequences of conceiving from rape, and the wild nature of men who rape. *Sir Gowther* is a harsh reflection of the lived realities of some women and men in the Middle Ages, and, undoubtedly, this romance was shocking and conversation-stimulating to contemporaneous audiences.

Le Bone Florence of Rome[63]

The story of Florence is one of a heroine's suffering, endurance, and eventual marital reunion. To briefly summarize the plot, this narrative opens with the one-hundred-year-old king of Constantinople, Garcy, who is infatuated by stories of Florence, the daughter of Otes, king of Rome. However, she rejected him. Enraged, Garcy declares war on Rome, and two valiant Hungarian princes, Mylys and Emere, travel to Rome to fight for Otes. Florence and Emere immediately fall in love, and they have a marriage ceremony with the exchange of rings, but, critically, the marriage remains unconsummated. Emere bravely leaves for Constantinople and entrusts his brother, Mylys, to look after Florence. However, Mylys tries to trick Florence into marrying him by falsely telling her that Emere has died in combat. At this point, the hagiographical tendencies of the romance are intensified, as Florence vows to be a bride of Christ, and the following threats of rape are a test of her chastity. Mylys attempts to rape Florence twice, but due to divine intervention, he is unable to. In anger, he violently beats Florence and abandons her in the woods. Florence is rescued by another man, Sir Tyrry, who brings her to his house as a place of refuge. An evil knight, Machary, comes into Florence's bedroom in the middle of the night and attempts to rape her. Florence successfully defends herself, but, as revenge, Machary murders Tyrry's daughter and leaves the weapon in Florence's hand as she sleeps.

63 Extant in one Middle English manuscript (Cambridge, Cambridge University Library, MS ff. 2. 38, fols. 239c–254b,) likely dating from ca. 1500. It was based on the French *Chanson de Florence* which was popular in England from 1275–1325. See Heffernan, ed., *Le Bone Florence*, 7–8; Riddy, "Temporary Virginity and the Everyday Body," 199; Stavsky, *Le Bone Florence*, 14, 18, 27.

Florence is then exiled from Tyrry's home, at which point she is captured and sold to mariners. While at sea, Florence endures another threat of rape, and while attempting to fight off her attacker, a miraculous storm brews, and Florence happily awaits death, as she would rather die than loose her virginity (clearly parallelling virgin martyr narratives). Her virginity is saved by a miraculous storm which destroys the ship, and Florence safely washes ashore.

Seeking refuge in a convent, Florence gains healing abilities which become renowned. As word spreads of a magical healer, all her previous aggressors—Mylys, Machary and the sailor, who all happen to be suffering from diseases (leprosy, palsy, and a festering wound)—come to the convent to be healed. The mariner suffers from "suppurating"[64] genitals, which serves as a form of divine justice and echoes *Bracton*-era legal thought in that the convicted rapist should lose his testicles. Unbeknown to the men, Florence is the healer. Before she agrees to heal them, she demands that they all confess to the crimes they committed against her. After confessing, she heals them of their various ailments. Emere, also suffering from an infected battle wound, comes to the convent and is reunited with Florence. Since she is still a virgin, their union is finally made into a proper marriage, and they have a triumphant return to Rome, where they rule happily together. This is how the majority of continental versions end. However, the Middle English text goes further, stating that Emere, upon hearing of all the wicked crimes these men committed against his beloved, orders them all to be burned to death. This is rather remarkable, considering one of the condemned men is Mylys, his own brother. This works to emphasize the theme of divine justice and secular punishments for crimes in a highly moralizing tale. There are four scenes of attempted rape in *Le Bone Florence of Rome*, making this romance not just hint at sexual violence against women. Rather, threatened rape is central to the plot. What has yet to be fully acknowledged is the immense legal realism depicted in these rape scenes.

Before Garcy kills Otes, he tells the king that "with this blow I challenge Rome, / And your daughter [Florence], bright as bloom, / That brewed all this trouble, / When that I have laid with her, / And done her shame and violence, / Then I will of her no more, / But give her to my chamberlain."[65] Garcy promises to violently rape Florence and then offer her to his men. The subsequent attempted rapes of Florence are not only a crime against her

64 MED, "roten adj." article 1b.

65 *Le Bone Florence*, ll. 685–91.

but, equally, a threat to the political stability of Rome, as she is her father's only child. Echoing the treatment of rape and abduction of heiresses in the real world, rape is being represented here as a threat to the male patrimony.

Mylys's wicked nature is repeated throughout the narrative, as he is continually described as "false" and "evil." Mylys intentionally misleads Florence, further isolating her, until they reach a "deep gulley," where Mylys attempts to rape her:

> "Thou shall [see Emere] no more," / Then the lady sighed terribly, / And fell off her palfrey. / He [Mylys] beat her with his naked sword [*nakyd swyrde*], / And she cast up many woeful cries, / And said often, "oh woe / Shall I never my lord see? / No, by God that died on the cross," / The false traitor said. / Up he cast her and forth they rode, / Hastily without any abode, / This long summer's day. / They spent the night in a thick wood, / A lodge made [by] that wicked traitor, / Underneath a tree, / There he would have laid [*leyn*] by her, / And she made her prayer specially, / To God and Mary fair and free: / "Let never this false fiend / Shame nor disgrace [*schame nor schende*] never my body, / Almighty in majesty!" / His lust [*lykyng*] vanished all away.[66]

The sexual nature of the assault is illustrated by Myly's "naked sword." Florence's pain is explicit, as she cries out multiple times, demonstrating both her mental and verbal non-consent through raising the hue and cry. After the physical assault, Mylys then tries to rape her, but, through Marian intervention, his lust disappears. The narrative suggests that the worthy will be saved from rape, as Florence receives divine protection which saves her body from "shame" and "disgrace." This is reminiscent of the real debates amongst theologians concerning the degree of guilt and shame that raped maidens endure. These real social issues are demonstrated here, as Florence knows that if she is raped, the disgrace and dishonour is her burden. Much like the preaching of Augustine previously discussed, virginity is not something that can be restored, and once it is taken, the woman is considered forever changed. After setting a hermit on fire and threatening to burn Florence to death, Mylys tries to rape Florence again:

> And there he [Mylys] would by her have laid, / But she prayed to God to be her shield, / And right as he was going to, / His lust vanished [*lykyng vanyscht*] all away, / Through the might of Mary mild. / Timely as the day can dawn, / He led her through a fair thicket, / In woods waste and wild; / He alighted at mid-morning, / Down under a chestnut tree, / The fairest in that field. / He said "you have bewitched me, / I may not have my way with you,

66 *Le Bone Florence*, ll. 1422–44.

> / Undo [your spell] or you shall pay for it." / She answered him with mild mood, / "Through grace of Him that died on the cross, / False traitor you shall lie [dead]." / He bound her by the lock of her hair, / And hung her on a tree there, / That lady of fair body; / He beat her with a birch-tree branch, / Her naked flesh [*nakyd flesche*] until he was exhausted, / She gave many a rueful cries [*rewfull crye*].[67]

The blending of physical and sexual violence is explicit, much like the necessity of physical proof of non-consent as discussed in the secular *raptus* laws and treatises. Like hagiographical stories of the mutilation of virgin martyrs, Florence is saved from rape by divine intervention yet again, although this time it is at the expense of her earthly body. While allowing herself to be physically abused—as Florence is in a "mild mood"—she knows that her virginal body will prevail despite the harm to her physical flesh. Like the sources of evidence prescribed in *Glanvill*, *Bracton* and Westminster I, Florence has dishevelled hair, ripped and torn clothes, and bruises and bleeding flesh. The romance is repeating the written legal expectations of physical, bodily proof of non-consent to rape almost verbatim. Beyond coincidence or mere entertainment, these markers of violence on the female body ensure Florence's victim status from a contemporaneous legal perspective.

Florence raises the hue and cry, indicating her mental and verbal non-consent by screaming out to such a degree that Sir Tyrry "heard the cries of that fair lady, / There he went with his men."[68] Upon hearing the men approach, Mylys flees and abandons Florence in the woods with "the fairest palfrey he left there, / And herself hanging by her hair, / And her rich garments."[69] This suggests that Florence was naked when she was rescued by Sir Tyrry, which further works to substantiate her victim status. It is also reminiscent of the exposed and injured body of virgin martyrs. They untangle her hair to relieve her from the tree, and we are told about the severity of her injuries:

> She could not speak, the romance said, / On a litter they laid her, / And to the castle her led. / They bathed her in herbs often, / And made her sore sides soften, / For almost was she dead. / They fed her with full rich food, / And all things that she needed, / They served her in that spot.[70]

67 *Le Bone Florence*, ll. 1496–1518.

68 *Le Bone Florence*, ll. 1525–26.

69 *Le Bone Florence*, ll. 1531–33.

70 *Le Bone Florence*, ll. 1546–54.

The legal context is paramount to the audiences' interpretations of Florence, as she does everything correct from the legal perspective: she raises the hue and cry to alert others, she resists the rape, and she has extreme bodily injury to show as legal proof of her non-consent.

While recovering, Machary attempts to rape Florence. He watched Florence "day and night," stalking her like a predator until he finally made his move:

> In her chamber stood that maiden, / To her then he went to see; / He laid her down on her bed, / The lady wept sorely [*wepyd sore*] for dread [*dredd*], / She had no one to protect her there. / Before her bed lay a stone, / The lady took it up immediately, / And took it in a haste, / On the mouth she hit him, / That his front teeth out he spat, / Above and also beneath. / His mouth, his nose, bursting out [*braste owt*] blood, / Towards the chamber door he went, / For dread [*drede*] of more wrath;[71]

The physical injury is graphic. Florence hits Machary with the bed-stone, causing him to lose his upper and lower front teeth, and blood pores from his nose and mouth. The two consent models are evident: Florence's initial weeping is indicative of her mental non-consent and her subsequent use of the bed-stone ensures she physically proved her non-consent. The text uses the exact same word, *dredd*, to describe both Florence and Machary at different stages in the attempted rape. This literary repetition works to re-centre the narrative around Florence's acts of agency in the face of sexual violence, as she who initially felt dread imposes those feelings onto the attempted rapist.

While at sea, all the men onboard the ship thought that they could have sex with Florance "each one of them after the other was done."[72] The threat of group rape is obvious, and it is here that the final rape attempt is made:

> The mariner set her on his bed, / She had soon after a bitter spread, / The ship sailed vigorously; / He said, "Damsel I have bought you, / For you are so worthily shaped, / I will wed you as my wife." / She said, "No that shall not be ..." / In his arms he folded [*folde*] her, / Her ribs cracked [*rybbes crakyd*] as they would break, / In a struggle [*struglynge*] they engage. / She said, "Lady Mary free, / Now you have mercy on me, / ... That I take no shame [*schame*] today, / Nor lose my maidenhood [*maydynhede*]."[73]

---

71 *Le Bone Florence*, ll. 1598–1611.

72 *Le Bone Florence*, ll. 1829–30.

73 *Le Bone Florence*, ll. 1840–57.

The mariner explains that he is going to rape and marry Florence because of her physical beauty, exemplifying *Bracton*-era mentalities that men rape because of irresistible female beauty. Florence's verbal and mental non-consent is unambiguous, as she clearly says "no." Her verbal non-consent is immediately ignored by the mariner, as he physically grabs her with such force that he cracks her ribs. The physical altercation is described as "a struggle," indicating the expectation of women to physically resist rape. This reading suggests that verbal and mental non-consent will not protect women from sexual assault, but physical resistance is necessary. Adding to the didacticism of the scene, Florence states that if her virginity is taken from her, it is her shame to carry. Even though she did not verbally consent, and she is physically fighting to preserve her virginity, the potential burden of shame is, nonetheless, apparently hers to endure. This notion is referenced later in the narrative when Emere and Florence finally wed because she is "chaste and clean."[74] Rape is described in this romance repeatedly as disgraceful and dirty, but these connotations are applied to the woman rather than the rapists themselves. Like the use of *pollutionis* and *corruptam* in the secular laws and treatises, the romance reminds the audiences that rape leads to the corruptions and dishonour of the victim.

Emere is enraged by the attempted rapes of Florence, and in an extremely vengeful state, he orders the men to be burned at the stake. Out of the seven extant versions of the story, this burning scene appears in only four of them, including the Middle English Cambridge text. The Cambridge manuscript states that "He made a great fire, / And cast them in with all their attire, / Then was the lady woeful."[75] Despite the hagiographic tendencies of the romance, Emere demonstrates that even after confession and the healing of their diseases as proof of their atonement, he does not accept divine justice. Instead, Emere demands secular punishments for the crimes committed against his wife. As we have already seen with the case of Eleanor West, male kin could claim victim status for their female relative's rape and/ or abduction. Emere is claiming this by demanding secular justice for the crimes against him, Florence's husband. The "archetype" of the Middle English narrative roughly coincides with the time of transition from the Second Statute of Westminster to the Statute of Rapes.[76] This historical legal con-

74 *Le Bone Florence*, l. 2163.

75 *Le Bone Florence*, ll. 2119–21.

76 Even though the Cambridge manuscript dates from ca. 1480s, Stavsky argues that "the archetype of the Middle English poem" dates from as early as ca. 1350–1375. See Stavsky, *Le Bone Florence of Rome*, 19, 27.

text exposes lawmakers' potential fears about protecting male rights, male property, and male honour in *raptus* cases. The Statute of Rapes ensured that men had the legal capacity to demand justice for the (alleged) crimes against the bodies of women. The romance opens the space for medieval audiences to discuss Emere's right for vengeance around the same time that the English parliament was discussing the petition of Sir Thomas West.

The repeated emphasis on mental, verbal, and physical non-consent intricately acts as the connective tissue between contemporaneous *raptus* laws, treatises, ecclesiastical texts, and *Le Bone Florence of Rome*. The paradox of Florence's initial objectification as a rapeable body—in that she is solely the object of male desire—and her subsequent subjectivity and agency as a defiant heroine that preserves her virginal status concurs with medieval legal and cultural understandings of rape and (non-)consent. In the legal discourse of medieval England, married women received some legal subjectivity and agency through the objectification of rape, as it was (in theory) one of two crimes they could prosecute independently. Florence (a married woman) embodies this paradox as both a rapeable body and a resisting heroine who demonstrates subjectivity through her resistance to rape. Unlike Mylys and the mariner, who wanted to marry Florence, the second rape attempt is solely because of her striking beauty, reaffirming the continuum of lust and seduction leading to attempted rape. Florence is so beautiful that she can drive courtly men (Machary and Mylys are both knights) mad with the desire to rape.

Florence demonstrates the various consent models, as she offers verbal, mental, and physical non-consent. Notably, her verbal non-consent fails her every time. Her physical resistance saves her from Machary. However, it is Florence's mental non-consent, through spiritual resistance and prayers, which saves her from the attempted rape by Mylys and the mariner. This further highlights the paradox of Florence's resistance, which more often successfully manifests itself as a submission of her will to a higher power rather than through any overt individual action. In accepting her powerlessness, she exemplifies her true victim status, as Florence and real medieval women were generally believed in criminal courts due to their presumed powerlessness and their physical proof of non-consent.[77]

Florence does everything "right," but, ultimately, without divine intervention, her non-consent was futile. Is the narrative suggesting that women

---

77 Frances Ferguson discusses the connection between a rape victim's "lack of power" which could "guarantee her truthfulness." See Ferguson, "Rape and the Rise of the Novel," 97.

and girls should continue to defend themselves, but in the end only the worthy will be saved from rape? Florence's physical injuries are viewed as temporary and trivial compared to the preservation of her chastity for her husband. But there is more here than mere hagiographic rhetoric. When looking at the romance from the perspective of contemporaneous statutory laws and legal treatises, the physical injuries inflicted on Florence take on a much more important meaning beyond the traditional hagiographic motif of saints' lives and threatened rape. The romance appears to purposefully incorporate the legal requirement for physical proof of non-consent while reiterating the possibility of mental non-consent. Mylys beats her specifically on her naked flesh until he exhausts himself, causing her to have near-death injuries. He rips off Florence's clothing, presumably leaving them torn, and, later, the sailor breaks her ribs. The attacks by Mylys and the mariner fulfill all the prescribed proof of non-consent to rape that *Glanvill, Bracton*, and Westminster I needed, even though the rapes do not occur. *Le Bone Florence* makes it clear that all attempted rapes are by force and against her will, thus concurring with contemporaneous understandings of the crime all the way from *Glanvill* to the Statute of Rapes. Much like the actual case of Agnes Enovere (1287)—who at seven years old was violently beaten yet was able to preserve her virginity—fictional Florence emulates the expectations not only praised in hagiography but also evident in real court documents.[78] Unfortunately, this was a double-edged sword: young Agnes Enovere fought so bravely to preserve her virginity that, despite the severe injuries she showed the authorities, the crime was deemed a minor trespass because her virginity remained intact. Perhaps Agnes's story was not unique, and, just maybe, the story of Florence provided the space to debate such court rulings.

Past scholars have come to different conclusions about Florence's physical injuries than I have, often claiming that she is a secularized virgin martyr.[79] Although Florence is reminiscent of a secular saint—as these other scholars have suggested—the evidence suggests that the contextualization of the romance within secular *raptus* laws and treatises adds another layer of understanding to the narrative's unmistakable attention on Florence's physical and mental non-consent. Florence resists all three attempted rapes, and she proves her physical and mental non-consent by enduring violent

78 TNA, JUST1/328 m6. For a full discussion see Chapter 3.

79 Dunn, *Stolen Women*, 91–92; Heffernan, "*Raptus*," 173–79; Mehl, *The Middle English Romances of the Thirteenth and Fourteenth Centuries*, 140–42; Riddy, "Temporary Virginity and the Everyday Body," 203–6; Saunders, *Rape and Ravishment*, 203–6.

assaults. In the context of *raptus* laws, the focus on Florence's injuries physically proves her non-consent and thus make her a "real victim." Florence is the perfect role model for audience members, as she demonstrates women's legal responsibility to resist rape verbally, mentally, and physically.

Concluding Thoughts

The previous two chapters demonstrate that when one reads romance in conjunction with contemporaneous legal assumptions about rape and (non-)consent, there is the potential for more holistic interpretations of the actions of the fictional characters. Beyond hagiographic rhetoric or attempts to simply excite the audience, scenes of sexual violence are mimicking legal realities that the medieval audiences would have undoubtedly been aware of. These narratives offer opportunities to examine cultural attitudes towards the expectations of rape victims, the potential use of silence as indicative of non-consent, and the physical injuries that women may endure when they refuse male sexual advances. There are continual representations of a woman's verbal and mental non-consent as inadequate to stop rape, and she must physically resist as well. Romance implies that male lust can lead to seduction and rape much like the legal assumptions that men rape because of a woman's beauty. Rape and seduction are placed on the same continuum in both MER and medieval England's legal sources. Laws, cases, and literary sources often end this continuum of lust, seduction, and rape with the potential of marriage. Romance continually excuses masculine aggression, as we have seen with the fairy rapist knight (*Sir Degare*), the demonic hybrid (*Sir Gowther*), and the ravishing fairy king (*Sir Orfeo*). These violent tendencies are normalized in romance as if they are inevitable outcomes of women's beauty, isolation, and vulnerability. Although masculine aggression is condemnable in romance, as in the laws, it is, nonetheless, continually depicted as a display of masculine lust. These fictional metaphors of men are frequently committing felonious acts out of desire much like the stated reasoning for Belisaunt's malicious accusations (*Amis and Amiloun*). The duality of the laws—to protect innocent women from rape and to protect innocent men from vindictive women or loss of property—are represented throughout the romances under study here.

Prevailing medical thought about conception and consent, ecclesiastical demands of the conjugal debt, and the legal impossibility of marital rape are all real social issues which are represented through the princess (*Sir Degare*) and the duchess (*Sir Gowther*). Questions regarding malicious accusations of rape and the validity of the marriage clause in *raptus* cases are depicted through the actions of Belisaunt and her father (*Amis and Amiloun*). Florence (*Le Bone Florence of Rome*) is depicted as the perfect victim, as she has all the legal requirements of physical proof of non-consent while also exemplifying verbal and mental non-consent. Florence endures and Belisaunt threatens to self-inflict the visible markers of violence and non-consent which are the exact same tokens of proof stated in *Glanvill*, *Bracton*, and Westminster I. On the other hand, Orfeo, Belisaunt's father, and Emere display how the male next of kin can claim victim status of their wives' and daughters' rapes and/or abductions around the same time as when Sir Thomas West was petitioning similar claims in parliament. These fictional stories mirror real societal anxieties around feminine sexuality, bodily worth, rape, consent and non-consent, abduction, physical abuse, malicious accusations of rape, resistance to rape, and pregnancy from rape. These social concerns are addressed in the fictional romances to such a high degree of realism that they provide the space for the audiences to engage and debate these issues. These characters are enduring real-life problems which make them relatable to the audience, both medieval and modern.

The duality of mental and physical (non-)consent is addressed throughout the romances under study here. Heurodis (*Sir Orfeo*) and the princess (*Sir Degare*) express explicit verbal and mental non-consent while the narratives make it clear that physical resistance is futile. Belisaunt (*Amis and Amiloun*) projects fears of malicious rape accusations, as she threatens to provide proof of physical non-consent to substantiate her alleged rape. The duchess's (*Sir Gowther*) non-consent is implied from her silence and lack of expressed desire to have coitus with the fiend in-disguise, which opens the space for questions about marital rape and implied spousal consent. Gowther (*Sir Gowther*) himself rapes every class of victim according to contemporaneous statutory law, demonstrating the monstrosity of rapists. Lastly, Florence (*Le Bone Florence of Rome*) provides explicit mental, verbal, and physical non-consent. The various non-consent models within these texts suggests that despite the laws expectations of physical proof of non-consent and ecclesiastical debates about a divided mental and physical (non-)consent, the belief that the mind and body can, and should, act together to defend against rape (but at times bodily consent will take over) was seemingly upheld in popular opinion.

Conclusion

THE BODY OF PROOF AND THE RAPEABLE BODY

A YOUNG GIRL named Emma was violently abducted by a group of five men.[1] The men kidnapped little Emma and brought her to a sixth man's house, that of David le Carpentur, at which point one of the kidnappers, Walter de Carlaton, raped her, presumably under the voyeuristic spectatorship of the other five men. The courts indicted Walter, and the jurors believed that Emma was undoubtedly raped. But the jurors said something along the lines of "Emma was kidnapped and raped by Walter, but after the rape was done rumour has it that Emma consented to the rape, and she has now agreed to marry Walter." Essentially, no rape *really* happened here. But what about their marriage? Was it legal? The jurors discussed how young Emma was likely coerced into this marriage, so Walter was ordered to pay a small fine. Case closed.

Was Emma raped? The jurors said yes. Did she later consent to the rape? The jurors said yes. Are rape and consent mutually exclusive? Apparently not, as one can be raped and then consent to it afterwards. Can rape lead to a legally binding marriage? Yes. Was Emma coerced into the marriage? The jurors said most likely. Does coercion make the marriage illegal? Apparently not. Medieval English understandings of rape and (non-)consent were complex, context specific, and sometimes conflicting, and yet medieval English lawmakers, theologians, authors, and ordinary people cared deeply about these issues.

Medieval England sustained a rape culture through its continual reiteration of the duality of mental and physical (non-)consent. Kate Manne poignantly states that the combination of "misogynist aggression, serial sexual predation, and norms that enable and protect perpetrators: that is, rape culture."[2] The qualities of "aggression," physical strength, "serial sexual predation," and sexual proficiency are all part of idealized masculinity in medieval England. Of course, "men" cannot be classified as a single homogenous group, and what it meant to be masculine or feminine changed throughout

1 TNA, JUST1/137 m6d.

2 Manne, *Down Girl*, 199–200.

the Middle Ages. However, there are some traits that reappear in representations of medieval manhood, including violence, controlling women, and rationality.[3] The relative ease at which these qualities teetered into sexual violence against women is exemplified by the language in laws, literature, and ecclesiastical and medical texts which describe the uncontrollable lust of men who rape beautiful women. The threat of rape was always present in medieval English society; it was something women were told to be fearful of and men were told to control.

Conduct literature is explicit in idealizing feminine passivity. The popular fourteenth-century Middle English text *How the Good Wife Taught Her Daughter* reiterates the instructions that a wife should be meek and mild,[4] and states if one's husband be "wrath and angry / Look thou meekly answer him,"[5] suggesting that when a husband is "violently enraged,"[6] the wife is advised to remain meek. *Meke* is defined as "gentle, quiet, [and] unaggressive,"[7] furthering the notion that feminine passivity is expected even in times of masculine aggression and violence. In advising against partaking in masculine activities—such as wrestling and cock-shooting—the poem claims that a woman who engages in such activities is a "strumpet."[8] When a woman is involved in traditionally masculine activities, she is not referred to as manly or unwomanly, but as a whore.[9] The close connection between a woman's sexual *fama*, reputation, and her assumed truthfulness is reiterated in romance, conduct literature, ecclesiastical and texts and it undoubtedly influenced court proceedings.

In another popular fourteenth-century conduct text, *Book of the Knight of La Tour-Landry*, translated into Middle English in the fifteenth century, a young daughter ventured into "another land" where a great lord "saw her so fair" that he fell in love, igniting his passion to rape "in so much he took from her, her maidenhood."[10] The girl's kin murdered the rapist and his family "for the shame that they had of their sister." Reminiscent of romance narra-

3 Karras, *From Boys to Men*, 6, 10–12.

4 Salisbury, ed., "How the Goode Wife Taught Hyr Daughter," ll. 20, 37, 124, 168.

5 "How the Goode Wife Taught Hyr Daughter," ll. 36–37.

6 MED, "wroth," article 1b.

7 MED, "meke," article 1a.

8 "How the Goode Wife Taught Hyr Daughter," ll. 73–75.

9 MED, "strumpet," article 1a.

10 Wright, ed., *Book of the Knight of La Tour-Landry*, chap. 56, pp. 73–74. Translations are my own.

tives, the girl's isolation led to her vulnerability, teaching young women and girls the dangers of being alone. The trope of "man sees beautiful maiden, man loves maiden, man rapes maiden," as stated here, is identical to contemporaneous legal and literary sources. Notably, the brothers avenge their sister's shame; she is the one who is seemingly burdened with this disgrace, and, because of her, "more than a thousand men were slain." If the didacticism was lost on the medieval audiences, the conduct text makes it explicitly clear: "now look you and see, how by a foolish woman cometh many evils and damages."[11] She is to blame for exciting the rapist's passion to rape; she is foolish, and she is responsible for the deaths of many men. Due to her recklessness, the raped girl was "chopped in small pieces." Her dismemberment was justified because "so many [men] had been chopped and slain" to avenge her rape.[12] Clearly, rape was considered a man's problem and something that men could be victimized by, as further reflected in the evolving statutory laws. This conduct text devotes multiple chapters to instruct women that rape leads to the shame (and death) of the woman, not the rapist.[13] The text warns young girls to never be alone with a man, as "a woman ought to trust no man" because their "young tender flesh [*tendir flesshe*] when it is chased, it is easy to be tempted."[14] In a section devoted to wifely obedience, a husband was so angry at his wife that:

> [he] hit her with his fist down to the earth; and then with his foot he struck her in the face and broke her nose, and all her life after she had her nose crooked ... And therefore, the wife ought to suffer and let her husband have the words, and to be master, for that is her worship.[15]

The conduct text discusses how a disobedient wife ought to expect physical assault by her husband, and, in certain circumstances, she was subject to justifiable homicide.[16] The repetition of a woman's meekness is noteworthy, as it is even stated in the opening prologue to *Glanvill* that the king's law protects the *humilium et mansuetorum* (humble and meek). There was a continual cultural insistence in medieval England on a woman's meekness, on a martyr's willingness to suffer, and on a wife's passivity during spousal

---

11 *Book of the Knight*, chap. 56, p. 74.

12 *Book of the Knight*, chap. 56, p. 74.

13 *Book of the Knight*, chap. 56, pp. 73–74; chap. 71, pp. 93–94; chap. 58, pp. 76–77 details malicious rape accusations made against Joseph.

14 *Book of the Knight*, chap. 61, pp. 78–79.

15 *Book of the Knight*, chap. 18, p. 25.

16 *Book of the Knight*, chap. 19, pp. 27–28; chap. 63, pp. 84–85.

violence. But this passivity and endurance is entirely counter to the expectation of women's physical resistance during rape. The cognitive dissonance of ideal femininity (passive) and ideal rape victims (resistant) sustained a continual cultural suspicion of rape survivors.

The paradoxical expectations of women to willingly endure their suffering while simultaneously resisting the assault created a no-win situation for rape survivors. Women threatened with rape should resist but also be passive. This duality is indicative of medieval England's conflicting societal attitudes towards rape and (non-)consent in general. The expectation of feminine subordination and passivity, as highlighted in hagiography, conduct literature, and canon texts, operated in a cultural context that believed women to be sexual temptresses. Fearing malicious accusations of rape—used to trap "good" men into marriage—the ecclesiastical perspectives were complementary to secular criminal courts, creating a legal ethos of suspicion towards women's rape claims. This, interestingly, is perhaps most clearly seen not in the courts themselves but as a theme in Belisaunt's accusations of threatened rape in *Amis and Amiloun*.

The blurring of seduction and rape in laws, treatises, literature, case records, and ecclesiastical texts ensured that the non-consent of the woman was difficult to determine, as Ellen Rooney states, "rape is a sex crime that is not a crime when it looks like sex."[17] Medieval romance authors played with this blurred line between consensual coitus and rape, as we have seen in *Sir Degare* and *Sir Gowther*. Rape was considered a negative consequence of uncontrollable male lust. Certainly, rape was viewed legally as a crime in medieval England. But it was also viewed as an extreme, and condemnable, form of male seduction. Moreover, legal treatises, statutes, and plea rolls have the narrative trajectory of rape which can, and sometimes does, end in matrimony, much like romance literature.[18]

The duality of mental and physical (non-)consent was emphasized throughout the sources under study here. Medieval English legal sources view sexual (non-)consent primarily by the injuries (or lack thereof) on the woman's body while recognizing the potential of mental (non-)consent. The belief in mental non-consent and physical consent is fully discussed in medical and ecclesiastical texts, and this is reiterated in romance literature. Crucially, all sources place significance on the woman's body as the potential proof of physical (non-)consent to rape while acknowledging the possibility (and at times necessity) of mental non-consent.

---

17 Rooney, "'A Little More Than Persuading,'" 90.

18 For example, TNA, JUST1/1171 m3; JUST1/112 m13d; JUST1/877 m61d.

This concept begins with the examination of the five legal ages of *raptus*. The duality of the two consent models is continually hinted at, often highlighted, and even debated throughout all legal sources examined here. The woman can show bodily injury *or* cry out while at the same time there is the expectation that the woman has physical injury to initiate the appeal process. This means that mental non-consent (raising the hue and cry) alone would likely not guarantee a trial. *Glanvill* discusses the injury of the flesh, which is the cornerstone to a woman's appeal of both rape (her own flesh) and the murder of her husband (through *uno caro*). *Bracton* prioritizes the rape of virgins as the most serious offence, yet *Bracton* also outlines some of the most explicit laws concerning the culpability of group rape. Critically, *Bracton* explains how the supposed "ancient" laws upheld the woman's mental and verbal non-consent as legally paramount, and yet *Bracton* states that, in present-day thirteenth-century England, the woman must show bruising, bleeding, and torn or stained clothing to prove her allegations. Thus, while *Bracton* acknowledges the possibility of mental non-consent, the treatise quickly undermines its legitimacy within medieval England's criminal courts in favour of physical proof of non-consent, further adding to the complexity of the two consent models. *Glanvill* and *Bracton* repeatedly insist on the proof of resistance to rape as indicative of the woman's non-consent. The Statute of Westminster I gave the crown legal power to indict *raptus* at the king's suit. This can be seen as both serving justice—if a woman does not properly appeal within the forty-day time limit—but also interfering with the marriage clause—potentially overriding a woman's consent to marry her ravisher. Westminster I provides greater attention to mental (non-)consent than *Glanvill* or *Bracton*, as it prohibits coitus with minors, and yet the accompanying Office of the Coroner reiterates that physical bodily proof of non-consent is still essential to securing a trial. It is within the Office of the Coroner that the duality of mental and physical (non-)consent are positioned as an "either/or" construction: the woman can *either* show effusion of her blood *or* raise the hue and cry. This reaffirmation on the supposed conflicting consent models demonstrates the possibility that the mind and body of rape victims could be working in opposition to each other. During the legal age of Westminster II, the victim is not necessarily the woman herself but primarily her male kin. The displacement of victimhood away from the woman is not new with Westminster II but rather began with fears of malicious rape accusations, as stated in *Glanvill*. This shift of victim status is completed with the Statute of Rapes, in which women could no longer legally appeal their own rape. It is important to note that this is occurring at the same time as a general decline in felony appeals, as indictments became more commonplace. During the age of Westminster II, lawmakers were clearly debating the temporality of non-consent and the legal implications of verbal non-consent after the crime occurred. Despite this, the laws and treatises continually state that force and violence are necessary, and thus they uphold the expectation of physical proof of non-consent. As outlined in Westminster II, even if the woman's physical non-consent is evident immediately after the rape, the statute allows for the possibility of the woman's declaration of mental consent anytime after the crime.

From *Glanvill* to the Statute of Rapes, we see the evolving legal displacement of women as the victims of rape. This victimization of men in the crime of rape demonstrates the unsurprisingly long history of what Kate Manne terms *himpathy*: "excessive sympathy sometimes shown towards male perpetrators of sexual violence," in which the courts may "sympathize with him first, effectively making him into the victim of his own crimes."[19] Medieval "himpathy" is evident in not only the legal rights extended to male kin and the high acquittal rate in the EC but also in the sustained belief that rapists are victims to their own sexual impulses. Medieval English culture supported a persistent belief in the bodily victimization of both rapists and rape victims. The medieval biological medical theories of the female anatomy were aided by the ecclesiastical doctrine which preached that women are inherently burning with sexual desire. The woman's body could betray her mental and verbal non-consent. This bodily victimization was not exclusively a female problem, as men too were considered in need of sexual release, and if this could not be legally attained through marriage or sex work, it was feared that men will rape. Men, too (it was thought) could be victims of their body's sexual desires.

Case records demonstrate that criminal courts interpreted rape and (non-)consent through varying circumstantial methods. As we have seen through the cases analyzed here, a lack of physical injury allowed for doubts about the woman's (non-)consent and worked to downgrade the offence. Consent could be applied to a rape case retroactively, in which case charges were dropped or downgraded. A lack of full vaginal penetration was used as indicative of non-completed rape. A woman's pregnancy from rape was proof of physical consent of the flesh despite her mental non-consent. A woman's past consent to coitus with the alleged rapist could be used as justifiable grounds to belittle a rape accusation, resulting in the acquittal of the accused. That there are zero felony convictions in these cases suggests a

19 Manne, *Down Girl*, 197, 201.

strong reluctance to convict men of rape because of the severity of the punishment up to and including execution. The lack of any felony convictions is also the consequence of underlying socio-cultural attitudes regarding heterosexual encounters, competing understandings of mental and physical (non-)consent, and an expectation of physical and mental resistance, as seen in the romances.

One of the most important considerations that this research into the plea rolls provides is the shockingly common occurrence of group rape in medieval England. This is an extremely understudied field, and scholars have rightly pointed to the limited archival information to determine if a "gang" rape (by modern standards) did occur. It is true that the archives do not usually divulge such information, but that does not mean scholars should ignore or trivialize the other men and women accused of acting as accessories to the crime. Of the sixty-one rape cases studied here, ten of them mention multiple people accused of aiding or committing the rape, representing 16.39% of the cases. Jacques Rossiaud found that of the 125 rape cases in Dijon, recorded between 1436–1486, nighty-eight were group rapes, with an average group of six persons, and 20% had groups of ten or more. This led Rossiaud to conclude that "gang rape had a place at the borderline between culture and subculture."[20] Even if we do not know—due to the limited archival information—the exact nature of their involvement, it is time that we re-consider how we discuss rape as typically a one-on-one scenario. This is why I propose the term "group rape" instead of "gang rape." Scholarly silence on the frequent occurrence of group rape not only dismisses the depth of information that is available in the archives but also works to preserve a manufactured rape culture.[21]

The traumatizing experience that medieval women and young girls had to endure when going to trial has also received little scholarly attention. As Wendy Turner and Christina Lee note, medievalists are concerned about scholarly integrity when "back diagnosing," but we cannot ignore the fact that people in the Middle Ages experienced trauma.[22] A rape victim had to undergo numerous rounds of men and women—particularly the coroner and the "legal women"—scrutinizing their body. They also had to be present in court, where potential neighbour jurors and the alleged rapist would be in attendance, as a defendant had the right to see their accuser. Not much

---

20 Rossiaud, *Medieval Prostitution*, 13–14, 22.

21 For more of my discussion on this topic, see Cooper, "'Let's Bring the Boys In'"

22 Turner and Lee, "Conceptualizing Trauma for the Middle Ages," 8.

has changed today, as "for many the impact of testifying as a sexual assault complainant remains traumatizing and harmful."[23] In appeal cases, women have to "give voice publicly, over and over again, to violations of their sexual integrity," and for many of the young girls discussed in this book, this was their first sexual experience.[24] The re-traumatization of the appeal process has been briefly considered by *raptus* scholars, but it is not difficult to speculate how distressing the criminal trial process was for these women and young girls, especially with the threat of imprisonment always looming. The potentially devastating consequences of publicly accusing a man of rape, the repeated inspection of the woman's body, and the process of testifying in a criminal court of all men and standing near the very man that committed the rape would have undoubtedly negatively influenced the likelihood of a woman bringing an appeal forward, much like it does today. In cases of indictment, this trauma may have been even greater, as the woman did not willingly come to court and pursue an appeal. In these indictment cases, some women were forced to endure a trial against their will.

In medieval romances, conduct literature, and canon texts, we can clearly see that cultural symbols were regularly used in rape narratives: as woman as pure or polluted, virgin or temptress, innocent or guilty. As St. Lucy's *Legend* details, bodily "corruption" does not necessarily corrupt the mentally non-consenting victim, despite any rape that may occur. While Augustine employs the same cultural symbols and language as other ecclesiastics—such as Jerome—Augustine underlines the importance of mental non-consent to rape despite any physical "corruption." These cultural symbols are echoed and legitimized through tokens of "proof" in rape cases. Laws, treaties, canon texts, case records, and romances stress the importance of signs of physical force used to overpower the woman, and sources analyzed here reiterate the legal responsibilities of women to resist their own rape both physically and mentally. When they are not able to, the application of legal identities, repeated in the romances, is frequently used against them. Through an examination of the legal constructions of *raptus* cases, the performance of victimhood by complainants and defendants, and the physical proof of a crime, I have identified that the EC prescribed one of three legal identities onto women in rape cases: the innocent victim, the guilty woman, or the reluctant, but willing, accomplice to her own rape. The latter two of these identities essentially turn the woman from a complainant into a defen-

23 Craig, *Putting Trials on Trial*, 4.

24 Craig, *Putting Trials on Trial*, 8.

dant. These identities were not embodied by the women themselves, nor are they "roles" that the women performed. Rather, they are linguistically constructed identities that the criminal courts seemingly prescribed onto women as their legal subjecthood, or persona, and they could carry severe consequences. These legal identities are part of the patriarchal control of women in rape cases, and they illustrate the long history of both victim-blaming rape survivors and victimizing rapists. Crucially, these legal identities can also be seen in the medieval romances, demonstrating both their legal and social value to those utilizing them.

In victimizing rapists, *Bracton* perpetuates the assumption that male sexual urges are excessive and dangerous. Bodily urges leading to uncontrollable emotions or urge to rape implies that rape is percolating just below the surface of medieval English society. The *Book of the Knight* tells readers that some men are full of "lechery, enflamed, unmeasurable like wolves, or other wild beasts [*wyld beestis*]."[25] Indulgence of one's "fleshy appetite" is, according to the conduct text, the "life of a beast."[26] Conduct literature, romance narratives, and ecclesiastical and medical texts indicate that "strong men" can control their appetite of the flesh—their sexual impulses—and only "weak men" succumb to their hot lust. The notion that men temporarily lose their reason during rape was not only seen as a failure of masculinity, but it also obscured cultural understandings of what "a rapist looks like." In what Manne has termed "the honorable Brutus problem," we can see how a society perpetuates a stereotype that only certain, monstrous men rape, thus making it difficult to accept the fact that "a golden boy" can also be a rapist.[27] Medieval English society considered rapists as men who lost their reason and their ability to maintain bodily control. With that lack of reason, rapists could be positioned as beast-like, monstrous, less human even, and more like a "wildman" attacking a lady.[28] The rapist embodies the "wild" nature of the fictional serial rapist Sir Gowther. Rape or violent sex could even produce a monstrous offspring, as stated in *De secretis mulierum*.[29] Medieval scholars, such as Thomas Aquinas, state that sexual desires are a form of sickness that compromises a man's reason. Gratian reiterates this by stating that sexual temptation is a form of sickness, and that only "weak" individuals submit

25 *Book of the Knight*, chap. 37, p. 53.

26 *Book of the Knight*, chap. 89, p. 116.

27 Manne, *Down Girl*, 197–98.

28 As depicted in the Taymouth Hours illumination on the cover of this book.

29 Lemay, *Women's Secrets*, 114.

to it.[30] The body needs to be controlled. This includes men's bodies (which ought to be controlled by reason) and women's bodies (which also need reason but also male protection). Both men and women's bodies are capable of being the site of victimization; for men, it is their all-consuming hot lust, and for women, it is primarily their injured body from rape.

Both the male and female body were believed to be able to *do things* contrary to one's mind; for men, it was to lose one's mind leading to rape, and for women, it was the flesh which could consent independently of the mind during rape. The incongruency between the consent of the mind and the flesh opens the figurative space for the legal identity of the reluctant but willing accomplice. The agreement of opinion between the legal treatises of *Britton*, *Mirror of Justices*, and *Fleta* strongly suggests that, even though the laws make no mention of conception as equivalent to consent, judicial men were debating it amongst themselves in medieval England. When the male body operates independently of the mind in instances of rape, rape could be considered a momentary lapse in judgement. But for the woman, rape could be considered momentarily enjoyable to the female flesh. Either way, the chances of securing a conviction in the criminal courts are diminished when the body *does things* without the mind, because this introduces doubt into the case. Doubt, as *Britton* states, requires that "the judgement ought always" to be in the favour of the defendant.[31] In rape accusations with little bodily injury, justices and jurors were warned since the *Glanvill* age that the accusations could be malicious and, as such, any doubt in the accusation ought to aid the accused. I am not suggesting that the legal requirement of proving culpability beyond a reasonable doubt is itself unreasonable; rather, I am arguing that a lack of physical injury or a pregnancy from rape which introduced doubt into a rape accusation had devastating consequences, both then as well as now.[32]

The cognitive dissonance between the passivity of ladies and the resistance of rape survivors undoubtedly troubled medieval jurors, leading to doubts about the truthfulness of rape accusations. Gender norms and societal expectations are evident in the fact that, despite the statutes' stated indifferences to virginity, there is a continual emphasis in the EC plea rolls on a loss of virginity to secure a conviction. This had severe repercussions

---

30 *Decretum*, C. 25, q. 1.

31 *Britton*, vol. 1, pp. 32–33.

32 See Digeser, "Resistance, Rape, Recognition, and Aggression," 1–10; Murphy-Oikonen et al., "Unfounded Sexual Assault," 8933.

for women who were not deemed virgins at the time of the assault or who were virgins and managed to resist full-penetrative vaginal rape. Even today, the importance of so-called virginal "purity" and the belief that the rape of virgins is the most serious sexual offence is still discussed.[33] The importance of virginal status was paramount to medieval ecclesiastics, who debated the possibility of the increased holiness of rape survivors and the differences between mental and physical (non-)consent. The theological debates around consent of the flesh and consent of the mind are largely neglected by the secular laws, but they appear in romances such as *Le Bone Florence of Rome*, *Sir Degare*, and *Sir Gowther*. These connections between texts and ideas demonstrate that medieval English culture conceptualized sexual (non-)consent as both mental and physical.

When reading romance in conjunction with legal sources on rape, it becomes absolutely apparent that romance engages with the very same cultural fears and anxieties as the laws. The social attitudes around gender expectations, sexuality, and appropriate behaviour often go unwritten in sources such as chronicles and law codes, and thus it has often escaped the attention of modern legal scholars. It is in the fictional literature where such cultural practices can be gleaned. Violence against women in romance has long been noted by scholars as a plot device, but the legal realities of resistance and sexual (non-)consent within the romances have thus far escaped scholarly attention—until now. Too often these scenes are dismissed as hagiographical rhetoric to excite audiences, but this research has revealed that the scenes of sexual violence are mimicking a legal reality that the medieval audiences would have recognized. Through a close reading of the select romances, it is evident that real-life issues around rape and (non-)consent are represented, exploited, and manipulated in the fictional literature. Medieval medical debates about conception and consent, church expectations of the marital sexual debt, and the legal impossibility of martial rape are represented through the actions of the princess (*Sir Degare*) and the duchess (*Sir Gowther*). Fears of malicious rape accusations and the validity of the marriage clause through *raptus* are depicted through Belisaunt and her father (*Amis and Amiloun*). Florence (*Le Bone Florence*) is the "perfect rape victim," demonstrating the exact tokens of physical proof of non-consent as outlined in the legal sources and exemplifying the (futile) expectation of verbal and mental non-consent.

---

33 Sklar, "Welcome to Senator Bill Napoli's X-Rated Mind"; Valenti, *The Purity Myth*.

These romances stress the importance of the physical proof of non-consent to rape and the importance of mental (and in turn, verbal) non-consent. Heurodis (*Sir Orfeo*) and the princess (*Sir Degare*) have explicit verbal and mental non-consent, but both narratives demonstrate the ineffectiveness of such resistance. Belisaunt (*Amis and Amiloun*) threatens to make herself appear as having been raped, and she provides the exact signs of proof of physical non-consent as outlined in the legal sources. The duchess's silence (*Sir Gowther*) is indicative of her mental non-consent, and the narrative opens the space for questions about implied spousal consent. Beyond coincidence, Gowther himself rapes every class of "victim" as outlined in contemporaneous statutory law, demonstrating to the audiences his lack of reason, his wild nature, and the correlation between monstrosity and rapists. Florence (*Le Bone Florence*) epitomizes the varying consent models, as she provides explicit mental, verbal, and physical non-consent. Mental non-consent fails to protect Heurodis, the princess, the nuns (*Sir Gowther*), and Florence, thus sustaining the normative assumption that women ought to physically prove their non-consent through physical resistance and bodily injury. All the romances examined here show the legal responsibilities of women to resist their own rape, and when they are not able to, the application of legal identities is used—some by way of conception and marriage to "erase" the rapes. Clearly, the romances are engaging with popular assumptions about the mind and body of rape victims (and rapists) in a similar—although at times contradictory—fashion to the legal and ecclesiastical texts.

Through this combined literary and legal analysis, the actions of the characters are not random but appear to be imitating the legal realities and issues surrounding rape and (non-)consent in medieval England. These issues include sexuality, bodily autonomy, rape, consent and non-consent, abduction, physical abuse, marital rape, malicious accusations of rape, resistance to rape, victimization, and pregnancy from rape. By studying conduct literature, hagiography, medical texts, legal treatises, statutory laws, criminal court plea rolls, and romance narratives collectively, it becomes evident that rape survivors were entangled in a cultural discourse, in which the mind and body of rape victims and rapists could operate independently of one another.

Only when we consider the breadth of primary sources on sexual violence in high medieval England can we truly appreciate the pervasiveness of distrusting women's accusations of rape without physical proof of non-consent—and its implications for the present. The parallels between modern "bro culture" and rape culture and the medieval concepts of rape and (non-)consent, are striking. As Carissa Harris asked: "how far have we really come?"[34] I, too, believe that, in many ways, we are still living in the medieval past when it comes to sexual violence, legal justice, and persistent victim-blaming. Enshrined in medieval laws and mentalities, these concepts have had long-term impacts, as many of medieval England's rape mythologies are still present. Modern rape myths, such as "rape is a result of uncontrollable male passions" and that "women routinely lie about rape,"[35] echo *Bracton*-era attitudes. Lawmakers still debate whether pregnancy can occur in a "real rape" scenario, while punitive castration for convicted rapists is still practiced in the United States.[36] *Bracton* is still considered a legal authority by the Supreme Court of the United States, as the treatise was used to justify anti-abortion legislation.[37] Although many concepts presented in this book seem truly *medieval*, they continue to have profound influence. In many ways, we are living in the medieval past when it comes to how we treat survivors of sexual assault and opinions towards "real rape."[38]

The medieval cultural and legal attitudes of physical proof of non-consent ensured that the "body of proof" was entirely the burden of the rape survivor. The cultural excuse that rape is the result of succumbing to one's libido enabled a societal toleration of male entitlement towards women's bodies—particularly lower-class women who were viewed as rapeable bodies. The modern "rapeability logic" can easily be applied to the medieval past, because it is founded on the belief that rape is only perpetuated against sexually attractive yet passive women who are "fuckable" from the male heterosexual perspective.[39] According to this logic, vulnerable women, attractive women, and docile women are considered easily rapeable, both then and now. The duality of mental and physical (non-)consent to rape erodes the legal possibility in medieval England of silence and acquiescing as a

---

34 Harris, "800 Years of Rape Culture."

35 Payne et al., "Rape Myth Acceptance," 28, 30–31.

36 Blake, "Todd Akin, GOP Senate Candidate"; Breen, "Louisiana Man Sentences to 50 Years in Prison, Physical Castration for Raping Teen"; Franke-Ruta, "A Canard That Will Not Die."

37 Supreme Court of the United States, "Dobbs, State Health Officer of the Mississippi Department of Health, Et Al., V. Jackson Women's Health Organization Et Al.," 25.

38 For example: Acquaviva, Meeker, and O'Neal, "Blameworthy Suspects and 'Real Rape'"; Du Mont, Miller, and Myhr, "The Role of 'Real Rape' and 'Real Victim' Stereotypes in the Police Reporting Practices of Sexually Assaulted Women"; Estrich, *Real Rape*; Krahé, "Societal Responses to Sexual Violence Against Women," 676–84.

39 Andreasen, "'Rapeable' and 'Unrapeable' Women," 106–8; Jane, *Misogyny Online*, 10, 25.

trauma-response form of non-consent. Without physical resistance to the rape—made evident through bodily injury to prove non-consent—there was legal and cultural trepidation in believing rape survivors. As this research has shown, this has contributed to a long history of distrust and silencing of rape survivors, the consequences of which can still be felt today.

BIBLIOGRAPHY

Archival and Manuscript Material

Legal and Medical Manuscripts

Cambridge, Cambridge University Library, MS Gg.vi.7.
Cambridge, Cambridge Pembroke College, MS 271.
Cambridge, Harvard Law School Library, MS Dunn 41.
Cambridge, Harvard Law School Library, MS Dunn 51.
Dublin, Trinity College Dublin, MS E.5.11.
London, British Library, Cotton MS Julius B VIII.
London, British Library, MS Additional 18210.
London, British Library, MS Additional 24066.
London, British Library, MS Additional 25029.
London, British Library, MS Additional 31826.
London, British Library, MS Additional 32086.
London, British Museum, MS Additional 12056.
London, British Library, MS Harley 324.
London, British Library, MS Harley 453.
London, British Library, MS Harley 1119.
London, British Library, MS Harley 1807.
London, British Library, MS Harley 5146.
London, Lincoln's Inn Library, MS Hale 135.
London, Lincoln's Inn Library, MS Misc. 3.
London, Lincoln's Inn Library, MS Misc. 87.
London, Lincoln's Inn Library, MS Year Book, Edward I, A.
London, Lincoln's Inn Library, MS Year Book of the Time of Edward 1, 30–33.
Oxford, Bodleian Library, MS Ashmole 399.
Oxford, Bodleian Library, MS Ashmole 1396.
Oxford, Bodleian Library, MS Rawl. D.506.
Oxford, Bodleian Library, MS Tanner 13.
Oxford, Bodleian Library, MS Tanner 450.

Legal and Literary Manuscripts Held at Kew, The National Archives

Close Rolls

Kew, The National Archives, C54/93, m17.

Coroners' Rolls

Kew, The National Archives, JUST2/1 m1d.

Gaol Delivery Rolls

Kew, The National Archives, JUST3/174 m1d.

General Eyre Plea Rolls

Kew, The National Archives, JUST1/1 m4d.
Kew, The National Archives, JUST1/18 m4d.
Kew, The National Archives, JUST1/26 m28, m37d.
Kew, The National Archives, JUST1/37 m31d, m34d.
Kew, The National Archives, JUST1/38 m33.
Kew, The National Archives, JUST1/54 m15, m16d, m18d.
Kew, The National Archives, JUST1/62 m3, m5, m3d, m5d.
Kew, The National Archives, JUST1/112 m13d.
Kew, The National Archives, JUST1/133 m25.
Kew, The National Archives, JUST1/137 m2, m6, m8, m6d, m7d, m14d.
Kew, The National Archives, JUST1/174 m40, m32d.
Kew, The National Archives, JUST1/175 m44d.
Kew, The National Archives, JUST1/186 m39d.
Kew, The National Archives, JUST1/207 m48.
Kew, The National Archives, JUST1/213 m34, m49.
Kew, The National Archives, JUST1/242 m93d.
Kew, The National Archives, JUST1/328 m6.
Kew, The National Archives, JUST1/369 m31, m7d.
Kew, The National Archives, JUST1/413 m1, m13d.
Kew, The National Archives, JUST1/479 m8, m7, m1d.
Kew, The National Archives, JUST1/497 m48d.
Kew, The National Archives, JUST1/540 m18, m19, m22d.
Kew, The National Archives, JUST /1/547A m66d.
Kew, The National Archives, JUST1/579 m143, m32d.
Kew, The National Archives, JUST1/648 m17.
Kew, The National Archives, JUST1/669 m8d.
Kew, The National Archives, JUST1/696 m7.
Kew, The National Archives, JUST1/759 m28.
Kew, The National Archives, JUST1/784 m17d.
Kew, The National Archives, JUST1/789 m3, m11, m29, m21d.
Kew, The National Archives, JUST1/833 m33d.
Kew, The National Archives, JUST1/877 m61d.
Kew, The National Archives, JUST1/921 m14.
Kew, The National Archives, JUST1/924 m60d.
Kew, The National Archives, JUST1/1005 m142.
Kew, The National Archives, JUST1/1078 m60.
Kew, The National Archives, JUST1/1098, m76/7.
Kew, The National Archives, JUST1/1171 m3, m4.

King's Bench Rolls

Kew, The National Archives, KB27/240, m104d, Rex, m1d.
Kew, The National Archives, KB27/242, m1, m154.

Legal and Medical Manuscripts

Kew, The National Archives, PRO 31/7/109.
Kew, The National Archives, SC8/146, no. 7252.
Kew, The National Archives, SC8/147, no. 7347.

Literary Manuscripts

Cambridge, Cambridge University Library, MS Ff. 2. 38.
Edinburgh, National Library of Scotland, MS Advocates 19. 2. 1.
Edinburgh, National Library of Scotland, MS Advocates 19. 3. 1.
London, British Library, MS Harley 2386.
London, British Library, MS Royal 17. B. 43.
Oxford, Bodleian Library, MS Bodleian 21900.

Primary Sources

Legal and Medical Primary Sources in Translation or Edited

Anglo-American Legal Tradition. University of Huston Law Center. Last Modified August 2015. http://aalt.law.uh.edu/.

Bedfordshire Coroners' Rolls. Edited by R. F. Hunnisett. Vol. 41. Streatley: Bedfordshire Historical Record Society, 1961.

Bracton de Legibus et Consuetudinibus Regni Angliae. Edited by George E. Woodbine, vol. 1. New Haven: Yale University Press, 1932.

Bracton on the Laws and Customs of England. Edited and translated by Samuel E. Throne, 3 vols. Cambridge: Harvard University Press, 1968.

Bracton Online. Harvard Law School Library. Edited by Charles A. Donahue, Thomas R. Bruce, and Terry Martin. Last Modified April 2003. https://amesfoundation.law.harvard.edu/Bracton/.

Britton: The French Text Carefully Revised, with an English Translation. Edited and translated by Francis Morgan Nichols. 2 vols. Oxford: Clarendon, 1865. Reprint Holmes Beach: Graunt, 1983.

Calendar of Close Rolls Edward I, 1272–1279. London: Eyre and Spottiswoode, 1900.

Calendar of Patent Rolls, Richard II. Vol. 2. London: Eyre and Spottiswoode, 1897.

Coke, Edward. *The Second Part of the Institutes of the Laws of England.* London: Flesher and Young, 1642.

Decretum Magistri Gratiani. Edited by Emil Friedberg. Corpus Iuris Canonici 1. Leipzig: Tauchnitz, 1879. Reprint Graz: Akademische Druck-u. Verlagsanstalt, 1959.

Fleta. Edited and translated by John Selden, 2nd ed. London, 1685.

Glanvill, Ranulf de. *Tractatus de legibus et consuetudinibus regni Anglie qui Glanvilla vocatur [Treatise on the Laws and Customs of the Realm of England Commonly Called Glanvill].* Edited and translated by G. D. G. Hall. Oxford: Oxford University Press, 1993; reprint 2002.

Hale, Matthew. *The History of the Pleas of the Crown.* Vol. 1. London: Nutt and Gosling, 1736.

Horwood, Alfred J, ed. and trans. *Year Books of the Reign of Edward the First: Years 30 and 31.* Vol. 3. London: HMSO, 1863.

Lanfranco of Milan. *Lanfrank's Science of Cirurgie: Part 1.* Edited by Robert Von Fleischhacker. London: Paul, Trench, Trübner, 1894.

Lemay, Helen Rodnite. *Women's Secrets: A Translation of Pseudo-Albertus Magnus's de secretis mulierum with Commentaries.* Albany: SUNY Press, 1992.

Matthew Paris. *Chronica majora.* Edited by H. R. Luard, vol. 1. London: Longman, 1872.

Placita Corone, or La Corone Pledee devant les Justices. Edited and translated by J. M. Kaye. London: Quaritch, 1966.

Select Pleas of the Crown: Pleas Before the Justices in Eyre in the Reign of King John. Vol. 1. London: Selden Society, 1887.

The Mirror of Justices. Edited and translated by William Joseph Whittaker, with an introduction by Frederic William Maitland. London: Quaritch, 1895.

The Statutes of the Realm: Printed by Command of His Majesty King George the Third, in Pursuance of an Address of the House of Commons of Great Britain from Original Records and Authentic Manuscripts. 2 vols. Edited by Alexander Luders. London: Dawsons, 1810–1828; reprint 1963.

William of Conches. *Dragmaticon Philosophiae.* Corpus Christianorum: Continuatio Mediaevalis 152. Turnhout: Brepols, 1997.

Year Books of Edward II, vol. 5: The Eyre of Kent 6 & 7 Edward II 1313–1314. Edited by Frederic William Maitland, Leveson William Vernon Harcourt, and William Craddock Bolland. London: Quaritch, 1910.

Literary Primary Sources in Translation or Edited

"Amis and Amiloun." In *Amis and Amiloun, Robert of Cisyle, and Sir Amadace.* Edited by Edward Foster. Kalamazoo: Medieval Institute, 2007. https://d.lib.rochester.edu/teams/text/foster-amis-and-amiloun.

Augustine. *The City of God Against the Pagans.* Edited and translated by George E. McCracken, vol. 1. Cambridge: Harvard University Press, 1981.

——. *The City of God Against the Pagans.* Edited by Jeffrey Henderson and translated by Philip Levine, vol. 4. Cambridge: Harvard University Press, 1966.

The Book of the Knight of La Tour-Landry: Compiled for the Instruction of His Daughter. Edited with an introduction and notes by Thomas Wright. London: Paul, Trench, Trübner, 1906.

Le Bone Florence of Rome. Edited by Carol Falvo Heffernan. Manchester: Manchester University Press, 1976.

"How the Goode Wife Taught Hyr Daughter." In *The Trials and Joys of Marriage.* Edited by Eve Salisbury. TEAMS Middle English Text Series. Kalamazoo: Medieval Institute Publications, 2002. https://d.lib.rochester.edu/teams/text/salisbury-trials-and-joys-how-the-goode-wife-taught-hyr-doughter.

"Sir Degare." In *The Middle English Breton Lays.* Edited by Anne Laskaya and Eve Salisbury. TEAMS Middle English Text Series. Kalamazoo: Medieval Institute, 1995. https://d.lib.rochester.edu/teams/text/laskaya-and-salisbury-middle-english-breton-lays-sir-degare.

"Sir Gowther." In *The Middle English Breton Lays.* Edited by Anne Laskaya and Eve Salisbury. TEAMS Middle English Text Series. Kalamazoo: Medieval Institute, 1995. https://d.lib.rochester.edu/teams/text/laskaya-and-salisbury-middle-english-breton-lays-sir-gowther.

"Sir Orfeo." In *The Middle English Breton Lays.* Edited by Anne Laskaya and Eve Salisbury. TEAM Middle English Text Series. Kalamazoo: Medieval Institute, 1995. https://d.lib.rochester.edu/teams/text/laskaya-and-salisbury-middle-english-breton-lays-sir-orfeo.

Stavsky, Jonathan. *Le Bone Florence of Rome: A Critical Edition and Facing Translation of a Middle English Romance Analogous to Chaucer's Man of Law's Tale.* Cardiff: University of Wales Press, 2017.

de Voragine, Jacobus. *The Golden Legend: Readings on the Saints.* Translated by William Granger Ryan. Princeton: Princeton University Press, 2012.

Secondary Sources

Acquaviva, Brittany, Katherine Meeker, and Eryn Nicole O'Neal. "Blameworthy Suspects and 'Real Rape': Assessing Effects of Rape Culture-Specific Suspect Culpability Factors on the Police Decision to Arrest." *Violence Against Women* 28 (2022): 3866–85.

Ahmed, Sara. *Willful Subjects*. Durham: Duke University Press, 2014.

Akard, Lucia. "Unequal Power and Sexual Consent: The Case of Cassotte la Joye." *Studies in the Age of Chaucer* 44 (2022): 285–92.

Akard, Lucia, and Alice Raw. "Global Response: Futures of Medieval Consent." *Studies in the Age of Chaucer* 44 (2022): 363–67.

Andreasen, Maja Brandt. "'Rapeable' and "Unrapeable' Women: The Portrayal of Sexual Violence in Internet Memes About #MeToo." *Journal of Gender Studies* 30 (2021): 102–13.

Andrews, Bernice, Chris R. Brewin, and Suzanna Rose. "Gender, Social Support, and PTSD in Victims of Violent Crime." *Journal of Traumatic Stress* 16 (2003): 421–27.

Archibald, Elizabeth. *Incest and the Medieval Imagination*. Oxford: Clarendon, 2001.

Armstrong-Partida, Michelle. "Precarious Manhood: Adolescence and Group Rape in Late Medieval Europe." *Medieval Feminist Forum* 56 (2021): 125–75.

Ashton, Gail. *Medieval English Romance in Context*. London: Continuum, 2010.

Baechle, Sarah. "Speaking Survival: Chaucer Studies and the Discourses of Sexual Assault." *The Chaucer Review* 57 (2022): 463–74.

Baechle, Sarah, Carissa Harris, and Elizaveta Strakhov. "Introduction: Recovering the Pastourelle." In *Rape Culture and Female Resistance in Late Medieval Literature*, edited by Sarah Baechle, Carissa Harris, and Elizaveta Strakhov, 1–14. Pennsylvania: Pennsylvania University Press, 2022.

——. "Reassessing the Pastourelle: Rape Culture, #Metoo, and the Literature of Survival." In *Rape Culture and Female Resistance in Late Medieval Literature*, edited by Sarah Baechle, Carissa Harris, and Elizaveta Strakhov, 17–28. Pennsylvania: Pennsylvania University Press, 2022.

Bellamy, John. *Crime and Public Order in England in the Later Middle Ages*. London: Routledge, 1973.

——. *Criminal Trial in Later Medieval England: Felony before the Courts from Edward I to the Sixteenth Century*. Toronto: University of Toronto Press, 1998.

Bennett, Judith. *Women in the Medieval English Countryside: Gender and Household in Brigstock before the Plague*. Oxford: Oxford University Press, 1987.

Bernheimer, Richard. *Wild Men in the Middle Ages: A Study in Art, Sentiment, and Demonology*. Cambridge: Harvard University Press, 2014.

Blake, Aaron. "Todd Akin, GOP Senate Candidate: 'Legitimate Rape' Rarely Causes Pregnancy." *The Washington Post*. Last Modified August 19, 2012. https://www.washington post.com/news/the-fix/wp/2012/08/19/todd-akin-gop-senate-candidate-legitimate-rape-rarely-causes-pregnancy/.

Bloch, Howard R. *Medieval Misogyny and the Invention of Western Romantic Love*. Chicago: University of Chicago Press, 1991.

Breen, Kerry. "Louisiana Man Sentences to 50 Years in Prison, Physical Castration for Raping Teen." *CBS News*. Last Modified April 24, 2024. https://www.cbsnews.com/news/glenn-sullivan-jr-louisiana-sentenced-rape-prison-castration/.

Brewer, Derek. *Symbolic Stories: Traditional Narratives of the Family Drama in English Literature*. Cambridge: Brewer, 1980.

Brooke, Christopher. *The Medieval Idea of Marriage*. Oxford: Oxford University Press, 1991.

Brown, Linda. "*Inaudito exemplo*: The Abduction of Romsey's Abbess." *Historical Reflections* 42 (2016): 21–34.

Brownmiller, Susan. *Against our Will: Men, Women and Rape*. New York: Simon and Schuster, 1975.

Brundage, James. "Implied Consent to Intercourse." In *Consent and Coercion to Sex and Marriage in Ancient and Medieval Societies*, edited by Angeliki E. Laiou, 245–56. Washington, DC: Dumbarton Oaks, 1993.

——. *Law, Sex and Christian Society in Medieval Europe*. Chicago: University of Chicago Press, 1987.

——. "Rape and Seduction in the Medieval Canon Law." In *Sexual Practices and the Medieval Church*, edited by Vern L. Bullough and James Brundage, 141–48. Amherst: Prometheus, 1994.

——. "The Teaching and Study of Canon Law in the Law Schools." In *The History of Medieval Canon Law in the Classical Period, 1140–1234: From Gratian to the Decretals of Pope Gregory IX*, edited by Wilfried Hartman and Kenneth Pennington, 98–120. Washington, DC: Catholic University Press, 2008.

Burns, Jane. "Raping Men: What's Motherhood Got to Do With It?." In *Representing Rape in Medieval and Early Modern Literature*, edited by Elizabeth Robertson and Christine M. Rose, 127–60. New York: Palgrave, 2001.

Butler, Judith. *Gender Trouble: Feminism and the Subversion of Identity*. New York: Routledge, 1999.

——. *Undoing Gender*. New York: Routledge, 2004.

Butler, Sara M. *Divorce in Medieval England: From One to Two Persons in Law*. New York: Routledge, 2013.

——. *Forensic Medicine and Death Investigation in Medieval England*. New York: Routledge 2015.

——. "Getting Medieval on Steven Pinker: Violence and Medieval England." *Historical Reflection* 44 (2018): 29–40.

——. *The Language of Abuse: Martial Violence in Later Medieval England*. Leiden: Brill, 2007.

——. "More than Mothers: Juries of Matrons and Pleas of the Belly in Medieval England." *Law and History Review* 37 (2019): 353–96.

Cadden, Joan. *Meanings of Sex Difference in the Middle Ages: Medicine, Science and Culture*. New York: Cambridge University Press, 1993.

Canadian Resource Centre for Victims of Crime. *Victim Blaming*. August 2009. https://crcvc.ca/ docs/victim_blaming.pdf.

Cannon, Christopher. "*Raptus* in the Chaumpaigne Release and a Newly Discovered Document Concerning the Life of Geoffrey Chaucer." Speculum 68 (1993): 74–94.

——. "The Rights of Medieval English Women: Crime and the Issue of Representation." In *Medieval Crime and Social Control*, edited by Barbara Hanawalt and David Wallace, 154–85. Minneapolis: University of Minnesota Press, 1998.

Carter, John Marshall. *Rape in Medieval England: An Historical and Sociological Study*. Lanham: University Press of America, 1985.

The Catholic Library Project. "Jerome, *Commentariorum in Jonam Prophetam Liber Unus*." Accessed April 2024. https://catholiclibrary.org/.

Clanchy, Michael. "Further Reading." In *Tractatus de legibus et consuetudinibus regni Anglie qui Glanvilla vocatur* [*Treatise on the Laws and Customs of the Realm of England Commonly Called Glanvill*]. Edited and translated by G. D. G. Hall, lxxi–lxxxi. Oxford: Oxford University Press, 1993.

Classen, Albrecht, *Sexual Violence and Rape in the Middle Ages: A Critical Discourse in Premodern German and European Literature*. Berlin: De Gruyter, 2011.

Cohen, Jeffery Jerome. *Of Giants: Sex, Monsters and the Middle Ages*. Minneapolis: University of Minnesota Press, 1999.

Connell, Raewyn. *Masculinities*. 2nd ed. Cambridge: Polity, 1995.

Cooper, Helen. *The English Romance in Time: Transforming Motifs from Geoffrey Monmouth to the Death of Shakespeare*. Oxford: Oxford University Press, 2004.

Cooper, Mariah L. "'Let's Bring the Boys In': Group Rape and the Culture of Silence." *The Sundial*. Last Modified April 9, 2024. https://medium.com/the-sundial-acmrs/lets-bring-the-boys-in- group-rape-and-the-culture-of-silence-3ebd60ba4272.

——. "Re-Reading Medieval English Cases of *Raptus*: Group Rape and Homosociality." *Florilegium* 38 (2021) [To be printed 2024].

Craig, Elaine. *Putting Trials on Trial: Sexual Assault and the Failure of the Legal Profession*. Montreal: McGill-Queen's University Press, 2018.

Crook, David. *Records of the General Eyre*. London: HMSO, 1982.

Davis, Nathalie Zemon. *Fiction in the Archives: Pardon Tales and Their Tellers in Sixteenth- Century France*. Stanford: Stanford University Press, 1987.

Digeser, P. E. "Resistance, Rape, Recognition, and Aggression." *Women's Studies International Forum* 100 (2023): 1–10.

Dinshaw, Carolyn. *Chaucer's Sexual Poetics*. Madison: University of Wisconsin Press, 1989.

——. *Getting Medieval: Sexualities and Communities, Pre- and Postmodern*. Durham: Duke University Press, 1999.

Du Mont, Janice, Karen-Lee Miller, and Terri Myhr. "The Role of 'Real Rape' and 'Real Victim' Stereotypes in the Police Reporting Practices of Sexually Assaulted Women." *Violence Against Women* 9 (2003): 466–86.

Duby, Georges. *The Knight, the Lady and the Priest: The Making of Modern Marriage in Medieval France*. Translated by Barbara Bray. London: Penguin, 1984.

——. *Medieval Marriage: Two Models from Twelfth-Century France*. Translated by Elborg Forster. Baltimore: John Hopkins University Press, 1978.

Duffy, Eamon. "Introduction to the 2012 Edition." In Jacobus de Voragine, *The Golden Legend: Readings on Saints with an Introduction by Eamon Duffy*, translated by William Granger Ryan, xi–xx. Princeton: Princeton University Press, 2012.

Dunn, Caroline. "The Language of Ravishment in Medieval England." *Speculum* 86 (2011): 79–116.

——. *Stolen Women in Medieval England: Rape, Abduction and Adultery, 1100–1500*. Cambridge: Cambridge University Press, 2012.

Edwards, Suzanne. *The Afterlives of Rape in Medieval English Literature*. Hampshire: Palgrave, 2016.

——. "Beyond *Raptus*: Pedagogies and Fantasies of Sexual Violence in Late-Medieval England." PhD Dissertation. University of Chicago, 2006.

——. "Consent and Misogyny: Response to Sarah Baechle and Sara V. Torres." *Studies in the Age of Chaucer* 44 (2022): 335–36.

——. "The Rhetoric of Rape and the Politics of Gender in the Wife of Bath's Tale and the 1382 Statute of Rapes." *Exemplaria* 23 (2011): 3–26.

Estrich, Susan. *Real Rape*. Cambridge: Harvard University Press, 1987.

Falk, Oren. "The Son of Orfeo: Kingship and Compromise in a Middle English Romance." *Journal of Medieval and Early Modern Studies* 30 (2000): 247–74.

Ferguson, Frances. "Rape and the Rise of the Novel." *Representations* 1 (1987): 88–112.

Ferzan, Kimberly Kessler, and Peter Westen. "How to Think (Like a Lawyer) About Rape." *Criminal Law and Philosophy* 11 (2017): 759–800.

Florschuetz, Angela. *Marking Maternity in Middle English Romance: Mothers, Identity and Contamination*. New York: Palgrave, 2014.

Franke-Ruta, Garance. "A Canard That Will Not Die: 'Legitimate Rape' Doesn't Cause Pregnancy." *The Atlantic*. Last Modified August 19, 2012. https://www.theatlantic.co/politics/archive/2012/08/a-canard-that-will-not-die-legitimate-rape-doesnt-cause-pregnancy/261303/.

Franklin, Sophie, Hannah Piercy, Arya Thampuran, and Rebecca White, eds. *Consent: Legacies, Representations, and Frameworks for the Future*. Abingdon: Routledge, 2024.

Fraser, Heather, and Kate Seymour. *Understanding Violence and Abuse: An Anti-Oppressive Practice Perspective*. Winnipeg: Fernwood, 2017.

Furrow, Melissa. *Expectations of Romance: The Reception of a Genre in Medieval England*. Cambridge: Brewer, 2009.

Galliano, Grace, Linda Noble, Linda Travis, and Carol Puechl. "Victim Reactions During Rape/Sexual Assault: A Preliminary Study of the Immobility Response and Its Correlates." *Journal of Interpersonal Violence* 8 (1993): 109–14.

Galloway, Andrew. *Medieval Literature and Culture*. New York: Continuum, 2006.

Gavey, Nicola. *Just Sex? The Cultural Scaffolding of Rape*. New York: Routledge, 2005.

Goldberg, P. J. P. "Echoes, Whispers, Ventriloquism: On Recovering Women's Voices from the Court of York in the Later Middle Ages." In *Women, Agency, and the Law, 1300–1700*, edited by Bronach Kane and Fiona Williamson, 31–41. London: Pickering & Chatto, 2013.

Goodich, Michael. "Introduction." In *Voices from the Bench: The Narratives of Lesser Folk in Medieval Trials*, edited by Michael Goodich, 1–14. New York: Palgrave, 2006.

Gravdal, Kathryn. "Camouflaging Rape: The Rhetoric of Sexual Violence in the Medieval Pastourelle." *Romanic Review* 76 (1985): 361–73.

——. *Ravishing Maidens: Writing Rape in Medieval French Literature and Law*. Philadelphia: University of Pennsylvania Press, 1991.

Green, Monica H. *Making Women's Medicine Masculine: The Rise of Male Authority in Pre-Modern Gynaecology*. Oxford: Oxford University Press, 2008.

Green, Thomas A. "Societal Concepts of Criminal Liability for Homicide in Medieval England." *Speculum* 47 (1972): 669–94.

——. *Verdict According to Conscience: Perspectives on the English Criminal Trial Jury, 1200–1800*. Chicago: University of Chicago Press, 1985.

Groot, Roger D. "The Crime of Rape temp. Richard I and John." *The Journal of Legal History* 9 (1988): 324–34.

Grubb, Amy, and Emily Turner. "Attribution of Blame in Rape Cases: A Review of the Impact of Rape Myth Acceptance, Gender Role Conformity and Substance Use on Victim Blaming." *Aggression and Violent Behavior* 17 (2021): 443–52.

Hanawalt, Barbara. *Crime and Conflict in English Communities 1300–1348*. Cambridge: Harvard University Press, 1979.
——. "The Female Felon in Fourteenth-Century England." *Viator* 5 (1974): 253–68.
——. "Whose Story was This? Rape Narratives in Medieval English Courts." In *"Of Good and Ill Repute": Gender and Social Control in Medieval England*, 124–41. Oxford: Oxford University Press, 1998.
——. "Women Before the Law: Females as Felons and Prey in Fourteenth-Century England." In *Women and the Law: A Social Historical Perspective, vol. 1: Women and the Criminal Law*, edited by Kelly Weisberg, 165–96. Cambridge: Schenkman, 1982.
Harris, Carissa. "'A Drunken Cunt Hath no Porter': Medieval Histories of Intoxication and Consent." *Medieval Feminist Forum* 45 (2018): 109–34.
——. *Obscene Pedagogies: Transgressive Talk and Sexual Education in Late Medieval Britain*. Ithaca: Cornell University Press, 2018.
——. "On Servant Women, Rape Culture, and Endurance." *The Chaucer Review* 57 (2022): 457–83.
——. "Pastourelle Fictionalities." *New Literary History* 51 (2020): 239–42.
——. "800 Years of Rape Culture." *AEON*. Last Modified May 24, 2021. https://aeon.co/essays/the-hypocrisies-of-rape-culture-have-medieval-roots.
Harris, Carissa, and Fiona Somerset, eds. "Colloquium: Historicizing Consent: Bodies, Wills, Desires." *Studies in the Age of Chaucer* 44 (2022): 268–367.
——. "Introduction." *Studies in the Age of Chaucer* 44 (2022): 268–71.
Harvey, Katherine. *The Fires of Lust: Sex in the Middle Ages*. London: Reaktion, 2021.
Hawkes, Emma. "Preliminary Notes on Consent in the 1382 Rape and Ravishment Laws of Richard II." *Legal History* 11 (2007): 117–32.
——. "'She Was Ravished against Her Will, What so Ever She Say': Female Consent in Rape and Ravishment in Late-Medieval England." *Limina* 1 (1995): 47–53.
de Heer, Brooke, and Lynn Jones. "Tonic Immobility as a Defensive Trauma Response to Rape: Bridging Public Health and Law." *Violence Against Women* (2023): 1–29.
Heffernan, Carol Falvo. "*Raptus*: A Note on Crime and Punishment in *Le Bone Florence of Rome*." In *Medieval Studies in Honor of Lillian Herlands Hornstein*, edited by Jess B. Bessinger, Jr. and Robert R. Raymo, 173–79. New York: New York University Press, 1976.
Higgins, Lynn A., and Brenda R. Silver, eds. *Rape and Representation*. New York: Columbia University Press, 1991.
Histed, Elise Bennet. "Medieval Rape: A Conceivable Defence?." *Cambridge Law Journal* 63 (2004): 743–69.
Hopkins, Amanda, Robert Allen Rouse, and Cory James Rushton, eds. *Sexual Culture in the Literature of Medieval Britain*. Cambridge: Brewer, 2014.
Hopkins, Andrea. *The Sinful Knights: A Study of Middle English Penitential Romance*. Oxford: Clarendon, 1990.
Horner, Shari. "Spiritual Truth and Sexual Violence: The Old English 'Juliana,' Anglo-Saxon Nuns, and the Discourse of Female Monastic Enclosure." *Signs* 19 (1994): 658–75.
Innes-Parker, Catherine. "Sexual Violence and the Female Reader: Symbolic 'Rape' in the Saints' Lives of the Katherine Group." *Women's Studies* 24 (1995): 205–17.
Jacquart, Danielle, and Claude Thomasset. *Sexuality and Medicine in the Middle Ages*. Translated by Matthew Adamson. Princeton: Princeton University Press, 1988.

Jager, Eric. *The Last Duel: A True Story of Crime, Scandal, and Trial by Combat in Medieval France*. New York: Broadway, 2004.

Jane, Emma. *Misogyny Online: A Shorty (And Brutish) History*. London: Sage, 2017.

Kaeuper, Richard. *Chivalry and Violence in Medieval Europe*. Oxford: Oxford University Press, 1999.

Kamali, Elizabeth Papp. *Felony and the Guilty Mind in Medieval England*. Cambridge: Cambridge University Press, 2019.

Kane, Bronach. "Men and Women in Love: Courtship, Marriage and Gender in Late Medieval England." In *The Routledge Companion to Romantic Love*, edited by Ann Brooks, 36–47. New York: Routledge, 2022.

——. *Popular Memory and Gender in Medieval England: Men, Women and Testimony in Church Courts, 1200–1500*. Woodbridge: Boydell, 2019.

Kane, Bronach, and Fiona Williamson. "Introduction." In *Women, Agency, and the Law, 1300–1700*, edited by Bronach Kane and Fiona Williamson, 1–16. London: Pickering & Chatto, 2013.

Kantorowicz, E. H. "The Prologue to *Fleta*." *Speculum* 32 (1957): 231–249.

Karras, Ruth Mazo. *Common Women: Prostitution and Sexuality in Medieval England*. New York: Oxford University Press, 1996.

——. *From Boys to Men: Formations of Masculinity in Late Medieval Europe*. Philadelphia: University of Pennsylvania Press, 2003.

——. *Sexuality in Medieval Europe: Doing unto Others*. London: Routledge, 2012.

Kelly, Henry Ansgar. "Meanings and Uses of *Raptus* in Chaucer's Time." *The New Chaucer Society* 20 (1998): 101–65.

——. "Statute of Rapes and Alleged Ravishers of Wives: A Context for the Charges against Thomas Malory, Knight." *Viator* 28 (1997): 361–419.

Kelly, Kathleen Coyne. *Performing Virginity and Testing Chastity in the Middle Ages*. London: Routledge, 2000.

Kittel, Ruth. "Rape in Thirteenth-Century England: A Study of the Common-Law Courts." In *Women and the Law: A Social Historical Perspective, vol. 2: Property, Family and the Legal Profession*, edited by Kelly Weisberg, 101–16. Cambridge: Schenkman, 1982.

Klerman, Daniel. "Women Prosecutors in Thirteenth-Century England." *Yale Journal of Law & Humanities* 14 (2002): 271–319.

Krahé, Barbara. "Societal Responses to Sexual Violence Against Women: Rape Myths and the 'Real Rape' Stereotype." In *Women and Children as Victims and Offenders: Background, Prevention, Reintegration*, edited by Helmut Kury, Sławomir Redo, and Evelyn Shea, 671–700. Cham: Springer, 2016.

Kümper, Hiram. "Learned Men and Skilful Matrons: Medical Expertise and the Forensics of Rape in the Middle Ages." In *Medicine and the Law in the Middle Ages*, edited by Wendy Turner and Sara Butler, 88–108. Leiden: Brill, 2014.

Leach, Elizabeth Eva. *Sung Birds: Music, Nature, and Poetry in the Later Middle Ages*. Ithaca: Cornell University Press, 2018.

Lett, Didier. "Women Victims of Sexual Assault and Rape: Evidence From the Criminal Courts of Bologna (Fourteenth-Fifteenth Centuries)." Translated by Marian Rothstein. *Clio: Women, Gender, History* no. 52 (2020): 45–70.

Manne, Kate. *Down Girl: The Logic of Misogyny*. Oxford: Oxford University Press, 2018.

Mardorossian, Carine M. *Framing the Rape Victim: Gender and Agency Reconsidered*. New Brunswick: Rutgers University Press, 2014.

McAvoy, Liz Herbert. *The Enclosed Garden and the Medieval Religious Imaginary.* Woodbridge: Boydell & Brewer, 2021.

McDonald, Nicola. "A Polemic Introduction." In *Pulp Fictions of Medieval England: Essays in Popular Romance*, edited by Nicola McDonald, 1–21. Manchester: Manchester University Press, 2004.

McSweeney, Thomas. *Priests of the Law: Roman Law and the Making of the Common Law's First Professionals.* Oxford: Oxford University Press, 2019.

McVitty, Amanda. *Treason and Masculinity in Medieval England: Gender, Law and Political Culture.* Woodbridge: Boydell & Brewer, 2020.

Meale, Carol, ed. *Women and Literature in Britain, 1150–1500.* Cambridge: Cambridge University Press, 1993.

Mehl, Dieter. *The Middle English Romances of the Thirteenth and Fourteenth Centuries.* London: Routledge, 1968.

Meyerson, Mark D., Daniel Thiery, and Oren Falk, eds. *"A Great Effusion of Blood"?: Medieval Violence.* Toronto: University of Toronto Press, 2004.

Morton, Vera, and Jocelyn Wogan-Browne. *Guidance for Women in Twelfth-Century Convents.* Cambridge: Brewer, 2003.

Moss, Rachel. "#NotAllMen: In Conversation with Lucia Akard and Samantha Katz Seal." *Studies in the Age of Chaucer* 44 (2022): 293–95.

Murphy-Oikonen, Jodie, Karen McQueen, Ainsley Miller, Lori Chambers, and Alexa Hiebert. "Unfounded Sexual Assault: Women's Experiences of Not Being Believed by the Police." *Journal of Interpersonal Violence* 37 (2022): 8916–40.

Musson, Anthony. "Crossing Boundaries: Attitudes to Rape in Late Medieval England." In *Boundaries of the Law: Geography, Gender and Jurisdiction in Medieval and Early Modern Europe*, edited by Anthony Musson, 84–101. New York: Routledge, 2005.

——. *Medieval Law in Context: The Growth of Legal Consciousness from Magna Carta to the Peasants' Revolt.* Manchester: Manchester University Press, 2001.

Neville, Cynthia. "Common Knowledge of the Common Law in Later Medieval England." *Canadian Journal of History* 29 (1994): 461–78.

Nicholls, Tracey. *Dismantling Rape Culture: The Peacebuilding Power of "Me Too."* London: Routledge, 2020.

Orr, Patricia. "Men's Theory and Women's Reality: Rape Prosecutions in the English Royal Courts of Justice, 1194–1222." In *The Rusted Hauberk: Feudal Ideals of Order and Their Decline*, edited by Liam Purdon and Cindy Vitto, 121–62. Florida: University of Florida Press, 1994.

Payne, Diana, Kimberly Lonsway, and Louise Fitzgerald. "Rape Myth Acceptance: Exploration of Its Structure and Its Measurement Using the Illinois Rape Myth Acceptance Scale." *Journal of Research in Personality* 33 (1999): 27–68.

Peters, Julie Stone. *Law as Performance: Theatricality, Spectatorship, and the Making of Law in Ancient, Medieval, and Early Modern Europe.* Oxford: Oxford University Press, 2022.

Phillips, Kim. "The Breasts of Virgins: Sexual Reputation and Young Women's Bodies in Medieval Culture and Society." *Cultural and Social History* 15 (2018): 1–19.

——. "Desiring Virgins: Maidens, Martyrs and Femininity in Late Medieval England." In *Youth in the Middle Ages*, edited by P. J. P. Goldberg and Felicity Riddy, 45–60. Suffolk: University of York Press, 2004.

——. "Written on the Body: Reading Rape from the Twelfth to Fifteenth Centuries." In *Medieval Women and the Law*, edited by Noël James Menuge, 125–44. Woodbridge: Boydell, 2000.

Piercy, Hannah. *Resistance to Love in Medieval English Romance: Negotiating Consent, Gender, and Desire*. Woodbridge: Boydell & Brewer, 2023.

Plucknett, Theodore F. T. *A Concise History of the Common Law*. 5th ed. Boston: Little Brown, 1956. Reprint Clark: Lawbook Exchange, 2010.

——. *Legislation of Edward I: The Ford Lectures Delivered in the University of Oxford in Hilary Term 1947*. Oxford: Clarendon, 1962.

Pollock, Frederick, and Frederic William Maitland. *The History of the English Law Before the Time of Edward I*. 2nd ed., 2 vols. Cambridge: Cambridge University Press, 1968.

Pope, Julia, and Shannon McSheffrey. "Ravishment, Legal Narratives, and Chivalric Culture in Fifteenth-Century England." *The Journal of British Studies* 48 (2009): 818–36.

Post, J. B. "Ravishment of Women and the Statutes of Westminster." In *Legal Records and the Historian: Papers Presented to the Cambridge Legal History Conference, 7–10 July, 1975, and in Lincoln's Inn Old Hall on 3 July 1974*, edited by J. H. Baker, 150–64. London: Swift Printers, 1978.

——. "Sir Thomas West and the Statute of Rapes 1382." *Bulletin of the Institute of Historical Research* 53 (1980): 24–30.

Pugh, Ralph. "The Duration of Criminal Trials in Medieval England." In *Law, Litigants and the Legal Profession*, edited by Eric Ives and Anthony Manchester, 104–15. London: R. H. S., 1983.

Putter, Ad, and Jane Gilbert, eds. *The Spirit of Medieval English Popular Romance*. Toronto: Pearson Education, 2000.

Raw, Alice. "Readers Then and Now: Coerced Consent in Dame Sirith." *Studies in the Age of Chaucer* 44 (2022): 307–14.

Riddle, John M. *Contraception and Abortion from the Ancient World to the Renaissance*. Cambridge: Harvard University Press, 1994.

Riddy, Felicity. "Temporary Virginity and the Everyday Body: *Le Bone Florence of Rome* and Bourgeois Self-Making." In *Pulp Fictions of Medieval England*, edited by Nicola McDonald, 197–216. Manchester: Manchester University Press, 2004.

Robertson, Elizabeth, and Christine M. Rose, eds. *Representing Rape in Medieval and Early Modern Literature*. New York: Palgrave, 2001.

Robson, Margaret. "How's Your Father? Sex and the Adolescent Girl in *Sir Degare*." In *The Erotic in the Literature of Medieval Britain*, edited by Amanda Hopkins and Cory James Rushton, 82–93. Cambridge: Brewer, 2007.

Roger, Euan, and Sebastian Sobecki. "Geoffrey Chaucer, Cecily Chaumpaigne, and the Statute of Laborers: New Records and Old Evidence Reconsidered." *The Chaucer Review* 57 (2022): 407–37.

Rooney, Ellen. "Criticism and the Subject of Sexual Violence." *Modern Language Notes* 98 (1983): 1269–77.

——. "A Little More than Persuading: Tess and the Subject of Sexual Violence." In *Rape and Representation*, edited by Lynn A. Higgins and Brenda R. Silver, 87–114. New York: Columbia University Press, 1991.

Rose, Mary Beth, ed. *Women in the Middle Ages and the Renaissance: Literary and Historical Perspectives*. Syracuse: Syracuse University Press, 1986.

Rossiaud, Jacques. *Medieval Prostitution*. New York: Blackwell, 1988.

Sagui, Samantha. "The Hue and Cry in Medieval English Towns." *Historical Research* 87 (2014): 179–93.

Saunders, Corinne. "Erotic Magic: The Enchantress in Middle English Romance." In *The Erotic in the Literature of Medieval Britain*, edited by Amanda Hopkins and Cory James Rushton, 38–52. Cambridge: Brewer, 2007.

——. "A Matter of Consent: Middle English Romance and the Law of *raptus*." In *Medieval Women and the Law*, edited by Noël James Menuge, 105–24. Woodbridge: Boydell, 2000.

——. *Rape and Ravishment in the Literature of Medieval England*. Cambridge: Brewer, 2001.

Sayles, G. O. *The Court of the King's Bench in Law and History*. London: Quaritch 1959.

Schneebeck, Herold. "The Law of Felony in Medieval England from the Accession of Edward I until the Mid 14th century." 2 vols. PhD Dissertation. University of Iowa, 1973.

Schulenburg, Jane Tibbets. "The Heroics of Virginity: Brides of Christ and Sacrificial Mutilation." In *Women in the Middle Ages and Renaissance: Literary and Historical Perspectives*, edited by Mary Beth Rose, 29–72. Syracuse: Syracuse University Press, 1986.

Schwebel, Leah. "Chaucer and the Fantasy of Retroactive Consent." *Studies in the Age of Chaucer* 44 (2022): 337–45.

Scott, Joan Wallach. "Gender: A Useful Category of Historical Analysis." In *Gender and the Politics of History*, 28–52. New York: Columbia University Press, 1988.

Seabourne, Gwen. "Drugs, Deceit and Damage in Thirteenth-Century Herefordshire: New Perspectives on Medieval Surgery, Sex and the Law." *Social History of Medicine* 30 (2017): 255–76.

——. *Imprisoning Medieval Women: The Non-Judicial Confinement and Abduction of Women in England, c. 1170–1509*. Farnham: Ashgate, 2011.

——. "Rape and Law in Medieval Western Europe." In *A Companion to Crime and Deviance in the Middle Ages*, edited by Hannah Skoda, 342–57. Leeds: Arc Humanities, 2023.

——. *Women in the Medieval Common Law c. 1200–1500*. New York: Routledge, 2021.

Seal, Samantha Katz. "Chasing the Consent of Alice Chaucer." *Studies in the Age of Chaucer* 44 (2022): 273–83.

——. "Whose Chaucer? On Cecily Chaumpaigne, Cancellation, and the English Literary Canon." *The Chaucer Review* 57 (2022) 484–97.

Skinner, Patricia. "Marking the Face, Curing the Soul? Reading the Disfigurement of Women in the Later Middle Ages." In *Medicine, Religion and Gender in Medieval Culture*, edited by Naoë Kukita Yoshikawa, 181–201. Woodbridge: Boydell & Brewer, 2015.

Sklar, Rachel. "Welcome to Senator Bill Napoli's X-Rated Mind." *HuffPost*. Last Modified May 25, 2011. https://www.huffpost.com/entry/welcome-to-senator-bill-n_b_17669.

Somerset, Fiona. "Consent/Assent." In *A New Companion to Critical Thinking on Chaucer*, edited by Stephanie Batkie, Matthew Irvin, and Lynn Shutters, 27–41. Leeds: Arc Humanities, 2021.

Stevens, John. *Medieval Romance: Themes and Approaches*. London: Hutchinson University Library, 1973.

Story, Robin. "Malicious Indictments of Clergy in the Fifteenth Century." In *Medieval Ecclesiastical Studies in Honour of Dorothy M. Owen*, edited by M. J. Franklin and Christopher Harper-Bill, 221–40. Woodbridge: Boydell, 1995.

Supreme Court of the United States. "Dobbs, State Health Officer of the Mississippi Department of Health, et al., V. Jackson Women's Health Organization Et Al." *Justia U.S. Supreme Court*. Last Modified June 24, 2022. https://supreme.justia.com/cases/federal/us/597/19-1392/.

Sylvester, Louise M. *Medieval Romance and the Construction of Heterosexuality*. New York: Palgrave, 2008.

Thorne, S. E. *Essays in English Legal History*. London: Hambledon, 1985.

Toner, Barbara. *The Facts of Rape*. London: Hutchinson, 1977.

Torres, Sara V., and Rebecca F. McNamara. "Female Consent and Affective Resistance in Romance: Medieval Pedagogy and #MeToo." *New Chaucer Studies: Pedagogy and Profession* 2 (2021): 34–49.

Turner, Wendy. "The Leper and the Prostitute: Forensic Examination of Rape in Medieval England." In *Trauma in Medieval Society*, edited by Wendy Turner and Christina Lee, 122–47. Leiden: Brill, 2018.

Turner, Wendy, and Christina Lee. "Conceptualizing Trauma for the Middle Ages." In *Trauma in Medieval Society*, edited by Wendy Turner and Christina Lee, 3–12. Leiden: Brill, 2018.

Urban Artists Association. "Banksy Quotes." Last Modified January 17, 2014. https://urbanart association.com/thread/112810/banksy-quotes.

Valenti, Jessica. *The Purity Myth: How America's Obsession with Virginity is Hurting Youn Women*. New York: Basic, 2009.

Verner, Lisa. *The Epistemology of the Monstrous in the Middle Ages*. Abingdon: Routledge, 2005.

Vines, Amy. "Invisible Woman: Rape as Chivalric Necessity in Medieval Romance." In *Sexual Culture in the Literature of Medieval Britain*, edited by Amanda Hopkins, Robert Allen Rouse, and Cory James Rushton, 161–80. Cambridge: Brewer, 2014.

Wade, James. *Fairies in Medieval Romance*. New York: Palgrave, 2011.

Walker, Sue Sheriden. "Common Law Juries and Feudal Marriage Customs in Medieval England: The Pleas of Ravishment." *University of Illinois Law Review* 3 (1984): 705–18.

——. "Punishing Convicted Ravishers: Statuary Strictures and Actual Practice in Thirteenth and Fourteenth-Century England." *Journal of Medieval History* 13 (1987): 237–50.

——. "Wrongdoing and Compensation: The Pleas of Wardship in Thirteenth and Fourteenth Century England." *Journal of Legal History* 9 (1988): 267–307.

Weiss, Judith, Jennifer Fellows, and Morgan Dickson, eds. *Medieval Insular Romance: Translation and Innovation*. Cambridge: Brewer, 2000.

Wicher, Andrzej. "Geoffrey Chaucer's *The Merchant's Tale*, Giovanni Boccaccio's *The Tale of the Enchanted Pear-Tree*, and *Sir Orfeo* Viewed as Eroticized Versions of the Folktales about Supernatural Wives." *Text Matters* 3 (2013): 42–57.

Wilson, Laura C., and Amie R. Newins. "Attitudes Toward Men and Rejection of Rape Myths: The Impact on Survivor Rape Acknowledgment." *Journal of Interpersonal Violence* (2020): 1–18.

Wolfthal, Diane. *Images of Rape: The "Heroic" Tradition and Its Alternatives*. Cambridge: Cambridge University Press, 1999.

York, Ernest. "Isolt's Trial in Béroul and *La Folie Tristan d'Oxford*." In *Medieval Hagiography and Romance*, Edited by Paul Maurice Clogan, vol. 6, 157–62. Medievalia et Humanistica: Studies in Medieval & Renaissance Culture. Cambridge: Cambridge University Press, 1975.

Youngs, Deborah. "Reading Ravishment: Gender and 'Will' Power in Early Tudor Star Chamber, 1500–50." In *Star Chamber Matters: An Early Modern Court and its Records*, edited by Krista Kesselring and Natalie Mears, 41–60. London: University of London Press, 2021.

Dictionaries and Reference Material

Cassell's Latin Dictionary. Edited by D. P. Simpson. New York: Macmillan, 1959.

Dictionary of Medieval Latin from British Sources. Edited by Ronald Edward Latham, David R. Howlett, and Richard Ashdowne. Turnhout: Brepols, 2015.

Farmer, David. "Ebbe the Younger." In *The Oxford Dictionary of Saints*, 5th ed. Oxford: Oxford University Press, 2011.

Lewis, Charlton T., and Charles Short. *A Latin Dictionary*. New York: Harper and Brothers, 1879.

Middle English Dictionary. Edited by Frances McSparran et al. Ann Arbor: University of Michigan Library, 2000–2018. https://quod.lib.umich.edu/m/middle-english-dictionary/dictionary.

Niermeyer, J. F. *Mediae Latinitatis Lexicon Minus*. Leiden: Brill, 1954–2001.

Oxford English Dictionary. Chief Editor Michael Proffitt. Oxford University Press. Accessed February 2024. https://www.oed.com/?tl=true.

INDEX

Place and county names are in England unless otherwise stated.

Printed and bound by CPI Group (UK) Ltd, Croydon, CR0 4YY

13/09/2026

14961067-0002